Semiotics at the Circus

Semiotics, Communication and Cognition 3

Editors

Paul Cobley
Kalevi Kull

De Gruyter Mouton

Semiotics at the Circus

By
Paul Bouissac

De Gruyter Mouton

ISBN 978-3-11-021830-5 pb
ISBN 978-3-11-021829-9 hc
e-ISBN 978-3-11-021831-2
ISSN 1867-0873

Library of Congress Cataloging-in-Publication Data

Bouissac, Paul.
Semiotics at the circus / by Paul Bouissac.
p. cm. – (Semiotics, communication and cognition; 3)
Includes bibliographical references and index.
ISBN 978-3-11-021829-9 (alk. paper)
ISBN 978-3-11-021830-5 (pbk. : alk. paper)
1. Circus – Social aspects. 2. Performing arts – Semiotics. 3. Performing arts – Audiences. 4. Visual communication. I. Title.
GV815.B68 2010
791.3–dc22
2010017153

Bibliographic information published by the Deutsche Nationalbibliothek

The Deutsche Nationalbibliothek lists this publication in the Deutsche Nationalbibliografie; detailed bibliographic data are available in the Internet at http://dnb.d-nb.de.

Cover design based on a design by Martin Zech, Bremen
Typesetting: PTP-Berlin Protago-TEX-Production GmbH, Berlin
Printing: Hubert & Co. GmbH & Co. KG, Göttingen
∞ Printed on acid-free paper

Printed in Germany

www.degruyter.com

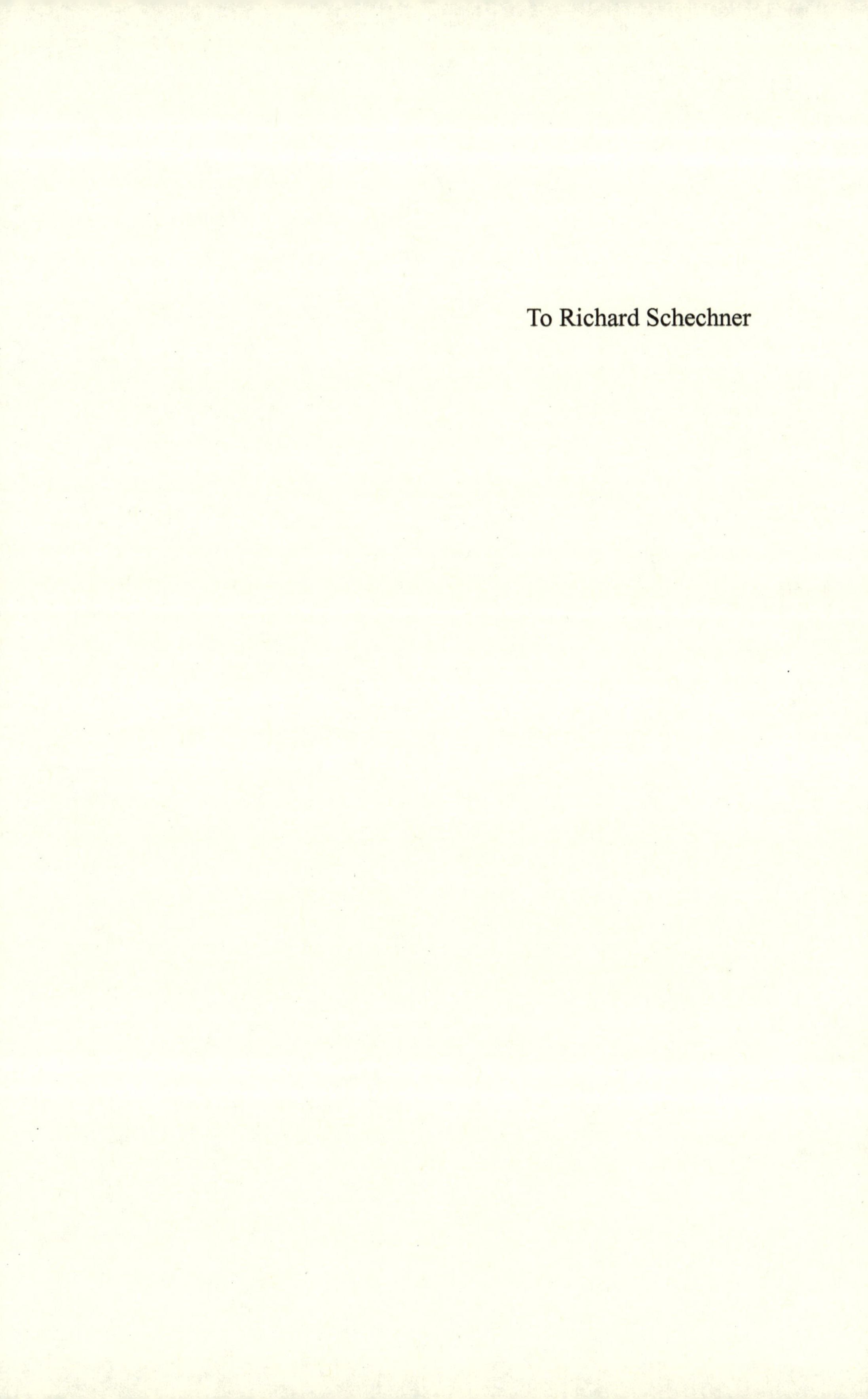

To Richard Schechner

Contents

Introduction
A semiotician at the circus 1

Chapter 1. The production of circus space 11
1.1. The constraints of nomadic life 11
1.2. The spatial algorithm of the circus 14
1.3. Squaring the circle 16
1.4. Olli and Illi: playing with space and desire 18

Chapter 2. The time of the circus. Cognitive and emotional dimensions of acrobatics and other circus acts 21
2.1. Circus acts as texts 22
2.2. A brain to brain affair 24
2.3. Another kind of time 29
2.4. The timeless tools of time 34
2.5. Clowns at work: the melodic structure of social interactions 38
2.6. Concluding remarks: circus time and cognition 43

Chapter 3. In what sense is a circus animal performing? 44
3.1. Meaning, text, and context 44
3.2. The civilized animal 46
3.3. A symphony of signs: the art of deceit and the pitfalls of self-deception 50

Chapter 4. Horses' feathers: from tacit knowledge to circus metaphors 55
4.1. A theoretical prelude 55
4.2. Birds, horses, and feathers 58
4.3. Horses, ostriches, and chorus girls 60
4.4. Circus horses in times of cultural changes 65

Chapter 5. Circus and cycles 68
5.1. Horse and bicycle: preliminary analogies 68
5.2. History, cultural evolution, and the circus 71
5.3. The introduction of the bicycle in circus spectacles 72
5.4. Pondering the strange history of the bicycle 75
5.5. The semiotics of the bicycle 78
5.6. The bicycle enters the kingdom of the horse 80

Chapter 6. The pyramid and the wheel: the visual discourse of circus acrobatics 82
6.1. The representation of law and anarchy 83
6.2. The language of the pyramid 84
6.3. The Tangier troupe: from order to chaos and back 86
6.4. The staging of acrobatics as social metaphors 89
6.5. Revolution(s) on a trampoline 90
6.6. Triumph and tragedy: the semiotics of fear and danger 92
6.7. Under the semiotic magnifying lens 94
6.8. Gender economy and tacit rules: norms and transgressions in the air 95
6.9. The predictive power of semiotics 100
6.10. Order and chaos on wheels 101

Chapter 7. The logic of clown faces 103
7.1. The structure of European clowns' make-up 104
7.2. From structuralism to biosemiotics 106
7.3. Icons of biomorphology 108
7.4. White faces and white patches: the management of leucosignals in clown make-up 110
7.5. A cross-cultural probe of clown make-up and its transformations 113
7.6. Expanding the scope: toward a global semiotic theory of clown make-up 117

Chapter 8. Incident, accident, failure: life and death at the circus 120
8.1. The representation of negative experience in performance 121
8.2. A science of the individual 122
8.3. Toward a model of negative experience 125
8.4. When failure means success: the staging of a negative experience 127
8.5. The semiotic dissection of George Carl's comic act 132
8.6. Anatomy of a negative masterpiece 134
8.7. Subjective vs. objective situations 136
8.8. A lady in danger 141

Chapter 9. There's no business like show business: the marketing of performance 149
9.1. Marketing the performing arts 149
9.2. The golden rules of performance 154
9.3. How to capture an audience 155
9.4. The power of stories 158

Chapter 10. The researcher as spectator: the pragmatics of circus performances 162
10.1. Toward a theory of live performances 163
10.2. The predicaments of description 166
10.3. The rules of performance 170
10.4. How to make a verbal copy 172
10.5. From rules of performance to rules of description 175

Conclusion
Circus in perspective 177

References 185
Subject index 195
Author index 197

Introduction
A semiotician at the circus

Euston Station, Thursday morning, June 26. The train that will take me from London to Lancashire, first to Preston, then to Blackpool, is due to leave at 9:00 am. I do not linger for breakfast in the hotel just across the street. My bag was packed last night. I know I will have to wait for thirty minutes in the railway station, standing in front of the information board, waiting for the departure platform to be announced. And here I am, more anxious than I should be, with a certain dose of elation and irrational excitement: I am going to the circus.

The Blackpool Tower Circus has been a hot spot of the circus arts for more than a century. Built between the four legs of a diminutive Eiffel Tower, it was inaugurated in 1894, and remained ever since a magnet for those who are passionately attracted to this spectacular ritual of modern times. No other circus in the world can match the temple atmosphere created by Frank Matcham's decoration, its gilded cast iron pillars and freezes, the deep red of its walls and seat rows, the intimacy conveyed by the proximity of the public to the ring. As the train speeds past Crewe, I anticipate finding my place on the steep pitch of the seats, leafing through the illustrated program, scanning the space above to identify the riggings that will be deployed for the aerial acts listed in the booklet, waiting for the circus to get dimmer and dimmer before the sudden burst of the orchestra and the formal entrance of the Master of Ceremonies, flooded by all the spotlights, immediately connected with the intensely focused spectators coiled tightly around the ring.

In the taxi which rushes me through the rain to the hotel, I could wonder why someone who has seen a thousand and one circuses in his life keeps checking his watch to make sure that he will not miss the next show. But I do not waste time asking myself such a silly question. I am entirely focused on "going to the circus", aroused by the forthcoming experience as if it were a date with the unknown.

This question, however, forms the core of this book. How can we account for the intensity and resilience of the meaning making power of the circus? For centuries, actually millennia, audiences have flocked to contemplate tight rope walkers, jugglers, tumblers, jokers, feats of horsemanship and wild animal training. All these performers from immemorial times have relied on the same techniques to survive the physical and social challenges to which they confront themselves. Their programs unfold with remarkable precision and predictability. Failures are the exception. Yet, the fascination they cause seems to be inexhaustible. They eke out a living from providing an ephemeral commodity as essential as bread and water, something that can be watched, and watched again when the desire returns, intact, to feed the eyes and the mind with the wonders of their arts.

Like a ritual that could be invalidated by some fatal misstep with dreaded consequences, the spectacle captures all my attention and emotion. Seated on the eighth row, I cannot see the faces of the five jugglers who keep fifteen clubs flying from hands to hands. They wear Venetian masks that reveal only their smiles. But their tight Harlequin costumes and the festive Italian tunes to which they harmonize their quick and supple movements, make their young bodies intimately present. Seven distinct and self-contained episodes that blend juggling and acrobatics are punctuated by gracious pauses or dance interludes which allow them to catch their breath and rest their muscles. The semiotician in me is silent. The first performance is always purely for the pleasure. So is often also the second, and even sometimes the third one. Then, once I have almost perfectly memorized the successive segments of this act to the point that I can anticipate each of them, I can ask myself, at last, why my attention is still totally absorbed and my emotion as intense as when I watched the first show.

In the cafeteria of the hotel, while the summer dusk is slowly falling on misty Blackpool, I attempt to retrace in writing the unfolding of the juggling act. It will take several more attentive viewings, adding notes to my rough written description, a sort of "verbal copy" that I will improve with details as time goes. I will not capture, though, in my semiotic net, the miracle of the body presence of the artists and the colors of my emotions. But I will manage to reconstruct the architecture of this act through a kind of reverse semiotic engineering. I will try to make explicit the kind of meaning that is forged every day by these performers by tracing back the performance to its tacit score. In so doing I will unearth the cultural symbols, both those which are rather obvious and those which are less so, that make their performance so relevant and so moving for their popular audience. I will be astonished at the quantity of biological and cultural information that is tightly packed in this collective juggling act, as in any other acts. I will understand why the artistic director has chosen it to open this year's program. I will also empathize with the overwhelming emotional reaction of the public for which it will have been a one-time experience until perhaps the following year but with an entirely new program.

From this brief existential and methodological sample, it should be clear what the experience of a semiotician at the circus is. The result of this fine-grained observation is certainly not to dampen the emotions with stifling analyses. It consists, in a way, of doubling the enjoyment by reconstructing the score which is materially absent like in any traditional art, but is nevertheless robustly inscribed in the memory of successive generations of circus artists, and takes an existence of its own in their audience. It paradoxically creates a kind of uncertain anticipation: we know more or less precisely how the actions we witness will unfold but we cannot be entirely sure that the outcome will meet both ours and the artists' expectations. In this juggling act, no club should be allowed to fall to the ground but this outcome is constantly threatened. This allows the contemplating of what could be called the unstable architecture of particular circus acts, an architecture that is provided in part by an immemorial artistic tradition, in part by the creative interpretations of individual artists who succeed in adding a surplus of meaning.

But the semiotic enterprise also goes deeper. Back at the circus, this time at closer range of the ring, I notice how much the Venetian masks unleash the erotic power of this juggling act. The spontaneous tendency to scan faces in human encounters is frustrated. What is fore-grounded is the body of each artist, their rhythmic and seductive movements, and the constant flashing of their smiles, a universal signal of willingness to engage in interaction. They broadcast an implicit invitation to join them in the dance, in the anonymous farandole in which social identities are dissolved and behavior could turn dissolute without shame. They are five, an odd number that precludes stable couples. The men wear tight pants and the women have very short skirts spiced up by black and red garters. They have woven into their technical actions discreet sexual displays, unilateral knee-bents for the men, reclining postures and side glances for the women. They recombine various configurations among themselves to achieve the launching and catching of an increasing number of brightly colored clubs that match the decoration of their costumes. One of the men, the one who seems to consistently perform the most difficult feats, catches a club between his legs, and marks a brief pause so that the phallic allusion which is congruent with the carnival theme cannot be missed by the audience.

The hotel lounge is a bit noisy with some people chatting about their day at the Pleasure Beach, children chasing each others, and a background music dating from a quarter of a century ago. I try to organize the notes taken on the spur of the moment during the last performance. I focus on the first act which, upon reflection, is more complex than it first appeared. It turns out that it implements a narrative of sort. The younger man who was a mere part of the team during the first half of the act progressively emerges as a special individual. The catching of a club between his legs, after having juggled more clubs that anybody else in the group, has set him apart both as the most skilled artist in the group and a transgressor who dares to visually produce a sexual joke. In the concluding segment, he positions himself facing at a distance the four other jugglers who stand in a row. The resident clown brings a pile of colorful plastic plates that he obviously intends to give to the lone juggler but trips and lets all the plates scatter on the ground. The audience can assess the large number of items which the clown picks up and eventually hands to the juggler as a challenge. After some quick plate juggling, the younger man will attempt to catch all the plates one after the other as the other members of the group send them toward him at an increasing speed. The first attempt is a failure: he misses the last catch and all the plates once again are scattered on the ground. The resident clown comes back and mockingly picks up again the plates. This time, he is not the one who failed his task. He asks the audience: "Do you want him to try again?" The audience shouts "Yes". They said "No", quips the clown as he leaves the ring. The exercise resumes and the juggler succeeds in catching all the plates. Having met this ultimate challenge which pitted him against the other jugglers and the irony of the clown, he briefly enjoys a hero's triumph before reintegrating the rest of the troupe to leave the ring. With gracious acknowledgements of the public's applauses, they exit backward facing the audience until they reach the red curtain behind which they disappear.

During the week, I have seen this act six times. The concluding segment is always the same. The failure is staged. It is an essential part of the narrative. The emergence of the hero from the group comes at a cost: the clown has mocked his ambition and has underlined his early failure. But the hero has eventually overcome both the physical and the social challenges, and, everyday, his achievements are being publicly recognized by loud hand clapping.

At dinner, I share a table with a vacationer who had noticed my scribbling at the circus, and had inquired whether I was a journalist. I had to briefly explain what a semiotician does. She had heard of Roland Barthes and Umberto Eco but had never connected semiotics with the circus. She had seen the performance once. I was very interested in knowing her reactions to this show, to this act in particular. "They were all very good", she says, "but the young man was really super". Here comes my own challenge: can a semiotician successfully communicate his analytic discourse to a regular spectator? I try. She had not noticed some of the details I point out. She thought that the failure of catching all the plates at the first attempt was indeed genuine. "They were so fast!" she insists. Then she comes to admire the performing skill of the juggler who made it look so natural, at the same time unexpected and expectable. She had empathized and experienced some anxiety. The eventual success had made her very happy. "He seemed such a nice guy!" Some of the things I say seem pretty obvious to her, although she had not thought of it during the performance. This of course does not mean that she had not processed the information subconsciously. She agrees to this. There comes my reward: "I must see that show again. I think I will enjoy it more", she says.

Two days later. My circus research stint in Blackpool is drawing to a close. After an early walk on the deserted North pier, I am now at the Library checking my email on a public computer. I am surprised to find a message from Shirley. She had returned to the circus after our conversation. All this had made sense to her because, some years ago, she had taken a course in film studies at London Metropolitan University. She had been trained to look behind immediate experience, so to speak. She wonders why the clown interferes with the juggling act. Good question. I had not raised it myself because I had taken it for granted that clowns often intervene in this manner. But for a semiotician the most challenging problems are precisely those experiences that are taken for granted as making sense "naturally". This is a great opportunity to articulate a tentative explanation: this clown is already known to the audience because he was the first spectacular event in the program. He was the primal act before the first formal act. As soon as the show is ready to start, he unexpectedly appears in the wing at the top of a side stairs among the public, drawing a broom, shouting "Hello, hello everybody!" The Master of Ceremonies, who represents the etiquette of the circus, reprimands him for troubling the good order of the spectacle which is supposed to take place in the ring. The clown does not obey and continues his antics, asking a spectator what his name is, introducing himself formally, then repeating the same question to another spectator a few rows below. Now he introduces the two spectators to each other, with some innuendos. As he climbs down the stairs, tripping at times, stealing a pop corn from a child, pretending that he does not understand what the authoritarian man says, he makes the audience laugh. He eventually reaches the ring, produces a farting noise as he climbs over it, and finds himself face to face with an angry Mister Law and Order. It will take a few more arguments and hilarious turns of events between the two before the clown leaves the ring and the juggling act can formally start.

From the beginning, as a kind of foundational gesture, this clown has defined himself as a rule breaker. He has mocked good manners. He has transgressed even the circus code of which he is a part. But his tricks have made people happy. He has denounced the arbitrariness of authority. When the Master of Ceremonies wants to throw him out of the ring, the audience spontaneously boos him. Note that his intervening in the juggling act comes at the precise moment when one of the artists emerges with a claim to heroic status. The clown puts him down. Seeking eminence first exposes an individual to the group hostility. The jester reminds the king of his vulnerability. At the end, the triumph of the juggling hero will be both physical and social but his eventual reintegration into the group will have been facilitated by the framing provided by the clown.

These remarks can lead to a reflection on the intertextual nature of the circus enjoyment. In this program the clown and the juggling acts are connected to each other and both refer to outside elements which are essential to their understanding: respectively, to the civil manners of the contextual culture (which are transgressed) and to the visual and musical stereotypes of a Venetian carnival (which are iconically implemented). For whoever has a previous experience of circus, such a juggling act is contextualized by a rich paradigm going from solo artists to fairly large teams using a variety of artifacts and a diversity of throwing and catching techniques but also a range of ethnic and cultural themes that anchor these skills in suggestive contexts. Like in many other circus acts, the tension between individual claims to stardom and group imperatives is poignantly represented but, in this case, with a particular emphasis because a team juggling act is an embodiment of absolute social harmony. Each member of the team indeed must time his or her actions very precisely with respect to the others' while all the successive exercises unfold at a fast pace on vivacious musical themes.

On the train back to Preston to catch the London Express, I leaf through the printed program. I try to decipher the notes I made in the margins and enter them in the notebook I kept during these few circus days. But focusing on field notes is not easy. I always feel sad when leaving Blackpool, its Lancashire congeniality, its permanent carnival atmosphere, shines or rains, rooted in two centuries of popular entertainment, its daytime leisurely loafers along the endless promenades, its pubs and clubs, and the hectic and festive young crowd that fills the street most of the nights until dawn. Tomorrow, I will compile my notes, and I will draft the blueprint of a book that will summarize thirty years of the experience and reflections of a semiotician at the circus.

Opposite my seat in the train I board in Preston is an Indian student who just graduated in computer sciences at the University of Birmingham. He has never heard of semiotics but soon declares that it obviously is what he has been doing all the time for his courses. I mention my earlier fieldwork in Indian circuses during the 1980s. He was not born yet. He had never been to a circus in his life but he supports the banishing of wild animals from this sort of show. "Why do you have to watch a circus act so many times? It is not very economical. A video tape could do the trick." I have to explain that there are at least two reasons: "Most circuses do not allow this and trying to obtain permissions would mean endless red tape. But this is not the whole story. A tape would give me only one version of an act from a single point of view." – "You can move the camera around" – "Then, I would lose the vantage point of a single spectator and my 'text' would be something that nobody has experienced in the audience. It would be a film, not a circus act. What I try to achieve is a reliable verbal copy which is a true synthesis of the spectacle as it is perceived by the public." – "It seems a lot of effort. There must be a way of doing this more quickly." I decide to bring forth two more arguments. I point out that successive performances are not absolutely identical. There are interesting variations. Some are just an expression of free play within the technical constraints of an act, or some personal experiments on the part of the artist. Other modifications are caused by outside events: the act has to be shortened, a prop may be broken, a partner may be sick. These circumstances force adaptations on the fly and, at the same time, demand that some kind of spectacular integrity be preserved. All these changes are very informative when your goal is to uncover the code that is at play. My interlocutor is perceptive. He sees the point I am trying to make but he is not someone who gives up easily: "Then, you will never be finished with your task. You have to stop sooner or later. You will always have missed something." I concede that all research has its limits and that knowledge cannot be absolute. As a conciliatory gesture, he anticipates my second argument: "Of course, you could also say that when people know that they are filmed, they become self-conscious and they behave somewhat differently. – Of course, they tend to perform for the camera and they are not as much attuned to the feedback of the public – But I still think that there must be a way of doing what you do more efficiently – Perhaps". What else can I say?

As the train rushes past Crewe through heavy rain, I ponder a final argument. I keep it to myself, though. Rajesh is totally absorbed in his laptop. I should try to express it some day in more theoretical terms. I will call it, for the time being, the pleasure factor. I let my inner voice develop it. Like for many, circus is for me a source of sought for emotions. The successive viewings of the same live performance are not redundant experiences. This allows me after a while to contemplate the particular beauty of a segment because I can anticipate its beginning, enjoy its deployment in time and space, and keep its ephemeral beauty in my memory. I am not any longer harassed by the fast tempo of the incoming information as is the case during the first performance I witness. Now I can savor its meaning in the form of an emotion because I can recognize it. I can hold it, even briefly, in aesthetic consciousness.

Circus is indeed an aesthetic object. Its semiotic analysis provides not only the means to reflexively understand its syntax, semantics, poetics and rhetoric, but also to appreciate its beauty. Not all circus programs are equally well balanced, not all acts achieve the same technical perfection and deliver the same aesthetic pleasure. Many factors are at play. Théophile Gautier, the 19th century French romantic poet and critic, called the circus "the opera of the eyes". It is true that circus is a prominently visual art but like a ballet it is unthinkable without the music that harmonizes with the movements and sets the mood of each act mainly if it is a live band that attunes itself to the beat of the acrobatic movements, even if it is a single drum that sets the rhythm and underlines the danger. I am not sure that the juggling troupe which opened the program at the Blackpool Tower Circus would fare as well as they did without the evocative Italian tune of "Funiculi, funicula". Technically, it was really a run-of-the-mill act. There must be criteria of what a good performance is.

However, cross-cultural comparisons are in order. Each cultural area in the world has its own performance traditions and aesthetic standards. As the train leaves the countryside to enter the outskirts of London, I remember the nun from Bombay. A flash back some twenty years ago when Bombay had not yet reverted to Mumbai. I am in a suburban district of Toronto, waiting in a bus shelter after a performance of Circus Vargas, a typical American three-ring show. A middle-aged Indian lady inquires about the bus schedule. She has seen the circus. She hails from Bombay to spend her vacation with family members who have migrated to Canada. She is a Catholic nun. She likes circus. Her order in India let the nuns go to a circus once a year. I was in Bombay the year before. I saw Apollo Circus there at Church Gate. She knows that circus. I was very disappointed the first time I saw it the day after I arrived. A former student of mine, Duccio Canestrini, had come to assist me in a research on the Indian circus. As we left the tent, he looked at me: "You made me travel from Italy for that?" Nothing seemed right to us. The slow pace, the informality of the presentation, the loose fit between the music and the performance, the sheer abundance of acts that succeeded each other in apparently haphazard order, the laid back attitude of the performers, some items that simply did not make sense to us. I tell the nun: "So, now, you have seen a real circus here! What do you think of the show?" I was expecting an expression of wonderment. "Yes, yes, she said, but it was not as good as Apollo Circus." Then she lists all the shortcomings of the Vargas program which, on the whole, was not presented as a circus should be. She missed this and that. It was too boisterous and somewhat vacuous. Elephants did not do this or that. The trainer did not put his head in the lion's mouth. The jokers were not as funny as they are in India.

Actually, Duccio and I had gradually come to appreciate the Indian circus on its own terms. After the first three shows, we started growing fond of this experience. We were no longer frustrated by its apparent lack of etiquette. We had learned its performance code as we had become comfortable with other aspects of the Indian way of life. Now, every time we meet, after so many years, we fondly remember details of some of the acts we saw at Church Gate. They have stayed alive in our joint memory. We still faintly visualize them. We hear, at a distance, the quaint music that fitted them so well and within which they are now preserved.

The first chapters of this volume deal quite naturally with space and time. Going to the circus means first of all crossing a threshold and accessing a heterotopic universe that beats at the rhythms of its own temporal structures. Next, we will enter the world of circus animals with a focus on horses which are from immemorial times intimately associated with the circus nomadic mode of life as well as with its spectacular feats of horsemanship. Acrobatics come next: trapeze, pyramid, tumbling, and bicycle, this modern substitute for horses, will be the topic of the two following chapters. Then, the clowns: their make-up, their garb, their nonsensical behavior. These chapters will try to answer the vexed question of what is there to be understood and why we laugh... or not. Finally, the problem of how to market a performance, and the semiotic issues it raises, will be addressed. This will lead us to the pragmatic sphere. Analyzing a circus show is not only a matter of identifying the spectacular signs and structures it uses. It consists also and foremost of understanding the dynamic nature of performance itself, its contractual nature, its articulation to the socio-semiotics of its cultural context. The coda will glance at the performers' bodies, and will somersault over evolutionary time to ask a challenging question: where does the circus come from?

The ambition of this book is above all to understand how so much meaning is produced for so many circus audiences the world over, how circus, in its numerous cultural forms, stirs emotions and activates cognition, how both are combined in elusive exhilarating experiences. Ultimately, I will have succeeded if its reading enhances the pleasure of "going to the circus." The book is grounded on thirty years of enjoyable research in Europe, Asia and the Americas. It is based on multiple viewings of circus performances and their verbal copies, at times helped by audio recordings, interviews, and photographs. It is concerned with the interface between the performance and the audience rather than backstage information to which the general public has no access. All this fieldwork would not have been possible without the support of the Social Sciences and Humanities Research Council of Canada, the John Simon Guggenheim Foundation, the Wenner-Gren Foundation for Anthropological Research, the Connaught Foundation and the Killam Foundation. My gratitude goes also to my university, in particular Victoria College in the University of Toronto, which has consistently supported me through multiple smaller grants "to go to the circus". Thanks to them, I was able to visit distant places such as Cannanore and Feroke (India), Semarang and Surakarta (Indonesia), and to discover there new facets of this popular performing art in the midst of cultures with which I was not familiar. My gratitude also goes to Professor Mahesh Mangalat, who was a graduate student in performance studies when he guided me through his native Kerala on the pursuit of circuses both big and small, and to Eko Setyo

Utomo, now a magazine editor in Jakarta, who was studying semiotics at the Universitas Indonesia when he helped me communicate with the Punakawans, the clowns of the Wayang Orang, in his native Java.

Finally, this volume would not have taken shape without the kind invitation of the editors of the SCC series, in particular Professor Paul Cobley whose kind encouragements and enlightened editorial advice are gratefully acknowledged. Any errors that may be found in the text remains, of course, entirely mine.

Although none of the chapters in this book is a mere reprinting of previously published material, some chapters makes extensive use of the contents of articles which appeared during the last decades either in English or in French. This applies particularly to Chapters 2, 3, 6, 8, and 9 which are based in part on articles or book chapters which first appeared respectively in *Communication and Cognition*, vol. 14 (pp. 132–152); *The Annals of the New York Academy of Sciences*, vol. 364 (pp. 18–26); *Anthropologica*, vol. 27 (pp. 101–121); *Multimedial Communication*, vol. 2 (pp. 63–75); *Approaches to Semiotics 96: Beyond Goffman* (pp. 409–443). The permission of the editors is gratefully acknowledged.

The drawings which illustrate some of the chapters in this book are not meant to represent actual acts or artist. Their purpose is to convey in schematic forms the most important types of circus acts that are discussed in the chapters in which they are featured. These composite renderings have been elaborated from sets of photographs taken by the author during his fieldwork research between 1980 and 2008.

Last but not least, I dedicate this volume to the memory of my early mentors: Firmin Bouglione (1905–1980) and Claude Lévi-Strauss (1908–2009).

Chapter 1
The production of circus space

My friend Nigel thinks he has arranged a meeting for me to become acquainted with the resident clown of the Blackpool Tower Circus. I have published several articles about his predecessor, the celebrated Charlie Cairoli, and I am planning to interview the new clown for this book. Nigel has secured two seats on the front row. We arrive early and he suggests that we go immediately backstage so that we can introduce ourselves before the show starts. He leaves me on the side, negotiates with the attendant who guards the access, and rushes to see the administrator who reigns behind the red curtain. Nigel soon comes back. He looks embarrassed. Interviews are granted only for radio or television, and have to be scheduled in advance. So said the clown's mother who is the overseer of this circus's inner world. We go back to our cramped seats. Nigel is disappointed. He thought that his involvement with circus friends associations would give him some degree of access privilege. Never mind. I understand. I know the rules. Nigel relaxes. As the show begins, Nigel, who is taller than I am, extends his legs and puts his feet on the ring curb. After the first act, comes the clown who starts his antics. He soon walks toward Nigel. "Are you an artist?" The tone is deceivingly polite. It sounds as if it's a part of the welcoming routine. "No" – "Then, get your feet out of the ring!" The voice is now loud and aggressive. It is a very public reprimand, an undiplomatic reminder that circus space is not to be tampered with. Some other clowns might have been less rude and more funny, and have handled the situation with more subtlety but this anecdote forcefully brings to the fore that within the circus confines the audience must know what its proper place is.

1.1. The constraints of nomadic life

No human group is nomadic by choice. This mode of existence with respect to space is an adaptation to the distribution over vast territories of the resources which a particular group needs for its subsistence. It applies to resources that can be exploited directly or indirectly through the mediation of other groups. This ecological principle must be kept in mind when considering the relationship of the circus to space. It is crucial for understanding the way in which the circus has generated over its long existence a *sui generis* spatial semiotics.

In the midst of millennia-old sedentary cultures, the circus is a vivid reminder of another way of life that characterized the mode of existence of prehistoric populations and which still survives among some hunter-gatherer and pastoralist tribes. Nowadays a literary tradition and a strong promotional narrative construe circus life as an existential choice that embodies a dream-like freedom for city dwellers caught in the shackles of their daily routines. This romancing of the circus is largely a modern fallacy. Running away with the circus sounds both heroic and liberating. The actual nomadic condition is more ambiguous and challenging than the poetic themes it has spawned as it is rooted in ethnic discrimination. The circus originally was a strategy of ephemeral acceptance and precarious survival devised by ethnic minorities that were not allowed to settle for business in villages and towns. They were providing instead for short durations of time a variety of exotic services among which were extraordinary entertainments. In industrial and post-industrial societies the circus became progressively one of the performing arts that define culture. Its status as an artistic genre that commands respect is a recent phenomenon. Today's relative gentrification of the circus in the form of national institutions, heritage monuments, official festivals, and multinational enterprises, emerged in parallel to the perpetuation of an ancestral nomadic way of life that, for many circus families, still consists of eking a living out of the social environment by performing spectacular feats. The most successful among these nomadic lineages may now legitimately own lands and buildings but their trading in a symbolic commodity such as circus performances requires a constant or at least seasonal traveling. To be effective, the wonders they cater for cannot breed familiarity. This implies a particularly constraining relationship to space that generates some contradictions that must be negotiated.

The first contradiction concerns the ratio space / demography. Circus needs free space and an audience in order to draw its resources from its social environment. Its target must be areas with higher population densities. But these areas are also those in which space has become a rare commodity. Urban centers are spatially saturated. Most modern cities have replaced their polyvalent fairgrounds and market squares with commercial malls and parking lots or buildings. Often, the spatial constraints tend to decrease as the population spreads toward the periphery of the cities, but when the population is widely distributed over large areas, the challenge is then to attract the public to the circus from further and further away. Performing in sparsely populated regions demands additional traveling at a cost that is not necessarily compensated by larger audiences. Optimally, a traveling circus must therefore operate in a conveniently located space at a price that is much less than the income it receives from its public. City space is rare and can be secured only for a limited time and for a high daily rent. Peripheral space is more affordable but involves the risk of being out of reach. Ironically, it may happen that a circus pitches its tent on a parking lot but the public fails to show up because of the resulting lack of parking space in the vicinity. In any case, the circus always temporarily disrupts the spatial economy and semiotics of the urban fabric into which it inserts itself, causing displacements and detours, upsetting the meaningful civil landscape by re-centering public attention to itself, its own pace, space and architecture.

The second spatial contradiction is inherent to the mode of operation of the circus: It must both show and hide the wonders it contains. It is indeed essential to protect from public sight the performance which must be seen only in exchange of a payment commensurate with the visibility afforded by the location of the seat in the tent. But it must also reveal enough of the performance to convince a potential audience that paying for an admission ticket is a fair deal. Hence the monumental display of signs – in both the commercial and theoretical sense of the term – which purport to freely disclose the extraordinary nature of the spectacle to be seen inside without delivering too much of the actual experience. This priming strategy involves drastic spatial constraints for a nomadic enterprise because the border between the two cannot be purely symbolic. There must be plenty of fences and screens to compensate for the irresistible enticement of the external displays. But these obstacles to public permeability must be easily portable and constructible, hence their relative fragility. This is why they can be effective only if they are supported by a strong semiotic system of spatial values which makes such fences and screens symbolically forbidding, and the paths between the two strictly regulated.

There is a third characteristic of the specific spatial semiotics of the circus as it has become a part of modern cultures. This condition does not generate an inner contradiction but a signifying visual contrast. It opposes an ephemeral conical or pyramidal architecture to the immutable rectangular patterns of cityscapes. The enclosed space of the circus evokes the yurts and the tents of nomadic populations. There is no discontinuity of functions and structural imperatives between, on the one hand, these shelters adapted to the geographical and climatic features of the steppes and deserts, and, on the other, the circus's demands for a flexible, portable, and protective shell that is able to counter meteorological hazards such as rain and wind as well as protect from the sun.

The presence of a traveling circus in a city or a village is immediately signaled by this irruption of an alien morphology closer to the natural forms of dunes and hills than the cubic shapes that are the mark of urban landscapes. When permanent circuses have been built in towns, the architects usually preserved a basic circular form and a more or less conical roof.

But this spatial delimitation through fencing out a portion of territory and constructing an envelope of canvass or plastic is only the first step in the creation of the space of the circus: its inner world is structured according to a rigorous algorithm.

1.2. The spatial algorithm of the circus

The first gesture of a circus as it reaches the lot which has been assigned to it through a previous negotiation with the city or a private land owner is to mark out various portions of this space. The team in charge of this task drives there ahead of the convoys and traces whitewash lines on the ground so that the trucks can park in predetermined slots as they arrive and do not block the areas that are needed for the main tent and other temporary constructions. The team applies a general algorithm and adapts it to the particular conditions of the new lot. This algorithm involves a small number of instructions that are used to draft a kind of blueprint on the ground that adumbrates the manner in which the circus will be built on this lot with both invariant dimensions, proportions, and relations as well some free variations which may be required in view of the properties of the area that has been allotted. It may be a sport field, a parking lot, a city square or a pasture, each with different geometrical and resistance qualities that must be factored in the mode of implantation of the circus topology which possesses its own pragmatic and symbolic constraints.

The focus of this topology is the circus ring with respect to which the whole construction will be organized, but no less important is the selection of an axis which will serve as the absolute spatial reference for the inner structure of the whole circus. This axis will determine where the entrance to the ring will be located. Ideally this axis will be aligned, in the opposite direction, with the main entrance gate for the public, a very sensitive locus as it will be the interface with the population at large. This is often a monumental front decorated with enticing banners and painted panels showing vivid images of circus icons purporting to visually convey the contents of the performance. However, local constraints may force the circus surveyors to distort this axis in a way that preserves only the symbolic diametric opposition between the entrance of the public and the entrance of the artists.

The circus algorithm indeed generates a set of topological oppositions that produces spatial meanings. There are four basic relations of opposition: (1) the space of the circus is disjointed from the urban space within which it is implanted; (2) the space of the performance is disjointed from the space of the audience which has secured access to the circus space through the payment of an admission fee; (3) within the circus space, the space reserved to the audience is disjointed from the private space of the circus population, and (4) the space of the performance is disjointed from both the audience space and the circus private space. All these spaces are related in ways that can be represented by the successive embedding of these different areas, each one being related to the others by paths that are strictly controlled both by material and human enforcements, and by symbolic, quasi-taboo values. The sharp reaction of the clown of the Blackpool Tower Circus which I reported in the initial anecdote of this chapter bears witness to the fundamental distinction that exists between these marked spaces: by casually resting his feet on the ring curb my friend Nigel showed disrespect for the performance space and transgressed, albeit minimally, a meaningful boundary. The public has no business putting its feet in the ring. This could be a serious hazard if it happened to interfere with a dangerous performance but, perhaps more importantly, it would violate the symbolic integrity of this special space which is defined by its redundant opposition to three embedded zones.

In practice, each zone, with the exception of the ring, can be variously morphed, either shrunk or dilated in order to adapt to circumstances. In traditional circuses, in which acrobatic horsemanship dictates an invariant radius that is optimal for this specialty, the diameter is approximately 13 meters long. This constant is generally observed mainly in circuses which feature animal acts. All other areas can be expanded or reduced as needed but the topological relations between them do not change. When the lot is too small for the whole compact circus territory, parts of its animal and human population are located in pockets outside the main periphery but the basic topology remains the same.

For the spectators, experiencing circus space is markedly different from simply covering some distances as it would be the case if they were crossing the city square or wandering in the field before the circus pitches its tent and erects its fences. Spectators are confronted by an unusual density of thresholds as if it were, *mutatis mutandis*, a private home. Access and paths are regulated as is the time at which some gates can be crossed under specified conditions. The spectators navigate a new geography through corridors bordered by forbidden zones. Dangers may be lurking behind canvasses and between trucks much like they are in the narrow streets of an unfamiliar town. A previously homogeneous pedestrian space has been turned into an alien complex place. The usual itineraries are subverted by inner detours and the free exploration of this space is strongly discouraged. The interpersonal distance which normally ensures the fluidity of the pedestrian traffic is most of the times transformed within the circus into the packed crowd mode and, when a show is sold out, the private seating space of each individual in the most affordable categories is reduced to a bare minimum.

The fine line between proximity and promiscuity may create a sense of ritualistic fusing of differences.

But there is more. Not only is this space visually, acoustically, and haptically saturated but it is also endowed with specific olfactory qualities. The smell of a place is an important dimension of spatial semiotics. In circuses which feature animals the air is imbued with their acidic and sulfuric olfactory presence that blends with the sweeter smell of the quasi ritualistic food consumed by the audience such as candy floss and popcorn. In addition, the fresh sawdust that is traditionally spread inside the ring and, sometimes, the earth of the field upon which the tent is erected combine to create unusual effluvia – the smell of the circus which awakens childhood memories in the audience. This typical property of the circus atmosphere functions both as an aggressive territorial marker in as much as it is an irrepressible sign of otherness, and as a regressive invitation to what psychoanalysts would call a return to the anal stage of human development (see R.A. Lewin 1999).

For the audience, the backstage that envelops the circus public space is rather undifferentiated. But for the circus folks who populate this space, it is rigorously structured like a city with its exclusive quarters, working class dwellings, and specialized premises. The circus hierarchy is mapped onto the lot. Between the animal enclosures at the back and the directorial family trailers, often ostentatiously located at the front, distinct areas are staked out and invisible fences prevent undesirable mingling. This inner political geography has been implemented in advance by the early surveyors who assigned every emplacement according to their technical and socio-cultural algorithms. This may vary, of course, with the scale of the circus, and the type of organization and social culture that characterize it.

Somewhat in the same manner, the socio-cultural differences among the spectators are mapped onto the audience space. City officials and media stars are often granted invitations and are seated in the VIP area among those who can afford the most expensive admission tickets. Loggias and individual chairs are numbered. The other categories are priced according to the degree of comfort and visibility they afford, with the cheapest reserved for narrow planks at the top of the side bleachers. The crowd is filtered by a uniformed team and everyone is directed to the category of seat where he or she belongs.

1.3. Squaring the circle

The whole circus architecture is organized with respect to the ring which is the redundantly marked focus of all the other activities, its semiotic center of gravity.

It is a perfect circle on the ground and it is used as such by the performers. But from the point of view of the spectators it is necessarily perceived as an ellipse which appears to be more elongated as it is seen from further away on its periphery. To understand the way in which the audience follows the unfolding of the performance requires taking perspective into consideration while keeping in mind that, cognitively, the perception is corrected by the knowledge that the circus arena is circular. Naturally, the closer one is to the ground, the more flattened the circle appears; and the higher one is located in the circus the more the ring looks like a circle. There is a give and take between perceiving the details and processing the whole in a single vista. It is actually equally interesting to visually experience a circus spectacle from both ends of the scale. But on average the audience interprets the movements they follow in the ring as taking place in a circular space.

However, it is relevant to note that from the point of view of perception, the ellipse formed by the ring corresponds to the very shape of the fovea in the eyes. This is precisely where visual information is first processed with maximal accuracy with the highest sensitivity to details and colors. This is also where all the action is concentrated and all the spotlights are focused. It is an optimal apparatus for experiencing the complex dynamics of the successive displays in a circus program.

The ring is a space strongly marked by its mostly symbolic enclosure. It offers a space that is, so to speak, put between parentheses. From an information theory point of view, it is noise-free. Each successive act saturates the information channel created by the ring. Everything in it is meaningful. At the end of each act, nothing is left. It is again a clean slate, ready for the next one.

But the space of the ring is not purely passive. It is not neutral. It is constituted by a set of binary geometrical oppositions that play the role of spatial algorithms for the construction of significant categories of location and movement. These virtual oppositions include: (1) inside versus outside the ring; (2) its center versus its periphery; (3) diametric versus circular movement; (4) horizontal plane versus the vertical dimension. These topological operators can combine and contribute to the elaboration of meaningful positions, displacements, and transformations in as much as they add oppositional values to what would otherwise be a simple progress along a bi- or tri-dimensional continuum. Of course, technically, circus artists deal with the continuum of the physical space with its actual distances and gravitational forces, but for the production of spectacular meaning they exploit discrete semiotic categories such as the ones listed above. The effective staging of a circus act consists of blending the two as seamlessly as possible.

For the purpose of analysis, the algorithms that were proposed by Greimas in the elaboration of his semio-linguistic theory (1987, 1989) can prove to be useful conceptual tools. The ordering of concepts through their relations of contradiction and contrariness, usually graphically represented as logical squares, can apply to any semantic domain. Whether they are the ultimate limit for understanding how meaning is articulated in any medium is an issue that remains to be further probed. But they provide a productive approach for conceptualizing what does happen in a circus ring when any moves and actions by the performers, both humans and animals, make sense beyond their mere physicality. The subtitle of this section, "the squaring of the circle" refers to the semiotic processing of the continuous space of the ring as a set of oppositional values such as the ones that stand between the sides or between the angles of a quadrilateral figure. This virtual square is super-imposed upon the continuous surface of the circus ring as a cognitive structure that can generate sense in the form of meaningful actions and interactions. A displacement from the periphery to the center, or the reverse, causes a change of status, as does a movement on the vertical axis, or the crossing from the public space to the performing space.

1.4. Olli and Illi: playing with space and desire

A typical example will illustrate the way in which the space of performance itself operates in a clown act. Olli and Illi are two clowns who were a part of the program of the Swiss circus Knie when they were observed in (1984). They presented several acts during the show. The "bird" act will now be described and analyzed in view of the above remarks.

In the dimmed light that followed the end of the previous act, the song of a mysterious bird is heard coming from the top of the tent. Olli, a man, emerges from the audience space under a bright spotlight and walks down toward the ring from the left side of the ring with respect to the diametric axis that originates with the performers' normal entrance. He carries a long green ladder and proceeds while repeatedly calling "Little bird! Little bird"! Illi, a woman, enters the ring holding a very large bird cage made of reed. As he sees her with the cage, Olli changes his calling to "Big bird! Big bird! " As soon as the two meet in the center of the ring, they endeavor to catch the invisible bird which seems to be high above. They each climb the ladder in turn while the other holds it vertical. But a series of mishaps prevent them from achieving their goal: they fall from the ladder, some rungs break under their weight, the sides come apart and "hurt" them, and they eventually fight each other when they fail to put the ladder back together. Then the woman, Illi, gets another ladder from backstage. Olli, the man, starts climbing it and they decide to play some music in order to attract the bird. Olli climbs down, is given an accordion and climbs up again, but this time with his back toward the ladder while Illi holds it. Suddenly, Illi declares that she wants to play some music too and leaves the ring. The ladder is not supported any longer but Olli keeps it vertical as he is also a balancing acrobat who can maintain his composure, standing on the top of an unsupported ladder. He keeps playing his accordion in this position. Illi comes back and wants to hand over the big cage to Olli, reminding him that their goal is to catch the bird. She throws the cage to Olli who catches it but after some awkward attempts at reaching for the invisible bird he drops the cage that falls on Illi. As the cage has no bottom, Illi is now within the cage. She mimics with her arms the fluttering of wings. Olli jumps from the ladder, holds the cage and triumphantly says "Bird!" His quest is over. They exit the ring together while the audience applauds.

This was not the only act produced by Olli and Illi in this program. In the two other interludes that preceded the "bird" act, they performed gags as a couple whose activities were complementary. This act starts with a markedly different situation: Their respective spaces are disjointed since the man is wandering in the public space while the woman enters the ring by the normal way. When they eventually meet in the center of the ring their relationship is dysfunctional as the successive gags consist of failures by Olli to capture the out-of-reach object of his desire. Her help is, to say the least, ambiguous and even turns to symbolic hostility when they mimic a gun fight with the rungs of the collapsed first ladder. Perpendicular to their "down to earth" interactions in the center of the ring, the vertical axis leads to an invisible and unreachable object of desire that is assumed to reside in the upper region of the circus tent, the bird whose seductive song is heard. There is, therefore, a second spatial disjunction along the vertical dimension. Two means are used in order to attempt to overcome the vertical distance: the ladder, which makes it possible to proceed toward the top, and the music, which is used to try to attract the bird toward the bottom. But they both prove to be obstacles rather than helping. It is very significant that the cage brought by Illi is grossly disproportionate with respect to the usual size of a songbird which could easily escape even if it was caught. It is a spatial metaphor bearing upon the relation between container and content or between desire and satisfaction. The visual conclusion of this lofty quest is that what Olli wanted to capture is what he already had: that is, Illi, who actually fits the dimension of the cage and stands on the same plane as he does. The realization of this "happy ending" is achieved by a vertical descent to the ground. Illi and Olli leave the ring through the normal way to the backstage holding each other again as a couple. This fable of a lost and found again harmony between a man and a woman was implemented by articulating its semiotic unfolding entirely by visual means. It has used the system of oppositions provided by the spatial matrix of the circus to signify both the problem and its resolution. The only words uttered were "little bird" and "big bird". In fact, these words were redundant since the sound and the artifact are sufficient to convey the contrast.

To better understand the use of spatial categories in the producing of such an act, let us pay attention to what was not done. Olli did not enter the ring through the normal entrance, nor even along the normal axis. His movement was devious (coming sideways) and transgressive (crossing the symbolic boundary of the ring curb from the public to the performance space). But he did not move along the inside periphery of the ring which is the path of animals, a potentially demeaning trajectory. He entered the ring and stood with his ladder at the very center, thus occupying with Illi the place of heroes where pitfalls are usually more tragic than comic.

Some aspects of this descriptive interpretation can certainly be considered as a kind of reverse semiotic engineering. Clowns know very well what they are doing and their mostly unwritten scripts are very precise even though they allow for minor variations according to contexts and circumstances. But a large part of this unwritten script is based on the spatial code of the circus which, like the grammar of spoken languages, is implicitly known by whoever utters a sentence. These spatial categories that are meaningfully manipulated in circus acts are the same as the ones that are cognitively alive in everyday life. But the prism of the circus makes them more salient because it concentrates them in a strongly bounded space whose whole matrix can be perceived in a single vista. In the following chapters, we will encounter many examples of the ways in which the technical constraints that govern circus acts combine with these spatial semiotic categories to produce meaningful displays of skills moulded into dramatic visual narratives.

Chapter 2
The time of the circus. Cognitive and emotional dimensions of acrobatics and other circus acts

As the train enters the outskirts of Duisburg, old memories flock to my mind. I am due to meet there an old friend, the juggler Chris Christiansen who performs this year at the German circus Busch-Roland. I have known Christian for more than a decade during which I witnessed several ups and down in his artistic career. Obsessed with perfection, as many solo jugglers are, he has been through a succession of crises when he thought that he should renounce juggling. Then he had bounced back again and again. Now his act has become a kind of quintessence of the art: paradoxically, he juggles with a single ball.

Christian welcomes me on the platform and picks up the conversation where we left it three years earlier. This past year, he has read Genet's Le Funambule *and Nietzsche's* The Birth of Tragedy, *and he has become acquainted with a star, or rather a saint of juggling, the great Francis Brunn, who pinpointed all his technical errors; he stopped working for six months, just busking from time to time in order to meet his basic survival needs; he started again from scratch; he purified his act: only a white handball, like his mentor, and the ping pong balls with which he concludes his act; but this latter trick, which consists of projecting and catching these small balls with his mouth, is strictly for the public; the big white ball is for himself; presently he works in this circus but he is very unhappy; they pay him well although, in his opinion, his act as it stands now is not worth it; last night, he has been terrible; he is so depressed; I should not expect anything great; perhaps in ten years if he lives long enough; and so on. I am used to Christian's self-deprecating laments. I had decided to visit him in Duisburg because it is always a great pleasure meeting him when an opportunity arises and I wanted to take some photos of his act which I was planning to analyze in an article. As he drives me to the circus lot, I hears about his latest philosophical discovery, Heinrich von Kleist's* The Puppet Theatre *which he had found by chance in a French translation. And, again, he complains how bad his act still is. As to the photos, he has secured for me a front row seat.*

The performance starts in the dark. As the recorded Schoenberg quartet he has chosen for this latest version of his juggling act fills the tent with weightless music, the spotlight reveals Christian in a crouched position in the centre of the ring. All in white, his body slowly unfolds and the white ball emerges and becomes alive, running along his arms and legs, jumping here and there with constant speed, taking to the air to land apparently on a place of its choice, his elbow, the tip of a foot, a finger, his soles after he does a somersault while the ball is alight. Body and ball glide around each other, effortlessly, as if gravity had been conquered and transposed in another dimension. My eyes are filled with tears. It is an epiphany. I do not think of picking up the camera. Absolute beauty cannot be captured as an object lest it becomes trivial. It might even have dissolved at the first flash.

After the show, Christian apologizes for his poor performance. In the third routine his leg was not as straight as it should be. Then he goes on about journalists and circus folks who do not see the difference. What puzzles him most is that in every town the circus visited, his act was the only one that was mentioned in the newspapers to the dismay of the other artists who were teasing him, joking that he could not even juggle two balls.

2.1. Circus acts as texts

In my earlier book on *Circus and Culture* (1976), I elaborated a semiotic model whose purpose was to account for all observable components of circus acts that could be understood as signs. I also analyzed the implicit narrative structures holding those elements together. Central to this attempt was the Lotmanian concept of a multi-media message construed as a "text", i.e., a finite set of elements having the status of signs and being logically inter-connected so as to form an intelligible whole, relevant to some aspects of their contextual culture (Lotman 1977 [1970]; Bouissac 1976: 90–91, 126–127). The level of observation on which this analysis was conducted remained close to the experience of an attentive spectator immersed in the circus performance situation. The only difference between such an involvement in the spontaneous understanding of circus spectacles and the kind of semiotic approach I have developed, is that in the latter some time is allotted to reconsidering what has taken place in the ring in order to sort out and classify whatever identifiable "objects" were used, and to become aware of which aspects of the "objects" were actualized by combining with each other as well as which transformations these "objects" underwent in the process. By "objects" I meant any identifiable elements that contributed to the meaning of the acts, such as the style and color of the costumes; the gestures made by the performers; the props; the kind of music that accompanied the action; the species of the animals involved; the apparatuses; and the tricks that were displayed. The formulation of a descriptive theory of the circus was made possible by *ad hoc* borrowings from various linguistic, cybernetic, and anthropological models, inasmuch as the description of a cultural phenomenon in a terminology that is more general than the one used by the participants in this activity, enables one to grasp it as a sub-set of a more comprehensive whole of patterned social behaviors. This also makes it possible to determine its specificity.

For instance, the juggling act that was briefly described in the prefatory anecdote to this chapter could be analyzed with respect to the paradigm of juggling as a solo act as opposed to team work like the one we encountered in the introductory chapter. Since the technical difficulty of this circus genre is assumed to be commensurate with the number of balls or other objects that are kept in the air, juggling with a single ball is semiotically marked with respect to the code of the circus. Furthermore, achieving extraordinary feats of control and balance with this unique object and sustaining the interest of the audience involve an efficient construction of the act that unfolds in a progressive manner with increasingly sophisticated exercises blending ballet and acrobatic movements. These are complemented by the artistic lighting, the classicism of the costume and the high culture music that accompanies the act. The minimalist style is underlined by the choice of white for the costume and for the ball, itself an ordinary volley ball that belongs to the paradigm of sport and play artifacts, not to production of useful objects. Some of these features are the results of deliberate choices by the artist, some other belong to the cultural code of the circus and to other cultural institutions such as sport and music. Probing further the implications of this juggling act will lead to the tacit knowledge in which its deep meaning is grounded: the relation of actions to goods and services which jugglers invert, and the further transgression that represents in itself a solo action with respect to the social imperative since it is a gratuitous, useless solitary expense of energy (Bouissac 1976: 64–89).

However productive this model may be in providing a methodology for observing and explaining circus performances, two important aspects were overlooked, or at least taken for granted in this approach: first, the fact that even the simplest circus act must be ultimately described as a brain performing for other brains, that is, it involves a fundamental understanding of motor, cognitive and emotional functions; secondly, the fact that performance involves time in a particular capacity. In dealing with those two closely connected aspects this chapter will attempt to achieve further progress in the description and elucidation of circus acts and in the understanding of what constitutes their specific cross-cultural, perhaps pan-human significance.

For this, I will first rely on the concepts of "plans", "tools" and "actions", and focus on developmental cognition rather than structural calculus. This does not mean that the validity of the structural approach is denied. With a "text" as complex as a circus performance, several levels of interpretation are not only possible but also unavoidable. The way in which these various levels are inter-connected is not as yet obvious, but it should be pointed out that to set forth a comprehensive theory which would account for the totality of the possible interpretations of the circus would amount to producing a theory of culture, a goal which is still a challenging task in the present state of the art in cultural studies. In addition, it might be a fallacy to assume the possibility of producing a unified, all-encompassing, and consistent theory of circus performances, because the various responses of the brain's sub-systems to a spectacle as engrossing as the circus are somewhat anarchical. It is now well known that reactions of the most evolutionarily ancient parts of the brain such those that control fear, for instance, can be in conflict with more recent regions that process linguistic or cultural information. Our limbic system, our frontal lobes, our parietal regions are all involved in making biological and cultural sense of a circus act. As we will note in subsequent chapters, the advanced knowledge that a spectacular near miss is staged does not prevent an observer from experiencing anguish and fright. The discovery of mirror neurons, these motor neurons which fire both when we perform a movement and when we witness a movement performed by someone else, certainly account for our being deeply engaged by dangerous balancing or catching acts. Our capacity to empathize can trigger fear responses while our semantic memory recognizes allusions to classical sculptures in the poses taken by an acrobat or to folk narratives evoked by the costumes and the music.

Of course, it is difficult to sort out what is happening in each spectator's brain. At least, what can be considered certain is that, given the usual intensity of the responses of the audience, a very high number of diverse cognitive stimulations and semiotic operations must be at work during the reception of a circus performance. As my response in real time to Chris Christiansen's act showed in the anecdote told at the beginning of this chapter, cognition and emotion are entangled in such an intense, multi-modal experience that the best plans (such as taking photographs at pre-set moments) can be forgotten in the heat of the action. This chapter, will concern itself with only a few of these aspects, and will attempt to delineate the circus phenomenon with respect to two poles: cultural specificity and pan-human relevance.

2.2. A brain to brain affair

An acrobat's or an animal trainer's achievements are not primarily feats of physical strength and moral endurance: they involve also cognitive performances such as acute perceptions, selective memory, adaptive moves, efficient processing of feedback information, accurate assessments of situations, correct anticipations, and felicitous decision making from instant to instants, to list only a few of the many mental operations which have to be inferred if one is to account for those individuals' eventual survival of the tests with which they are confronted. The features listed above apply to the day-to-day completion of the circus acts in which these artists specialize, but we must not overlook the fact that they perform according to a pre-conceived "score" (in the musical sense) in view of which they have trained themselves and others (humans or animals). The successful negotiations of a circus act depends on both the blueprint of this act stored in the artist's memory and the relative flexibility of his/her skill during the application of the blueprint to real, ever-changing, conditions that may include variables involving climate and temperature which may significantly impact on the properties of their props; material conditions such as the quality of the ground on which the circus is built; social atmosphere that may or may not convey a sense of empathy; physical and emotional stress; human and equipment failures, and so on. Circus acts as conceptions and implementations of "programs" display events of rather high order of complexity that only brains of potentially similar capacity can follow and understand. The nature of this "understanding" deserves close scrutiny, because it is far from obvious that what even an articulate spectator is able to report verbally about his/her experience actually is what is the most cognitively relevant in processing all the information comprising this experience. A feeling of saturation is quite common when one has just left a circus performance, and it takes some time until some form of selective reporting can be made. It is also a common experience to discover upon a second viewing of a show that many details had been overlooked during the first one. This does not mean, of course, that the information has not been processed by the spectator's brain but simply that it has not registered as an explicit memory.

A reason for this feeling of information saturation is undoubtedly the fact that, in terms of communication theory, the channels conveying a circus performance are practically noiseless, that is, they are totally filled with relevant information to the point of creating an overload. In contrast with the everyday conditions in which we are accustomed to select only relevant information amidst a noisy flow, we are confronted in the circus with a much higher percentage of relevant information. In addition to this, the sophistication of the text structure and the cultural pertinence of the operations performed (in brief the purely semiotic nature of the experience) trigger so many decoding operations at such a fast pace that some are bound to be missed or to misfire.

All this implies that intellectual and cognitive maturation as well as sufficient acculturation are prerequisites for the understanding of circus performances in which numerous semiotic systems are entangled with each other. The supposedly essential link between children and circuses, although historically and culturally motivated, is nevertheless a misconception if it means that circus acts are made for children. It is a common place among circus artists to complain about afternoon audiences that are primarily made up of children, including very young ones, because children react mostly indiscriminately, don't understand, and therefore don't appreciate the technical complexity and aesthetic value of their acts on the level intended by their artistic creativity. However, the irresistible attraction that the circus holds for many children must be based on a definite, albeit less sophisticated kind of appreciation which involves multisensorial stimulations and the excitement of discovering a new environment. But children can hardly be blamed for a lack of connoisseurship which requires both maturation and education. The codes of the circus must indeed be learned as all other cultural codes.

As Piaget and his followers have demonstrated, all fundamental cognitive functions develop serially in time; crucial concepts and mental operations involved in the child's progressive construction of reality are necessary for the complete understanding of circus acts. This understanding requires indeed not only that the spatial and temporal fields as well as the elaboration of groups of displacements be acquired, but also that the concept of causality be fully developed and a logical universe be constructed. A textual and cultural competence is also required if the structure of a circus act and the cross-references it usually implies are to be followed. For instance, a Wagnerian melody may serve first as an introduction to an acrobatic act, thus setting a mood of seriousness and tragic grandeur, then a few acts later the same melody will be alluded to by a clown playing trumpet while another clown performs some antics, with a comical effect as a result of the incongruity of the musical accompaniment. Another example could be the graceful imitations by acrobats of the famous postures of classical sculptures such as the discus-thrower or the running Mercury. Numerous ethnic, folkloric, and literary allusions are commonly found in the performers' costumes and behavior. In Indian circuses, for instance, visual allusions to religious icons such as the dance of Shiva or the flute of Krishna are common occurrences.

It is symptomatic that for many children the circus is associated with some of its elements which are not necessarily essential to the acts performed, such as remarkable animals, the gross behavior of the clowns or even the smell and taste of popcorn and the acquisition of a balloon! An assessment such as the one expressed by psychologist Tarachow in "Circuses and clowns" (1951: 171–185) can be questioned as a misrepresentation of the art of clowning: "[The clown] engages in endless bickering or problems with another clown [...] One might endlessly break dishes, another eat enormous amounts of pie [...]". In fact, as we will see in the last section of this chapter, clown acts are dramatically structured and the actions they display are not haphazard. Plates are broken only in carefully constructed context and within a dialogical structure. But the meaningless behaviors listed by Tarachow may indeed be what children mostly perceive and remember until they eventually learn the code and can make better sense of clown antics. In the early stages of their cognitive development, children indeed seem to truly enjoy as a liberating experience the view of clowns who merrily indulge in precisely what children are prevented from doing by their caregivers and educators. Circus, specially clowning, often becomes a children's play theme. As we will see in Chapter 7, the kinds of make-up some clowns wear invite such a spontaneous identification because they integrate elements that are characteristic of the facial morphology of children and can thus invite empathy.

Adolescent and adult circus goers experience also a strong participatory feeling, a phenomenon that cannot be accounted for by mystical explanations even though they themselves refer to such vague terms as the magic of the circus or the supernatural power of the performers through lack of better means of expression. From this point of view, semiotic literacy can empower an audience to better appreciate the "text" and enhance the pleasure it creates. Obviously there is, in this case, a form of interaction whose factors can be analyzed. By shifting the focus of attention from the "objective components of the acts", or the "factors involved in a communication process", to the cognitive operations and the emotional responses that take place in both performers (human or animal) and spectators, I am attempting in this chapter to correct an approach which could lead to an illusory atomistic model. Once every observable element of a circus act has been isolated and categorized, will the same circus act be re-created by putting the elements back together? This is most doubtful, because the cognitive templates, without which any circus act is bound to be meaningless, would be lacking. Two aspects will now be discussed in order to make this point more explicit.

First it seems that all circus acts are primarily made up of successive situations, that is, a combination of factors relevant to an action or to a reaction. A situation is not formed by the sum total of the accessories but by their respective positions in relation to an observational and decision-making agent. The assessments and representations of these successive situations and their segmentation from both the point of view of the artist(s) and the spectator(s) are cognitive processes that at the very least overlap significantly. Situations are still more complex when they involve trained animals who are also, during the act, negotiating successive situations whose representations and assessments must overlap with their trainer's, an aspect which has been particularly well studied by Hediger (1935, 1955, 1967) and which we will consider in more details in the next chapter. Animals do not so much respond to individual stimuli, but process situations more or less flexibly in the light of past experience. To follow trained animal acts attentively implies that the spectator is able to represent to him/herself the situations as they are represented both from the point of view of the trainer and the animal(s); for a naïve spectator the interpretations of situations can be generally biased by the verbal comments printed in the program or made by the presenter. For instance, if "man-eating" is the qualification that has introduced a tiger act, every move made by the animals is bound to be viewed as suspect and threatening. In the same manner, non-verbal behavior produced by the trainer such as acting out as if he/she were constantly on his/her guard conveys an impression of imminent danger. Naturally, a trainer has to constantly monitor the movements and the moods of his/her animals but she/he may either emphasize these worries in order to enhance the drama or mask them through frequently smiling directed to both the audience and the animals. Given that to live means to constantly represent and assess situations with respect to plans and survival, these remarks should make the biological relevance of circus performances obvious, a point that will be fully discussed in the last chapter.

The second aspect, which also has to do with the audience's feeling of participation, is the timing or pacing of actions. The performers set indeed a certain visual rhythm, underlined by the accompanying music that forcefully overcomes the spectators' own time, tuning them in, so to speak, on the same sensorimotor wave length and framing their attention. The performance unfolds, alternating slow and fast rhythms, but maintaining a characteristic tempo until the climax of its conclusion. This phenomenon, which is easily observable if one turns one's attention toward the audience of a circus spectacle, is conditioned by the same neuro-plasticity which explains in part the charismatic power of leaders and the interactional dominance of those who, in every day experience, hold the floor, make the conversation, or steal the show. The circus writer who has most insightfully dealt with those factors is T.K. Pond, who analyzed in *Big Top Rhythms* (1937) the whole gamut of the circus acts from the perspective of muscle control, timing and rhythm. Pond observed performers during the first decades of the twentieth century, a time that is considered one of the golden ages of the circus. "Timeness" or timing is indeed a crucial factor in distinguishing "good" from "bad" circus acts; the spectator's appreciation should not be neglected as a merely "subjective" aspect, if only because the totality of the circus arts depends on the readiness of an audience to pay for "a seat at the circus"; a poor show means sparse audiences and the eventual disappearance of the circus which failed to effectively entertain its public. Most criticisms of circus acts I have heard from circus artists – who more often than not are also spectators – were incriminating the poor quality of the timing. One of my most lucid informants, the clown Charlie Cairoli, mentioned once a troupe of brilliant acrobats who, after years of success, were puzzled by the progressively milder reactions of audiences to their act; he showed them, by a video recording, that although they were performing the same feats as before, they had lost, through mindless routine, their initially excellent timing.

Timing can be defined as the steady pulsation which gives its "musical" unity to an act as if an invisible metronome was ticking in the ears of the performers. They are all on the same dynamic wave length and all their actions are coordinated like those of the musicians in an orchestra. When they enter the ring, acrobats "mark a time": they briefly stop and start again with the same step rhythm which will carry them through their act and will determine the precise relative length not only of the segments of their act but also of their gestures, pauses, and smiles. This integrated rhythm is communicative and it can be said that it carries the audience to the climax of the act.

This is not only true of acrobatics; Charlie Cairoli, in his own clown act, had to provide one of his partners with clues signaling exactly when to start doing the various parts for which he was responsible because this man lacked the sense of proper timing. A delay of a fraction of a second can indeed kill a gag. This aspect of the performance is all the more relevant to a semiotic study of the circus as it involves a factor that research in social inter-action considers to be essential. A circus act does not consist only of what is done in it but also – and in a prominent way – of how it is done with respect to time. However, as it will be suggested in the next section, this is not the only way in which time is involved in a circus act.

2.3. Another kind of time

The ways in which humans conceive and experience time are conditioned not only by a lengthy psychological maturation, but also by cultural inculcation Developmental psychologists (e.g., Piaget 1971a; Brandsträdter 2006) have pointed out that there is no such thing as an intuitive, immediate, pure perception of the flow of time but that, as for spatial organization, sequential steps are necessary towards the construction of personal and socio-cultural time. As put by Miller and Johnson-Laird: "The growth of a child's grasp of temporal relations and concept requires a number of years as Piaget has shown, and the final articulated system is likely to depend on the technology of the culture in which the child is raised" (1976: 76) or in Mair's words: "The perception of temporality itself is built into the (cultural) structure through which the individual awareness makes its path. We have so thoroughly taken over time that we can have no other concept of it than that of the cultural universe within which we are immersed (1978: 24).

Developmental psychologists have also convincingly demonstrated that such concepts of time are dependent on the perception of movement, hence of spatial organization (Piaget 1971b: 362–363). The child's "construction of reality" which slowly emerges from her/his progressive conceptualization of space, movement, speed, etc., comprises a time dimension that is sufficiently polymorphous for justifying cross-cultural investigations in a chronemic perspective, that is, the differential *use* of time according to cultures and sub-cultures, as well as from the point of view of cognition, that is, the various ways in which time is represented and conceived (Lloyd 1972: 76–84).

In western cultures, people alternatively rely on two opposite representations: a linear, irreversible time, and, as most cultures do, a circular, cyclic time. The former is explicit in mathematical thinking and mostly implicit in the serial representations that underlie the tense system of the verbs in languages such as English and French; the latter becomes obvious if we consider our temporal segmentation into recurring weeks, seasons, religious and national celebrations or if we study cosmologies based on cyclical changes. But between or beside those two concepts of time, another kind of time representation plays a prominent function in our "reality": *the time of actions*. As we move closer to intimate experience, fundamental aspects of our cognitive structures tend to become less apparent: we are indeed confronted with the passive resistance of tacit knowledge. Nevertheless there are good reasons to assume that the particular concept of time that is necessary to account for the concept of action is no less "constructed" than the other two. This was clearly evidenced by Piaget's experiments who related the concept of action to the conceptualization of time:

> To the extent, therefore, that action is made the subject of reflection and not merely of intuition, i.e. that reflective analysis replaces pure introspection, the results of the action, its rapidity, and the various events which constitute it, become fused into a coherent framework, in which the order of succession and the colligation of durations are interrelated in precisely the same way as they are in the case of physical time. (Piaget 1971: 262–263)

The concept of action is so central to our structuring of "reality" that it organizes most of the changes according to its principles, from the conception of the universe as a "creation" to the supposition of plots and conspiracies as explanations for minute disturbances in our everyday lives. The kind of time construct that underlies the concept of action is indeed intimately connected with the concepts of "plan" and, consequently, "tool". This perspective on time is also prominent in languages such as Mandarin Chinese and the Slavic tongues which foreground "aspects", that is, whether an action has been completed or is in progress (rather than the linear time of past, present, and future) in their verbal systems.

The importance of those concepts for the relevant segmentation of body movements and behavior was effectively pointed out by Mills, Galanter and Pribram in *Plans and the Structure of Behaviour*, a work which remains a basic reference in the developmental psychology of action (e.g., Brandsträdter 2006):

> The problem is to describe how actions are controlled by an organism's internal representation of its universe. If we consider what these actions are in the normal, freely ranging animal, we must be struck by the extent to which they are organized into patterns. Most psychologists maintain that these action patterns are punctuated by goals and sub-goals, but that does not concern us for the moment. We wish to call attention to the fact that the organization does exist – configuration is just as important a property of behavior as it is of perception. [. . .] What we must provide, therefore, is some way to map the cognitive representation into the appropriate *pattern* of activity. But how are we to analyze this flowing pattern of action into manageable parts? (1960).

One satisfactory answer is to identify plans, i.e., hierarchical processes in the organism "that can control the order in which a sequence of operations is to be performed". The relationship of "plans" to time in the construction of human reality is outlined as follows by Mair: "In both visual and auditory modes we have a process in time, scanning, which is segmented by plans which are timeless. [. . .] Human reality appears to consist of the stable states of achieved or perceived plans, and the paths by which they are achieved or perceived." (1980: 128–129, 1986: 141–142)

It is assumed in this chapter that, if indeed the concept of action results from the timely confluence of psychological maturation and social acculturation (or cultural socialization), it is necessary that at one given point the child grasp a model of "action" in relation to time, plan and tool – and that the instruments that engineer such a representation can only be "tools". No doubt that some toys play an important part in this respect. But there is an experience that very few children escape: most people remember having been taken, willy-nilly, to the circus at a young age. It is an interesting fact that visits to the circus are organized by families and schools, and are therefore to be considered a part of cultural transmission. It is significant that the better circus companies maintain educational activities enjoying general credibility among other pedagogical institutions. In this respect it is at the very least amusing to note that the cover of the Ballantine edition of Piaget's *The Construction of Reality in the Child* (1971) shows, as a superimposition on a young boy's head, some toys among which is an acrobatic clown engaged in a balancing act (specifically: riding a monocycle on a wire).

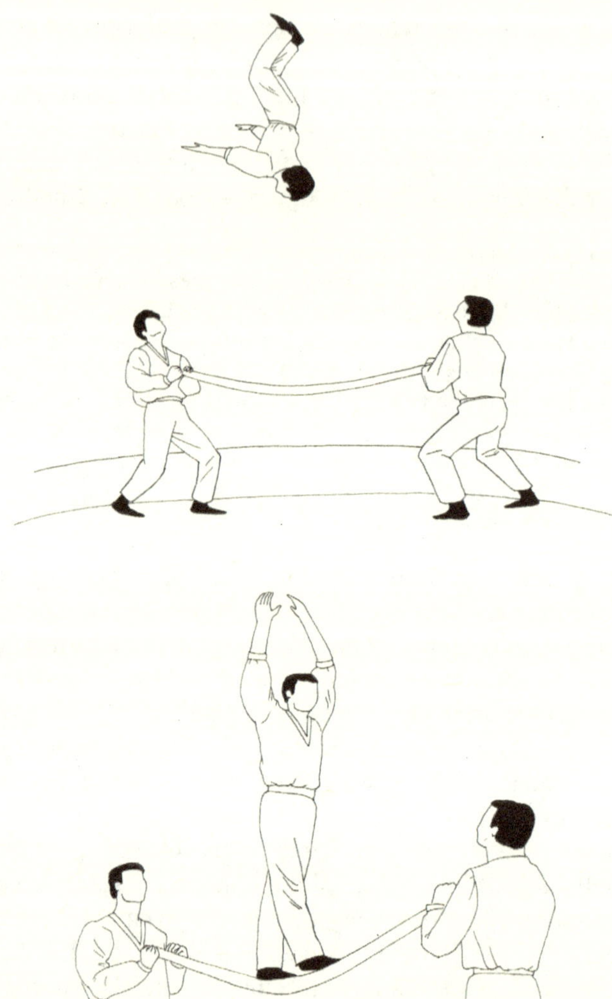

Figure 1. The tools of acrobatic actions can be as simple as a flexible bar, held by two persons, from which an acrobat takes off and upon which he or she lands after performing a somersault, or it can be as complex as a steel cable stretched between two platforms at the top of two metallic towers.

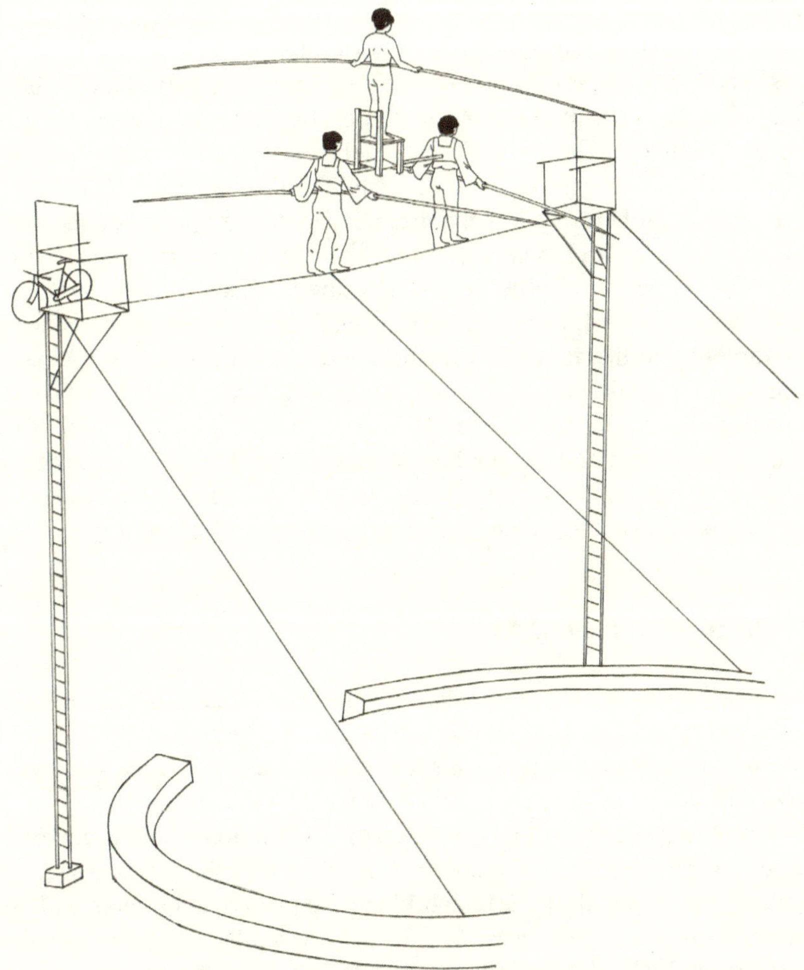

Figure 2. Various props such as a bicycle or a chair can add to the difficulty of successfully completing the crossing of the high wire. The action is facilitated by preventing excessive oscillations of the wire through cables anchored to the ground and balancing poles are used by the acrobats when their spectacular actions involve several participants combined into challenging constructions.

One may suspect that what remains in a child's memory (possibly what has been named by the adult: "look! here is a clown, here is an elephant" and so on) – is not what has actually been the most cognitively decisive in her/his experience of a circus performance. As I will try to demonstrate in the next section, the performances of acrobats and trainers are "pure actions". They consist of "passing tests", "achieving goals", or, in other words, "implementing plans". Their instruments, that is, the setting, the accessories, the artifacts through which they accomplish their feats of strength, balance, or timing are indeed the tools which produce nothing other than the particular kind of time implied in the concept of action. When a juggler throws a ball in the air this action makes sense with respect to the movements which will enable him or her to catch the ball in a particular position before it hits the ground. The time of action stops when the loop is closed. The plan has been enacted. The way the ball has been thrown has determined its speed and trajectory so that the juggler can anticipate the spatial and temporal coordinates of its anticipated point of impact on his/her body. The completion of the action is a feedforward phenomenon, an anticipation of a realized plan. Undoubtedly a very young child lacks the maturation that is necessary for competently understanding a circus act, but for a child of five or more a circus act can only have a formative value with respect to the conceptualization of actions and its subsequent result in constructing the substructures of later speech and socialized behavior as Piaget (1976) pointed out.

2.4. The timeless tools of time

An acrobat's apparatus is always custom-made according to the instructions given by the person who has conceived the act. It can be bought second hand in the case of traditional acts, but most of the time it will have to be adjusted to the size and weight of the participant(s) in the act. Its construction is governed by the rule of parsimony. All its parts are strictly functional and its decoration is reduced to a minimum so that it does not interfere with the apparatus's essential purpose which is to make a particular kind of actions both possible and visible. As an instrument that has been designed in view of a category of patterned movements and whose proportions are determined by those of its user(s), an acrobat's apparatus belongs to the class of objects that qualifies as *tools*: it cannot be understood independently from the plan whose implementation it makes possible. Its only difference from ordinary tools is that it is not aimed at transforming a portion of space but a portion of time. Indeed, it puts together the conditions for the performance of an action or a set of actions, by creating a topological configuration with respect to which a set of goals will be achieved in succession. It constructs a universe for the actions which it makes possible by determining their forms, and conversely it comes to full existence as a universe through the action(s) which – so to speak – bring(s) it to life. A trapeze hanging from the circus top is both as incomplete and as evocative of an action as a violin or a hammer lying on a table. Defined as conditions for the implementation of a plan, an acrobatic apparatus necessarily plays a part in the representation of the time of the action, that is, a subset of instants structured as a finite sequence of "now", "then" and "next" and forming a logical cluster of temporal values (the performing of a task) embedded in linear time, a phenomenon which amounts to a suspension of linear time (a phenomenon effectively labeled the "time trick" by Mair) or rather, as we have suggested earlier, the construction of a time different from both linear and cyclic representations of time.

Inasmuch as the acrobat's apparatus is instrumental in the performance and representation of "pure" action and consequently of the kind of time it implies, it can be said that such an apparatus is a tool aimed at a transformation of the representation of time into the "timeless time of action" (a view encapsulated in the title of this section for lack of a better expression). The conceptual unity formed by a tool and its tasks with the consequent involvement of memory and feedforward, is a neat symbol of what cognitive psychologists refer to as "plans", a concept introduced in the preceding section. In Leroi-Gourhan's words, "The functional synergy of tool and gesture presupposes the existence of the memory trace of a behavioral program" (1965: 36). The topological structures of an acrobat's apparatus with all its parts designed for making possible and efficient such basic functions as prehension, rotation, translation, and balance, are somewhat similar to musical instruments inasmuch as they are conceived in view of a gamut of actions within a certain domain of the sensorimotor universe. These apparatuses, by themselves atemporal tridimensional constructs, are sorts of stable "incomplete images of achievements". Their importance and meaning can be assessed only in view of perspectives such as the one expressed by Pribram and Luria, two pioneers in cognitive neuroscience, with respect to actions in general:

> The results of these experiments and observations showed that the motor regions of the cortex were critically involved in the control of neither individual muscles nor specific movements. Rather, the motor cortex seemed to play some higher order role in directing action – action defined not in terms of muscles but of achievement of an external representation of a psychological set or Plan. (Pribram 1971: 241)
>
> The ready question of how movement becomes transformed into action is that a sort of Imaginary process must occur in the motor cortex and that the Image is a momentary Image-of-Achievement which contains all input and outcome information necessary to the next step of that achievement. (Luria 1973).

As circus acts are performed in relation to an environment exclusively made for them, such actions are almost as clear as a logical formula because each component is isolated, then recombined in a sequence perfectly disentangled from the confusing complexity of the indefinite components of "reality". In addition, the actions displayed in the circus ring are totally explicit; there is no ellipsis whatsoever, contrary to actions represented in theatrical plays or in narratives in which time gaps and retrospections (flashback) are usual. Indeed, although the concept of action is central to our worldview, any given situation implying an action contains some ambiguous features regarding the degree of intention, freedom, vision of the outcome, assessment of the value of the result, to the extent that most "actions" are only *ex post facto* interpretations of events which were actually shaped to a certain extent by circumstances, pressure, and chance. Given that any outcome of an action is not in general an isolated, abstracted "object", but combines with other factors in a way that is hardly foreseeable, any decision implies a certain amount of gambling, if only the assumption that the state of the world will remain constant or that the rules of the game will remain valid. The micro-universe constructed in the circus ring in view of a sequence of typical actions involving a sub-set of human capacities (jumping, juggling, lifting, etc.) represents a finite set of conditions which are given as constant by hypothesis. It could even be said metaphorically, that a circus act has an axiomatic character and that the apparatuses and accessories are the stable symbols, the concrete scaffolding of this human algebra. This seems all the more likely since, as I have contended in previous works (e.g., Bouissac 1976: 130–132), natural objects (humans, animals, artifacts) undergo a process of *iconization* in the circus system, that is, the features of those objects which are relevant to the text in which they operate are redundantly enhanced and whatever could interfere as noise with those qualities is suppressed as much as possible. For instance, all the members of a flying trapeze act wear leotards of the same style and color because they display a kind of act that foregrounds team work. Flyers and catchers are equally necessary for the successful completion of the act. Although the acrobats might be very different from each other, this diversity of identities and appearances must not distract the audience which is required to focus on the actions themselves. In all acts the participants are carefully groomed so that signs of age or pain are masked as much as possible. The circus does not display life stories but actions by agents who are icons of their specialties and deeply engage their viewers neuro-motor competence (Wilson and Knoblich 2005).

It appears that this is not only true of the "object", i.e., the items comprising the "text" of an act, but it applies also to the actions performed, as it has been suggested above. All the components of our concept of Action (intention, freedom, plan, completion, achievement....) are enacted in ideal communication conditions. In a way, the circus operates similarly to the logicians of action by displaying sequences of well-defined symbols with very little room, if any, left for any ambiguity. In addition, the circus prominently represents coordinated actions by teams of agents, an essential aspect of the motor and socio-cognitive development of the child (e.g., Knoblich and Jordan 2003).

This is one of the reasons why current ways of filming or taping circus performances for media purposes are so much at odds with the very system of the circus which requires that a complete act be seen from only one particular point of view – whatever this may be. Note that the physical layout of circuses ensures that from any seat a spectator can perceive the totality of the movements performed and the setting within which they are performed. Indeed the symbols and their matrix have to be constant in their appearance and mutual relationships if the "formula" is to be visually and intellectually grasped. If the camera constantly changes its point of view, its distance and its focus, the sense of the logical totality of the sequence of movements is lost and the brain of the viewer is distracted by having to process multiple fragments to the extent that the advantage of the semiotic economy obtained through *iconization* is lost. For instance, Chris Christiansen juggling act could not be appreciated if the distance between the center of the ring where he performs and the spectator, wherever he/she may be located in the audience, were not constant. By focusing the camera on his anxious eyes, zooming on the frown that his make-up is designed to make invisible from a distance, following the ball as it ascends and losing the image of the full body in relation to the ball, the integrity of the action that is displayed would be deeply corrupted.

If these remarks are correct, it becomes clear that the circus provides ideal means for the cultural transmission – and reinforcement – of a normative concept that is crucial to the permanence of a worldview and its subsequent way of life. One could even wonder where else than in the circus such an iconized representation of pure "action" and consequently the generation of its correlative time, is performed so effectively. Certainly not in sport as a spectacle or a practice, because not only the concept of "action" must have been mastered in both cases as a prerequisite, but also because the whole system of sport is made far more complex by the introduction of the ludic and competitive factors, its open-endedness. Tales do not seem to be sufficient either to convey pure representation of actions because, as mentioned earlier, the conceptualization of action is a cognitive condition for the understanding of narratives. The adults' enjoyment of a circus act may be rooted in the unique possibility of contemplating ideal actions in a nutshell, similar to those described in treaties on ethics, i.e., comprising intention, free will, meaningful purpose, skill adjusted to well-defined and challenging goals, and eventual success, in brief the cornerstone of our humanistic ideology. For children, it is a learning experience.

2.5. Clowns at work: the melodic structure of social interactions

At least some clown performances can also be described as iconic representations of *actions*. A very popular specialty known as "musical clowns" possesses the characteristic of using musical instruments and tunes as metaphors of conflict situations. Dramatized interactions indeed take place within a template typical of the art of circus clowning. The process consists of translating into the musical code – or more generally the acoustic code – the most relevant relationships in a social system such as center and periphery, dominance and dependency, norm and deviance, fusion and fission, and so on. The claim that such an encoding is metaphorical relies on the assumption that the choice of the acoustic medium is motivated and not arbitrary. This latter point should be clarified before turning to some precise examples.

Current linguistic research is shifting the focus of inquiry from abstract syntactic structures to intonation patterns, thus integrating in the "linguistic object" some aspects of verbal communication which had been – and still are to some extent – expelled into the liminal field of paralinguistics or assigned to the realm of a different discipline, pragmatics. It seems more and more obvious that melodic structures should not be viewed as dispensable accompaniments of linguistic performances but must be assessed in terms of linguistic competence. Concurring with this approach, research in the structure of patterned social interactions tends to show that the organization of interactive processes is governed by melodic curves encompassing the totality of the media involved in such processes, including postures and gestures. In his early seminal paper entitled "The Melody of the Text" that was quoted earlier, Mair suggested that a melodic preeminence integrates all other dimensions:

> It is perhaps the precision of the integration of speech and movement within and between interactants that might give the game away... since they constitute a co-patterning rather than something added to each other in any retrospective sense, then we merely complicated our prospective cerebral organization by chopping up what happens into functions such as, for instance, expression, communication, illustration, and management of the environment. In describing the movement of spontaneous, rapport-full conversation, the common attitude words are curiously inadequate. This is a problem with faces too. One automatically looks to poetry to be adequate to the experience. Something about the way the words are arranged being more suitable... But that is precisely what is happening in the subjects we are studying – the melody of the text. (Mair 1980: 129)

Given that the "text" is in integrating function, the one who controls the melody, as Mair puts it, controls also the text. Note that the concept of melody has been applied to movements by Luria, a pioneer of the cognitive neurosciences, who used such expressions as "kinetic melodies" and "kinaesthetic melody" (Luria 1973: passim).

Therefore, if social interactions are patterned by melodic structures and if conflict processes can be described adequately as interferences of competitive melodies, then musical clowns deal with the very fundamentals of the dynamic processes which make up everyday life on the level of face-to-face interactions.

Two clown acts will now be analyzed in view of these remarks and the general approach illustrated by this chapter. The first example – the Fornasari clown act – follows a pattern often observed in musical clown acts, according to which the performance of a melody is interrupted again and again by a troublemaker who eventually makes his point and joins the group. The Fornassaris' interpretation of this scenario is very effective and emphasized some aspects that are particularly significant from the point of view of the hypothesis outlined above.

A whiteface clown, the embodiment of distinction and authority, elegantly dressed, introduces himself and his brother – and announces that they will play music for the audience. He starts playing a tune (A) on his trumpet and his brother accompanies him on the drums. His interpretation of tune A is personalized, that is, he introduces variations of his own, but his plan is clear to the audience: he intends to complete the familiar melody to its end. As he plays, another clown – a messy and grotesque character – enters the ring without being noticed by the two musicians. He carries a music-stand and a trumpet, puts his music-stand beside the other clowns and starts playing the trumpet, adding his own tune to the tune that is being performed. When the whiteface clown realizes that the cacophony is caused by someone else who is playing beside him, he stops playing, turns toward the new-comer, and pokes his arm to signal to him that he has to stop playing – then he sends him away. "You cannot play music here, you have to go outside – Luigi (his brother), let us continue!" – So they do as the interrupter leaves the ring for a short while, after which he returns but, this time, with two trumpets on which he plays simultaneously. The whiteface clown confiscates the two trumpets and tells him that he cannot have them back. "If you want to play music, you have to go to play outside." Then he confiscates his hat. There follows an argument during which seven hats are successively confiscated because, every time, the clown produces a new one that was hidden in his pocket or in his trousers. Eventually he leaves the ring shouting that he will go and buy another one. The two musicians resume their performance (tune A). The other clown returns with a new trumpet and interrupts their playing by performing, this time, a markedly different tune (B); he concludes by performing variations on the former tune (A). The whiteface clown pulls a gun and fires at his foot. One of his oversized shoes jumps in the air revealing an enormous foot on which a red bump starts to grow (in fact a balloon that he inflates by a special device). He leaves the ring crying as gushes of water come from his eyes. Near the exit, he mimes the movement of swimming. The two musicians then play a new tune (C) soon interrupted by the old trouble-maker who now arrives with a trombone and interferes aggressively with their performing, aiming at them the slide of his instrument (tune D). The whiteface clown tells him again that he cannot play here and hits his hands with a soft stick or a bladder several times until the victim deceives him by withdrawing his hand in time to avoid the stick, then he retires. The concert resumes (tune C). New interruption with a saxophone (tune D), and, as he is stopped, he takes off his jacket, exposes his backside, and fires several gun shots from a revolver which is fixed to his bottom. The two musicians are scared to death and temporarily leave the ring, returning only when the clown has walked out of the ring, imitating the proud and defiant gait of a gunman in traditional western movies. The concert resumes (tune E). The clown comes back with an oversized saxophone, whistles to signal his presence and shows the instrument; he is given permission to perform and tries to play but with little effect. He takes from inside the instrument a very small saxophone which he introduces as "a baby saxophone" on which, after having been given permission, he plays the same tune as in the beginning (A), but in a particularly brilliant manner. He stops playing because he feels a bite on his leg, then performs some antics, pretending that someone in the audience is watching his bare legs when he pulls up his trousers to look for the cause of his discomfort. Eventually he finds a mosquito, shoots it with a gun, and makes big steps towards the mosquito to finish it by crushing it under his foot. The drummer accompanies his steps with corresponding beats, but at the third one the drummer is tricked into playing the drums without there being any steps – and the clown makes the last noise himself by firing his gun. Then he goes on to finish his tune (A) on the small saxophone but soon after, the sheet which was on the music stand explodes reducing the musical score to pieces. At the same time he pulls a white flag from his pocket. Then he is asked by the whiteface clown "what are you going to do now?" and, as an answer, he gives the signal for a march as three other musicians carrying various kinds of drums enter the ring and join them. The old troublemaker now acts as the band conductor, but a last musician arrives with a very large tuba (bass horn) and starts interfering with the tune performed (tune F). This causes an argument with the clown, but the newcomer soon joins the group which makes its way to the exit while playing a last march (tune G) under the direction of the old clown.

The texture of this act is very rich but at least two aspects can be distinguished: First, a main sequence involving a conflict between two musical performers who intend to implement two competing plans; second, a series of conflicts imbedded in the main sequence (the hats, the shooting of guns, the stick and the mosquito bite); note that those events which do not involve musical performance are nevertheless consistent with the main sequence both syntactically and semantically. I will not deal with them in detail in this chapter. The reason for their methodological neglect is that comparisons with other acts of the same type shows that the main sequence follows a general pattern whereas those imbedded events can be considered as free forms, not only observable in other sequences but also being commonly substituted for other events. In addition, whenever clowns performing this act in a program are asked to make it shorter, they drop those episodes. Conversely they can insert a few more if they are requested to make their act last longer.

If we focus on the main sequence and eliminate its redundant episodes, we can easily identify the following functional phases:

1. An authoritative character plays a familiar melody (tune A), that is, he starts to implement a plan as it is clear that he intends to complete the tune to its end in his own terms.
2. An outsider interferes and attempts to join the performance of the melody (tune A) on his own terms. He is brutally rejected.
3. The same scene repeats itself several times with the outsider using various instruments.
4. The outsider interferes with a more aggressive instrument and plays another melody (tune B). He is again rejected.
5. The authoritative character plays another melody (tune C).
6. The outsider returns – showing more authority – and eventually plays better than his colleague the first melody (tune A) and wins his approval and admiration.
7. The outsider acts authoritatively, takes over the leading part and organizes the whole group which plays a march under his direction (tune G), thus completing his plan that is to complete a tune he fully controls since he is the conductor.

The embedded events are narrowly connected to this sequence: First, within (6) the piece of paper containing the score of the melody (presumably tune A) explodes and is reduced to pieces. Second, within (7), another outsider repeats tentatively the behavior of the first outsider once the latter has asserted his control of the group, but this last interference is reduced to a minimum as the tuba player soon joins the group for the final march.

In other words this act displays a conflict regarding the control of *a* melody, amounting to aiming at controlling *the* melody. This clown scenario enacts indeed a progressive taking over of the function of band leader, during which three phases can be observed: (1) several unsuccessful attempts; (2) a breaking point event in which the outsider takes over the melody and performs it more effectively. Note that this event is symbolically emphasized by the violent and sonorous destruction of the musical score. (3) The winner asserts his victory and becomes the bandleader. At this point he is himself challenged by another outsider but integrates him successfully in the group.

Mair insightfully pointed to a fundamental dimension of social interaction by focusing on the melody and emphasizing the fact that the most basic processes in human business are invisible to those who are immersed in them. If this is correct, then a clown act such as the one described above should indeed "speak" to our brains inasmuch as these brains must be subtle processors and identifiers of such conflictual melodic patterns that are so relevant to our social survival. The way this phenomenon is captured (abstracted, iconized, redundantly expressed) in circus clown acts is similar to the treatment of actions which we have observed in other types of circus acts. Note also that the time factor is involved exactly in the same capacity but applies to social actions. It means taking over the control of a group, i.e., a special case of the more general category of implementing a plan since it involves two mutually exclusive plans, and that the initially dominant one is taken over by the challenging one.

A short clown gag, which incidentally was observed in the same program as above, evidences very neatly the closeness of the two processes: implementing a plan and taking over the melody.

Rudy Dockey is introduced as a great violinist, and starts by trying several positions with his violin and bow. The plan is clearly stated: he will perform the "carnival of Venice", everybody keeps silent and listens (this is the most striking evidence that the audience is ready to submit to the melody). As he has some difficulty in finding the right position for playing, he ends up holding the violin on his back and plays the tune in the posture of a contortionist. The plan has been implemented in an original manner. But the Master of Ceremonies who had introduced him shows signs of disapproval and takes the instrument away from his hands, a drastic way of taking over the melody from him. Then Rudy Dockey finds in his pockets a balloon that he blows to a fairly large size and manages to perform the same tune – with a very similar sound quality – by expelling the air from the balloon through a little pipe. Therefore he has demonstrated his ability to implement his initial plans through an alternative strategy and at the same time he has taken over the melody again as the orchestra starts accompanying him. Finally he leaves the ring as a hero.

2.6. Concluding remarks: circus time and cognition

Obviously the analytical approach outlined in this chapter does not exhaust all the symbolic riches provided by circus spectacles. Other aspects will be explored in the following chapters. No mention has been made, for instance, of the complex semiotic operations through which some rules of the contextual culture are expressed, combined, and transformed in the various acts comprising a circus program. In the two clown scenarios which were considered in the last section the nature and connotations of the melodies that were used by the performers, as well as the details of their costumes, postures, dialogues, etc., were not taken into consideration. However the aspects of circus spectacles which I have attempted to analyze in this chapter are crucial with respect to the cognitive foundations that make circus spectacles, as well as other cultural phenomena, possible. More specifically, I have suggested that no other form of spectacle or ritual seems to be more apt than the circus to contribute decisive experiences to the cognitive development of children, although only a mature acculturated adult who is cognizant of the circus codes and traditions can fully enjoy its spectacles as complex multimodal texts and their intertextual dimensions.

But, fundamentally, a circus act is a prototype of social behavior providing a clear demonstration of what is (or should be?) an action, thus generating a specific concept of time in relation to the concepts of plans and tools. The demonstration is all the more effective since, through the *iconization* of the components of the situation it represents, the action itself – and consequently the concept of time it implies – are foregrounded. Thus, the circus artist's tools, those impressive apparatuses made of tubes, poles, rings, ropes, wires, etc., or those sets of objects (stools, barrel, balls, hoops, etc.), are indeed the signs of *atemporal* structures, denoting normative models of action, both as individual and team endeavors, to which one could certainly apply Victor Turner's remark:

> Temporal structure until at rest and therefore atemporal, is always tentative; there are always alternative goals and alternative means of attaining them. Since its foci are goals, psychological factors such as volition, motivation, span of attention, level of aspiration, and so on, are important in its analysis; contrastingly, in atemporal structures these are unimportant, for structures reveal themselves as already exhausted, achieved, or alternatively as axioms, self-evident cognitive or normative frames to which action is subsequent and subordinate. (Turner 1974)

Chapter 3
In what sense is a circus animal performing?

On my first day of work at the circus, I was assigned among other chores the twice a day watering of the tigers, eight superb adult felines that were either happily sleeping or pacing their spacious compartments when they were not rehearsing or performing in the steel arena. I had been warned about not leaving them without fresh water. I was also supposed to keep a safe distance between them and me by using a hose to provide them with their cool drink.

The most attractive of my charges was the tigress Domino, the only animal that my boss, the trainer Firmin Bouglione, could pet at close range when he was making his round and when he was presenting the group in the show. One day, as I was finishing the watering, an old circus hand who was always ready to teach me the ropes called my attention to Domino. She had suddenly jumped on her feet and was intently looking toward the crowd of visitors. "You see. It is always easy to know when the boss is around. She sees his hat before anyone else as soon as he enters the compound. She is truly in love with him." Her eyes were indeed focused in a particular direction and she had put up her paws on a bar to see better in the distance. It was not long until he appeared in front of us, reiterated his warning to me not to get too close, and started to scratch Domino's forehead while exchanging with her the signal of utmost trust in tiger language that can only be transcribed as "pfrrr", a transliteration that falls short of all the nuances with which it is uttered: softness, warmth, intensity, even passion. This is the reassuring vocal contact between a tigress and her cubs who readily reciprocate in similar fashion. Later, in a tiger life, it becomes a standard sign of comfort and affection. Some humans in circuses and zoos may also enjoy this privileged way of being told: "I am happy to see you".

3.1. Meaning, text, and context

The linguist and semiotician Roman Jakobson (1896–1982) reported in one of his most influential essays that a Russian actor with whom he was acquainted could utter the phrase "this evening" in fifty different ways with respect to intonation by varying intensity, pitch, rhythm, and juncture. The range was going from threat to fear, from order to submission, and from hate to passion as well as subtle combinations of all the above emotions. This actor was thus able to create fifty different messages that evoked in the mind of the listeners fifty different situations or contexts. The emotive cues combined with the semantic, morphologic, and syntactic components of this minimal linguistic message could easily be related by native speakers to culturally congruent social settings and psychological moods. This was later experimentally verified under the auspices of the Rockefeller Foundation (Jakobson 1960: 350–351).

Advances in the pragmatics of human communication have shown that social interaction in all its forms can be construed as a complex model whose parameters can be experimentally controlled. Such an analytical approach enables the observer to shift the focus from the message to its context and to study the covariations that may occur. Gestures and facial expressions in particular can modify the meaning of a message to the extent that mere paralinguistic variations can make a proposition mean exactly the opposite of what it explicitly states in words.

"Context" should be understood here as not only whatever immediately precedes and follows the linguistic message itself but also whatever is emitted simultaneously through all the other available channels; "situation" refers to the type of social interaction that is identified by the observer within a specified cultural domain, such as conversation between peers, confrontation between rivals, ritualized testing of the affective bond between lovers, and so forth. The spontaneous identification of the various categories of situations is an on-going business in everyday life and an important aspect of the cultural competence of any individual. Obviously these various situations are construed from some minimal cues that can be manipulated once they have been identified: respective class of age, sex, natural posture, role expectations, distance, place, and degree of normality or abnormality of the interaction. It would be theoretically possible to design an experiment inspired by the one recounted by Roman Jakobson, in which the utterance of the linguistic message would remain invariant and the context or the situation would vary, the hypothesis being that a given sign would convey various meanings depending on the manipulation of the context and situation of this sign. As a matter of fact, such experiments are performed daily in one of the most popular institutions of our culture, the circus. Performing animal acts are indeed patterned events that are two-sided. On the one hand, the trainers interact with their charges on the basis of their biosemiotic competence; on the other hand, they frame these interactions in particular situations relevant to the system of social interactions shared by the public for which they perform. Therefore all animal acts are the combination of a biologically patterned behavioral sequence and a constructed social situation. Once an animal is trained, the behavioral sequence can be considered as the equivalent of the invariant aspect of a message whose meaning can be modified, within certain limits, by the variations of the situational construct. This does not mean, naturally, that the behavioral sequence is produced independently from any situation but that the situation through which the behavioral sequence is elicited simply overlaps, sometimes minimally, with the situation outwardly constructed for the audience. Whether the presenter wears a costume that evokes a ballet dancer or the outfit of a gladiator, the imaginary context differently impacts upon the range of expectations and interpretations formed by the audience. It also provides a system of reference for the esthetic evaluation of the act.

For instance, in Alberto Zoppe's Rhesus Monkey act, one of the two trainers who present the act is dressed as a clown. He walks toward one of the monkeys that is standing on a platform and gestures with his hand as if he were starting an argument with "him". Suddenly, the monkey slaps the clown twice. This monkey wears a masculine garment. If it had been dressed as a woman and if the clown had whistled at "her," this patterned segment "slapping the man on the face" that is triggered by the trainer would have communicated a quite different meaning, shifting from a situation of confrontation between males of equal status to the expected reaction of a proper lady in response to an inappropriate behavior toward her by an ill-educated male. Such changes of frame for a given trick are common practice in the circus. In this case, the costume acts as a gender sign which is, of course, culture-dependent. By thus manipulating both the animal's behavior and the context of this behavior the trainer utilizes, at the same time, two different semiotic systems in a single segment of performance. As a result, such manipulation generates for the public, and to a lesser extent for the trainer, the illusion that the relevant context is the one they perceive and that the animals share this perception of the situation that is constructed in the ring. This chapter will attempt to show the generality of this semiotic illusion in the art of training and to point out the nature of the performing animal's performance without denying, however, that genuine emotions can bridge the divide between human and animals, thus emphasizing that the point of view of the animal should also be brought into the picture in order to form a comprehensive semiotic theory of performing animal acts.

3.2. The civilized animal

Let us take a few simple cases to further illustrate the point made by the example of the Alberto Zoppe's monkey act. In the 1970s and 1980s, Ursula Böttcher, a bear trainer from what was then the Democratic Republic of Germany, presented in European and North American circuses a remarkable act that featured ten polar bears. This impressive act was the highlight of the 1980 program of one of the traveling units of Ringing Brothers, Barnum and Bailey Circus. This is where the details reported below were observed. One of Ursula Böttcher's routines consisted of performing what is sometimes called "the kiss of death" with one of her charges. In this segment of her act, an animal left its stool, rose on its hind legs and walked across the ring until it stopped in front of the five-foot high woman whose head hardly reached the level of the animal's chest. The bear then lowered its head toward the woman's face until its mouth apparently touched her lips. Even those who were seated in the first rows of the audience could not notice that the trainer had discretely put in her mouth a piece of carrot, kept unobtrusively between her teeth because their attention was irresistibly drawn to the twelve-foot high polar bear that was "menacingly" proceeding toward the frail trainer standing helplessly, her hands behind her back. Once the bear had caught the carrot, or whatever other convenient bait was used, it was led back to its place in the steel arena. The illusion was completed by the fact that in the printed program a beautiful close-up photograph of this sequence did not show the bait, either because it had been artificially removed from the photograph or because the bear had already caught it with its tongue when the photographer took the shot. In any case, a careful examination of the photograph shows that the trainer had a pouch full of "goodies" attached to her belt.

It is obvious from this elementary example that the situation created to elicit this behavior from the bear who actually approached the trainer in order to obtain a delicacy, was different from the one created by the various cues provided to the public by the announcement, the music (from the musical *Kiss me Kate*), and the posture of the woman, which brought into focus the complex and powerful themes of bestiality, love, and death. Although this bear was a female whose name was Alaska, it was perceived as a male through the multimodal semiotic construct of this dramatic segment. Such semiotic gender plays are possible with animal species which are not characterized by a marked sexual dimorphism like the lions for instance in which the males display an abundant mane. Seen from a distance, male and female bears differ only in size. Gender play is also possible with animals that can be dressed up like the monkeys of the Alberto Zoppe act.

Incidentally, the Ursula Böttcher example shows why television more often than not tends to alter the semiotic efficacy of certain circus acts by constantly zooming back and forth, and varying the objects in focus, jumping for instance from the trainer to the animal, and thus losing the spatial dimension of the drama since the suspense increases as the distance between the woman and the bear becomes shorter and shorter. This is usually done with the best of intentions by cameramen in search of visual variety and interesting details, but the viewers are deprived of the constancy of the frames within which the relevant situations are constructed for the sake of the spectacle. Moreover, elements of the acts that are not congruent with these situations may be fore-grounded such as the actual direction of an animal's glance or the facial expression of a trainer that may contrast with her assumed mood and goal. The unfortunate result of this visual dismembering of the circus act is the dissolution of the semiotic illusion that was constructed with great care and risk by the trainer. This is also true of many acrobatic acts that make sense only if they are perceived in relation to the global situation created by the totality of the apparatus as we have seen in Chapter 2. Naturally, such filming techniques reveal valuable information on another semiotic level than the one intended for the circus audience.

The second example that will illustrate the point made in this chapter is a vivid childhood memory. At the end of a lion act, after the trainer had sent all the animals back to their individual cages in the backstage, a lioness remained on her stool, stubbornly refusing to leave the ring in spite of the shouting and whip cracking of the man. Then, at the suggestion of the ring master, the trainer put aside his whip and stick, and bowed while making a very polite gesture toward the lioness, as if he was inviting her to go through the exit before him. She immediately did so with utmost grace. There was no doubt in my ten-year-old mind that this event was still another proof of the deep and mysterious understanding between the daring trainers and their wonderful lions. Since then I have seen the same trick performed several hundred times by dozens of trainers. It is an excellent example of the minimal overlapping of two situations: on the one hand, a constructed context perceived as meaningful by the public at large and, on the other hand, a situation created by the trainer and negotiated by the animal.

There are several procedures to obtain this effect. I will describe three of them. As a rule, wild circus animals have an urge to return to their private territory, that is, their own individual cages. It is usually sufficient to open the door connecting through a tunnel the central steel arena to their cage for them to rush back there. As long as the door remains closed they will not dash for the exit. Therefore, the only valid auditory and visual cue for the animal is the opening of the door by the cage attendant, regardless of whatever else can be hinted at by the trainer's behavior. In the act I described above, the trainer was actually acting out as if he wanted the lioness to leave the ring while not allowing her to do so.

Another possibility is for the trainer to stand in the way of the exit and to crack the whip while shouting at the animal to leave. All that the animal perceives is the man as an obstacle which bars the way, regardless of what he says. A few moments later, it will be enough for the trainer to step aside while making his emphatically polite gesture to trigger the rush to the exit. For the animal, the relevant modification of the situation is that the path is now free of obstacles.

The audience interprets this segment of behavior as a way for the lioness of saying: "treat me as a lady and I will happily comply with your request that I leave the ring".

A third procedure consists of manipulating the flight distance, a phenomenon that has been thoroughly described and evidenced by early animal psychologists such as Hachet-Souplet (1905) and Hediger (1968) who have observed, and experimented with, circus animal training in order to understand the biological and psychological basis of this training. Any wild animal in a given environment tends to flee from man – this is a complex system with many variables that cannot be addressed in detail here. Suffice it to say that in the steel arena one of the most relevant dimensions of the man-animal interaction is the distance that is maintained between them. As long as the trainer remains at a sufficient distance, the animal will not budge whatever gesture is made and whatever words are shouted. But if the trainer steps up toward the animal, thus crossing the critical distance while leaving the shortest path toward the way out, the lioness will "flee" toward her cage.

The critical distance is both a specific and an individual factor as it can be modified by circumstances. Some tame animals accept and enjoy closer contact with humans. A case in point is the behavior of the tigress Domino that was described in the anecdote which introduced this chapter. As a cub, she had been abandoned at birth by her mother and the trainer had bottle-fed her. This had created a special bond of the kind that was documented by Lorenz regarding goslings and other animals, which is based on an early "imprinting" that modifies the subsequent natural behavior of the adults (1981: 274–281). These are individuals who are human-imprinted, that is, they consider their trainer as a conspecific rather than an alien. This phenomenon has vast consequences for the training process and beyond because it may involve some rough behavior that is common among playful young tigers or even among adult rivals. In general it is considered that for species like tigers and lions which are *altricial*, that is, in which the cubs need the presence of the mother if they are to survive not only for food but also for their basic education, notably regarding hunting, the possibility of being trained is an essential part of their genetic endowment. Actually, in nature, only a very small percentage of cubs reach adulthood. The most successful are usually the offspring of experienced mothers who can be very rough indeed in driving the points they want to make with respect to the various dangers that are encountered in the range of their territories. This is why the training of circus felines is possible as long as the animals are trained within the window of the few years that correspond to the period of time during which they learn from their mother in the wild. A tiger reaches adulthood at about seven.

But even imprinted and trained animals have deeply ingrained reflex behaviors that can be manipulated while, at the same time, constituting hazards for the trainers. For example, if they are startled they tend to bite whatever is within their reach. In his tiger act, the expert trainer Firmin Bouglione (1908–1980) had come to trust so much Domino that he let her use his own back as a path to ascend to the top of the highest pedestal in the ring. This was risky because tigers always attack from the back. This is why forest workers in Sumatra and other parts of Asia wear human masks on the back of their heads to protect themselves from such deadly attacks. Domino enjoyed the privilege of this exceptional trust until the day when, startled or driven by an irresistible visual cue, she grabbed her trainer's nape with her teeth but immediately released the pressure without causing any damage. No need to say that the stint was discontinued after this incident.

As we have seen above, another aspect of the biosemiotics of training is the use of proxemics (Watson 1970), that is, the particular significance of distance that exists for a species or an individual animal. Most of them have responses appropriate to the variations of the physical distance between self and others. Until the critical threshold is passed, they do not have any reason for reacting. They simply monitor the situation. If this threshold is transgressed, then they flee in the opposite direction. If they cannot flee – that is, if they are cornered – then they usually attack. To return to the case of the well-mannered lioness, the trainer will not cause her to move as long as he does not transgress the lioness's critical distance and cracks his whip sideways. But if he steps toward her while making the polite gesture, this reduction of the distance will trigger the flight reaction especially if it is combined with the opening of the exit door.

These examples clearly illustrate the two-level manipulation in which a circus trainer is engaged, and how s/he carefully constructs situations that are socially relevant for the spectators but include, as building blocks, so to speak, segments of interactions based on totally different biosemiotic systems.

3.3. A symphony of signs: the art of deceit and the pitfalls of self-deception

A first conclusion that could be drawn at this point is that circus trainers are professional deceivers. This is true at a certain level, but their imperfect knowledge of the ethology of their charges also leads them to what amounts to occasional self-deception, a phenomenon that accounts for the accidents, often tragic, occurring from time to time in the circus ring.

Many trainers tend to see themselves as teachers and may overlook the biosemiotic significance of some aspects of their interactions with the animals they train. From interviews that were conducted under the auspices of the *Research Center for Language and Semiotic Studies* at Indiana University, it transpired that their own understanding of the relation was often mediated by dangerous metaphors. This remark is not meant to question the practical knowledge of many experienced trainers who reliably manage to elicit complex behaviors on the part of their charges, but the situation they perceive in the very process of training may be at times quite different from what is known to be the ethological or biosemiotic meaning of the animals' behavior. For instance, tiger trainers appear to compete with each other regarding the number of tigers they can line up and make do a trick known as the "roll over". This consists of having the tigers lie down in front of the trainer then roll over laterally several times in perfect synchrony. I have witnessed training sessions that convinced me that some tigers seem prone to perform this trick whereas others are very reluctant to do so. A stubborn trainer I knew once spent many hours of exhausting effort trying to "make the tiger understand what he wanted it to do and to persuade it that it had better do so." The result was eventually a stressful poking game during which the tiger was enticed to roll over as a necessary segment of a defensive behavior aimed at catching the stick that the trainer lightly poked in its side. The contrast with the relative ease with which other tigers could "learn" this trick puzzled me until I read McDougal's book, *The Face of the Tiger* (1977), which is devoted entirely to the ethology and biosemiotics of this beautiful animal. It is clear from the many segments of natural behavior in context that are described in this book that the "roll over" belongs to the tiger's repertory of social behavior. It indicates submission and it is performed both by the mature tigress in the mating ritual and by cubs in front of adult animals. It has also been observed during chance encounters between subadults or transient males and the resident male tiger of a given territory. Its result is to prevent a fight. Having discussed this with some trainers, I found out that they were not aware of the fact and simply thought that their more successful colleagues had discovered a better pedagogical method than theirs or that they had come across some more obedient and intelligent animals. But these are anthropomorphic categories that do not take into consideration the respective age, sex, and rank within the tiger group of the individuals concerned.

True enough, most trainers are remarkably sensitive to the biological constraints of the situation they negotiate in their daily confrontations with those large predators, but their perception of these situations nevertheless is more often than not at odds with the animals' own perception of these situations. The last few decades have witnessed the emergence of a large body of knowledge derived from long term observations of wild animals in their natural environments, notably yielding information on their social behavior and the significance of their ritualized interactions. What makes training possible is only a slight behavioral overlapping between the two species, in this case humans and tigers. Both partially share the same *umwelt* and compete for the same prey. However, this very overlapping often causes misreadings and misgivings that entail fatal consequences. The chronicle of the circus is replete with accidents that bear witness to this fact. As a result, even the wisest of wild animal trainers seems to oscillate between a narcissistic and a paranoid attitude towards his animals. Whoever has once in his/her life enjoyed the playful but risky charge of a friendly young male lion can easily understand this double attitude. It is not uncommon to hear trainers calling their "pupils": "good boy!", "good girl!" with a paternal or maternal soft inflection of the voice, when the animals behave according to their plans. On the other hand, in their dealings with some of their most impressive and difficult animals, the same trainers may use the most abject insults. Both types of interactions are obviously experienced by these men and women as heavily anthropomorphized and strictly within the domain of the repertory of human values and emotions.

These latter remarks open up our perception of a circus act to the third dimension of the performance: the animal's point of view. In addition to the situation constructed for the audience and the one perceived and manipulated by the trainer interacting with the animals, there exists also, necessarily, a situation that is experienced and negotiated by the animals within their own biosemiotic system, that is, the system provided by the structure and programs of their genome. Although their adaptability enables them to survive in an artificial environment and to adjust accordingly their *ethogram*, that is, their behavioral repertory with respect to the environment in which they have evolved, such modifications nevertheless remain within the boundaries of a strict socio-biological code that forms an absolute obstacle to all attempts at cross-specific communication. Naturally, it would be ludicrous to deny that some form of interaction takes place first in the training process, then in the performance: attention is obtained, orders are obeyed, behavior is shaped by appropriate conditioning, cues are recognized, moods are sensed, and so forth. Hediger (1935) has brilliantly discussed the flow of information that circulates between the participants during the performance of an animal act. However, if one considers communication as the vicarious sharing of experience, a term other than "communication" should be used in order to describe adequately the sort of interaction that models an animal act. Crucial features of the training process such as the structure of attention, the establishment of a social hierarchy, and even the learning ability of the young belong to the species-specific competence of the animals that are used in circus acts. Tigers, for instance, are genetically programmed to learn patterned behavior relevant to their particular environment from their mothers during their first years. This is a condition for their survival. The fact that a trainer undertakes to model some aspects of their behavior when they are about one-year, imposes himself or herself as a leader and becomes the focus of their attention, makes sense "tigerwise." It is also in the order of things that later on, when the male tigers mature and reach full adulthood, the situation evolves from deference to confrontation; although the trainer may then manage to maintain his/her leadership – and this is not always the case – the same patterned behavior has a different meaning with respect to the social significance and biosemiotic chart of the animals. In this sense, a circus animal performs, i.e., negotiates social situations by relying on the repertory of ritualized behavior that characterizes its species. The ritualization may have been slightly modified by the human input during its learning stage, but far less than is usually thought. It seems obvious that the biological score according to which they perform is not the same as the one that the trainer has conceived and which he keeps perceiving. The trainer can elicit at will some segments of behavior and frame them in a situation of his/her choice, but the animal's behavior is never performed out of its own socio-biological context, which transcends the trainer's understanding of the animal's performance. In the Rhesus Monkey act mentioned earlier in this paper, the animal performers display most of their specific social repertory in the category of agonistic pattern and related movements, such as "submission and withdrawal," "threat, attack, and approach," and "affinitive movements," as they are listed and described in the pioneering work of Altman (1965). The trainers have built situations easily identifiable by their audience but these situations are mostly irrelevant to the monkey's concerns. However, these animals find themselves in a series of situations that they negotiate according to their own terms and through which they may be led to actual attacks if the trainers are not fully aware of the animal's point of view, as is often the case.

The psychologists who have attempted to educate some apes in order to test their nonverbal linguistic abilities have found themselves in the same situations as circus trainers. There are indeed indications that accidents are not infrequent, although they have never been publicized; the celebrated "Washoe" once attacked the psychologist Karl Pribram who lost a finger during the interaction (personal communication, 13 June 1980). This accident was undoubtedly triggered by a situation that was not perceived in the same manner by the chimpanzee and her human keepers and mentors. The semiotic overlap fallacy is at the root of most serious animal accidents that have occurred in the circus ring.

Trainers are not always aware of the discrepancies existing between their context of action and that of their charges, and situational overlapping often creates the illusion that a given context is fully shared. The fact that accidents occur unexpectedly has generated an abundant circus lore regarding the nature of wild animals, in which moral or psychological interpretations distort the ethological significance not only of the segment of behavior that is incriminated but also the totality of the animals' comportment in their daily routines. "Never trust a lion," some trainers will say, "because a lion always goes through an outburst of madness in its life." The concepts of "trust" or "madness" are totally irrelevant in this context, but it is through such concepts that trainers can cope with the biosemiotic otherness with which they are confronted daily, an otherness that poets have sometimes sensed and expressed in felicitous forms such as William Blake's "fearful symmetry" embodied by the tiger or Victor Hugo's lines referring to "la nuit qu'un lion a pour âme" (the dark night of a lion's soul), an expression that, incidentally, has found its way into some trainers' jargon (Thétard 1928) to express a fundamental communication gap that the best of signs can hardly bridge.

Chapter 4
Horses' feathers: from tacit knowledge to circus metaphors

When my friend Shinichi Nakazawa presented me with a book on the history of the Japanese circus, I excitedly leafed through the volume in search of illustrations. There were numerous finely drawn representations of performances, exquisitely colored posters that detailed the programs of circus shows that were presented in Edo or Kyoto, and early photographs of acrobats and animals. Many horses were shown in all the circus specialties with which I was familiar. Something, however, was missing. I was instinctively looking for feathers and could not see any.

As a child, if I wanted to draw a circus horse, the outline of the animal with its abundant mane and tail would be adorned with two big plumes, one on its head and one on its back. This was the seal of the circus stamped on a domestic animal that was otherwise prosaic. It magically elevated my awkward drawing from the trivial domain of the farm and the race track to the magic realm of the circus.

Curiously, the Japanese circus horses were wearing instead a kind of wide red belt with a large bow on their back. I asked my friend: what is this? – Oh, it is what the geishas used to wear, he said, with a matter of fact tone of voice.

I was left puzzling with this odd, unsettling feature of exoticism. Perhaps I had too easily taken the horses' feathers for granted. Perhaps, visual metaphors are no more innocent than linguistic ones?

4.1. A theoretical prelude

The circus presents an array of various species among the trained animals which are featured in its spectacles. In the previous chapter, we have considered wild animal acts which involve lions, tiger, and bears, and we have elucidated the complex communication processes which are at play in such performances. This chapter will focus on domestic animals which also form an essential part of circus programs but it will deal with the symbolic uses of these animals and the ways in which circus spectacles relate to the cultures in which they are observed. It will address more particularly the display of horses in one circus specialty: the "Liberty Horse Act", that is, an act that consists of a group of usually decorated horses which perform a variety of collective movements in the ring under the direction of a trainer. This genre is markedly different from acts which feature mounted horses either to make them "dance" or to execute acrobatics on them while they canter at various speeds. I have discussed elsewhere in detail the complex composition of a circus program that made use of the whole gamut of equestrian specialties (Bouissac 1991). I will turn in this chapter to the issue of the symbolic decoration of circus horses.

But the point of entry into this semiotic problem will be the puzzle presented by the Japanese anecdote which was recounted at the beginning of this chapter. The solution I will propose is based on a few theoretical assumptions that must be made explicit in order to clarify the method I will follow in order to answer the question: why does it seem so appropriate to us that circus horses wear plumes and why does this conjunction convey an impression of being truly felicitous. If semiotics can be considered as a form of cultural anthropology that addresses issues regarding our own culture rather than exotic ones, then many aspects of our daily life which we take for granted can be construed as challenging problems. An ethnographer who would encounter a society in which horses are consistently associated with birds through feather ornaments rather than with floral decorations in ritual-like performances, would certainly wonder why and would be looking into the system of categories that sustains the worldview of this culture. This is precisely the problem we are going to engage in this chapter.

Cognitive and linguistic functions have a complex relationship. They do not seem to exactly map unto each other. It is obvious that most of the time words appear to determine our perceptions and the way in which we categorize these perceptions. But sometimes it looks as if natural language and cognition were somewhat independent from each other. Linguistic forms encode only partially cognitive values. Often our lexicon falls short of the richness and diversity of our experiences and feelings. This is particularly obvious when we try to describe a smell, a flavor, or an odor. We are truly at a loss. Most of the time, we have to categorize it as the smell of a known object (fruit, flower, chemical) or as resembling the smell of such objects. The range of olfactory nuances which we discriminate in our practical life is infinitely wider than the lexicon of smell that is at our disposal. We are often reduced to having to decide between good and bad, or to say that what we experience is indefinable or elusive. Perfume specialists have developed a code of their own which is of little help in ordinary conversation. The same kind of problems arises when it comes to define moods and emotions.

Fortunately, discourse is not an exclusive privilege of the linguistic medium. Cognitive contents can be discursively combined and transformed through patterned manipulation of actions. A discourse as such is defined through its formal properties rather than the characteristics of its medium, even though within our culture it is institutionalized as a performance of a linguistic nature and denotes a communicative and/or expressive event in which the verbal component is emphasized. In previous works (e.g., Bouissac 1976) I have pointed out the autonomy of some discursive non-linguistic systems and the shortcomings of the natural language when it comes to verbally interpreting some of these systems. Using "non-linguistic" rather than "trans-linguistic" to characterize these types of discourses suggests that "discursiveness" as such is founded upon some principles alien to what is usually referred to as "universals of language". It foregrounds both concomitance and process instead of linearity, and it conveys information in a manner that is akin to the way in which we monitor our life environment. Although this early approach only attempted to enunciate *linguistically* some intuitive and programmatic propositions, it definitely questioned the theories which insisted upon founding the quasi-totality of the human meaningful universe on an implicit *glottocentrism*, that is, an epistemological attitude that takes language as the absolute model of reference. Instead, this approach shifted attention toward the biosemiotic notion of *umwelt,* understood here as the set of environmental cognitive features or, in other words, the information that is considered relevant to an individual's biological or social survival, or which is formally pertinent from the point of view of a systematic organization of differential qualities within a representational register or paradigm.

But if all 'semantic features' – that is, the meaning of words and sentences – are necessarily also 'cognitive features', the reverse is not true. Many cognitive features are not translatable into semantic features (i.e., linguistically) but are experienced usually – and in some cases exclusively – on the visual and practical levels. The semiotic universe within which we are immersed and which sustains our capacity to process information and make sense of most of it, transcends the linguistic grid which allows us to communicate about a fairly restricted range of concepts and situations. The non-verbalized cognitive domain seems nevertheless to be organized systematically as a complex network of relationships comprising code-like structures through which partial systems of cognitive features are related to one another, for instance in the form of equivalence of relationships. This 'translatability' of sub-systems of the cognitive domain one into the other accounts for the very possibility of all sorts of metaphors, and, by extension, of meta-discourses both verbal and non-verbal. It is often extremely difficult, if not impossible to describe in precise words the visual discourse of the circus which we nevertheless understand spontaneously. This is also true of many other domains such as artistic, emotional, and religious experiences. We have to construct meta-languages such as semiotics in order to articulate a theoretical account of these complex phenomena.

The purpose of this chapter is to explore, from this point of view, a recurring feature of traditional circus performances: the felicitous conjunction of horses and feathers. Indeed, if such patterned displays of objects and actions as circus horse acts can be considered as non-verbal discourses, the meaningful coupling of two classes of mutually exclusive natural objects which characterizes this discourse must be rooted in the cultural system in which this phenomenon is observed. The effect of *cognitive consistency* (effect of truth) which is produced can be explained, not in terms of pure aesthetics (necessarily redundant with respect to this effect) but in terms of semiotic operations within the cognitive structures of any appreciative audience broadly belonging to the same cultural sphere.

4.2. Birds, horses, and feathers

The use of colored feathers for decorating horses is indeed a readily observable phenomenon in the circus tradition, and it has been so for at least two hundred years as is witnessed by an abundant iconography. The last decades, though, have seen a marked shift toward a different decorative treatment of horses, a cultural phenomenon we will address in the last section of this chapter.

According to the tradition, plumes are fixed on the horses' heads, usually screwed on the top of a special halter that is connected to the rest of the trapping. Most of the time, plumes are also set on the horses' back, except when it is incompatible with the exercises performed, for instance if equestrians are balancing on the horses' backs. In popular iconography, advertisements, or children's drawings, plumes are consistently used as a diacritical sign that distinguishes circus horses from farm or sporting horses. Also, as observed in circus posters, the be-plumed head of a horse symbolizes the circus itself. There are instances which are at variance with this use, but the absence of plumes, in Liberty Horse Acts, or their replacement by some other type of decoration, were usually felt by circus audiences to be a stylistic transgression of a norm. In a few other cases, the absence of plumes could be explained on technical grounds, for instance if a part of an act consists of having the horses lying down or rolling over on their backs, something which tends to damage the plumes irreparably. Let us note finally that, within the paradigm of the traditional circus, horses and feathers appear to be congruent in some respect; their conjunction has an effect of felicitous naturalness, usually summarized, in journalistic accounts of circus performances, by the word "elegance", or other metaphorical expressions suggesting that a certain "truth" of the horse is set forth through this particular type of decorative association.

From an ethnological point of view, this recurrent feature appearing in a quasi-ritualistic phenomenon, such as the circus, raises a problem which can be formulated as follows: why a part of a certain type of animal (birds) so aptly combines with another type of animal (horses) to produce a cognitive consistency that does not seem to be accountable solely in terms of arbitrary habit? What motivation can possibly explain this phenomenon in terms of the cultural system where it is observed?

Of course, an immediate answer could relate this to the winged horse of Greek mythology, Pegasus. But such a historical explanation would be extremely weak, not only because plumes and wings are two different attributes – birds do not usually grow big plumes on their heads – but also because it is questionable to account for a productive phenomenon in one culture by an ancient myth from another culture, even if this myth shows some apparent resilience. In fact, there are some instances in the circus of jumping horses which are fitted with Pegasus wings. In this case it is as an explicitly mythical "quotation" from a dead past, a legendary figure, similar to the unicorn which is occasionally represented in the circus with horses wearing a decorative straight horn protruding from their forehead. This is comparable to the use made of these fantastic animals in the iconography of advertising or as a decorative or artistic theme.

Still more to the point, when the Pegasus theme is used in the circus context by fixing wings on the back of an individual horse that performs a high jump or a capriole, this horse does not wear plumes on its head or back. The use of Pegasus imagery is an erudite allusion to ancient mythology and, in the circus visual idiom, belongs to the same paradigm as acrobatic postures that imitate well-known classical statues, as we noted in Chapter 2.

Another possible explanation for the conjunction of horses and birds is suggested by Claude Lévi-Strauss's views on the respective positions of these two species in the structure through which western cultures organize the animals belonging to their ecological system, more specifically those to which we relate to the extent that we give them individual names: birds, dogs, cattle and racing horses (Lévi-Strauss 1962: 273–277). In this early structuralist essay, Lévi-Strauss attempts a comparative analysis of the types of names given to individual animals in each of these four categories. This leads to the construction of a three-dimensional model, bringing into play the categories of human vs. non-human with respect to apparent social organization, and metonymic vs. metaphorical with respect to the type of names used to designate (and address or call to attention) individual animals. According to Lévi-Strauss, birds and horses are in a complementary relationship because they represent the opposition society (birds) vs. anti-society (horses) and, at the same time, receive a metaphorical treatment as far as their given names are concerned. Therefore, it would be tempting to explain the conjunction of horses and feathers in the circus as an operation in which the metaphorical drive, that seems otherwise typical of the circus system, would neutralize the disjunction based on social status. This view would be all the more interesting since, as I have shown elsewhere (Bouissac 1991), the operations effectuated through the patterned exercises of a liberty horse act bear essentially upon the individual vs. society opposition. However, even though those contrasts have a function in the complex semiotic texts formed by circus horse acts, they do not account for all of their aspects. It should not be forgotten that Lévi-Strauss's idea was proposed in view of a restricted body of data which had been intuitively elaborated from the striking differences between the categories of names generally given to domestic animals according to contemporary French norms, and not in view of the problem I am addressing in this chapter. Note also that although birds are used in some circus acts, they very rarely, if ever, appear with horses with the occasional exception of pigeons and doves.

A more general theoretical view that is relevant to the symbolic status of horses was discussed by Leach (1964). In this essay, Leach takes as a starting point the particular attitudes of cultures concerning the edibility or non-edibility of horse meat. Leach explains the strong taboo observed in England by the fact that the horse is a pet and as such the equivalent of a "sister" with respect to the self. In France, even though horse meat is considered edible, it possesses a special status because it is sold in special shops and is credited with unique qualities that enhance strength and virility. Those two attitudes – the French one and the British one, which are often opposed – seem to be in fact variants of the same taboo with respect to an animal which is considered apt at providing metaphors for human status and relationships. If my hypothesis is correct, the strict prohibition in one case and the qualified one in the other case, could be interpreted as bearing upon the consumption of human flesh, taken literally in England and taken as a metaphor for non-institutionalized sexual indulgence in France following the well-known homology between the registers of sex and food. In both cases, horses appear to occupy a very sensitive position in the symbolic register of the two cultures.

4.3. Horses, ostriches, and chorus girls

In fact, it does not seem that the feathers worn by circus horses come directly from the ostriches that provide them. Although the ostriches could be conceived as the bird that is the closest analogue to a horse, this would be stretching too far the cognitive ground for the rapprochement. There is a shorter semiotic detour which is inspired by structuralism. The plumes are indeed identical to those used as head or garment decorations by dancing or chorus girls in cabarets or vaudevilles. Therefore the question is: what circus horses and chorus girls have in common, besides feathers, so that what is apt at decorating the former is also apt at decorating the latter? Indeed, the similarities between the two categories (girls and horses) are not limited to their preferred decorative elements; in the ring liberty horses perform patterns of collective movements or *solo* exercises similar in many respects to the ones seen in various kinds of ballets. They canter two by two, four by four, etc., sometimes twelve abreast; they pirouette individually or two by two accompanied by dance music; it is not uncommon that an act's last movement consists of the horses galloping around at the maximum possible speed while the band plays a French cancan, a musical icon of popular culture.

This relationship of equivalence between horses and dancing girls is confirmed if we consider another type of traditional equestrian act: the dancing horse (High School); the rider's relationship to his/her mount is specified first by the fact that whenever the rider is a female, she is often dressed as a man; secondly, the relationship is underlined by a familiar circus routine consisting of having a female dancer moving abreast with the horse and performing on its side the same steps as the horse does, exactly as if the horse was mirrored, or duplicated in the form of a female dancer. This is in striking contrast to the part played by showgirls in elephant acts in which they are complementary partners, to the extent of sometimes performing an exercise reminiscent of a typical position of human copulation with the woman lying under the lowered belly of the elephant. All this has nothing to do, of course, with the actual sex of the animal involved but with their symbolic values: most circus horses are stallions or geldings, and elephants are practically always females although they are referred to as "bulls" in circus parlance.

From these remarks, it is obvious that a certain form of equivalence between women and horses is posited in two types of traditional circus horse acts: liberty horse acts and High School acts. It should be added that in the ballets which some circus programs feature as brief transitions between the acts, female dancers sometimes wear equine attributes such as pony tails fixed on their lower back, even occasionally horse masks or wigs. It does not seem that this equivalence is based mainly on direct similarities such as length of hair, gait, and so on, or on a resemblance between riding and "possessing", because it would then apply to any horse act, which is not the case since there are many other acts in which horses play a quite different part.

Rather, this phenomenon seems to be specific to traditional Liberty Horse Acts and to some extent to High School displays. Mainly in the former, the equivalence is established through the correlation of two systems of contrastive cognitive features which can encode one another: first, the system comprising the various statuses of women in traditional western societies; secondly, the system organizing domestic animals. Both systems, although they are articulated in part in natural languages, seem to be characterized by tacit knowledge, that is, they are articulated principally through non-verbal discourse; such systems nevertheless have some sort of linguistic manifestation insofar as they produce poetic clichés, terms of abuse, proverbs, and metaphorical expressions. When we examine later the drastic changes which occurred in the symbolic treatment of circus horses during the last decades under strong societal pressures toward gender equality, we will observe a significant shift. In a pre-feminist context, the categories articulating the various statuses of women show the following oppositions: nubile women are either married or unmarried: the former are childless or mothers or grandmothers, the latter are seen as sexually active or sexually inactive. A category would comprise maidens (not yet married), spinsters and nuns; another category would be made up of non-remarried divorced women and widows; a third group would presumably include unattached and (assumed) sexually active women distinguished along a scale from professionals to prostitutes, chorus girls being perceived in the male imagination as straddling the latter two categories. Of course this is a cultural mapping dependent upon a traditional male-dominated society that had been integrated into the "natural" way of thinking as part of cultural common sense that still prevailed until the last decades of the twentieth century in western cultures. We have to remember that the modern circus created what is considered to be its folk tradition mostly during the nineteenth century in Europe. Naturally, these systems of classification are ill-defined, albeit rather constraining. They are only statistically stable and they are subject to cultural changes as we can observe nowadays, at least in western cultures. As the circus is a conservative form of popular entertainment, it is legitimate to rely on a traditional model for its investigation, keeping in mind that cultural revolutions such as feminism are bound to have an impact on its spectacles, as we will see in a moment.

The various relationships between statuses are aptly expressed by the system of domestic animals in which for instance sporting horses – entirely devoted to pleasure – are in strong opposition to cows exclusively defined by their usefulness as breeders and providers of milk and meat.

The system of domestic animals can also serve to encode other systems such as human qualities (lamb: gentleness; bitch: meanness; pig: vileness and gluttony, etc.). The terms of abuse are a window on the tacit knowledge of a culture as Leach (1964) and Tambiah (1969) have famously shown. With respect to the statuses of women, there is definitely in English a consistent, if partial, encoding, viz. the opposition between a "filly" (attractive unmarried woman, potentially available) and a "heifer" (not so attractive maiden, possibly homely, perceived in a breeding perspective). Kitten, chick, bird, dog, bitch, old cow, are other classificatory terms trivially applied to women in casual conversations among men; local slang would offer more examples. In French, an *oie blanche* [white goose] is opposed to a *poule* [hen], the former meaning a naïve maiden and the latter referring to a promiscuous woman, while *vieille chêvre* [old goat] may apply to an aging spinster. The purpose of this chapter is not to focus on those systems as such, but to point out that, if we follow Lévi-Strauss's early analysis (1962: 273–277), horses occupy a special position "beyond" the categories of both pets and cattle, outside the extended family cell (that is, on the borderline of society). Moreover they do not even constitute a society of their own on the model of humans as birds do. They could be defined adequately as "outcasts" or superfluous with respect to the system in which they nevertheless belong. On the other hand, Leach's study of animal systems suggests that there is a homology between the three sets which can be constructed with respect to "self": a) Self, Sister, Cousin, Neighbor, Stranger; b) Self, House, Farm, Field, Distant; c) Self, Pet, Livestock, Game, Wild animal. In accounting for various kinds and degrees of taboos, he locates horses in the category of pets, on the grounds that the pet quality of some horses determines the taboo values which apply to all horses. In fact, in the tables and diagrams he proposes, horses seem to be out of place; possibly because of their basically ambiguous position with respect to the other categories. Another reason may be that a cultural unit which another cultural unit is apt to encode because of their respective positions in two different systems becomes a cognitive component of this cultural unit. The horse is experienced not only as one of the terms of the system of domestic animals but also as an adequate sign or symbol for a particular status of women, namely the unattached, sexually active and potentially available women, a category epitomized in the "chorus girl"; note that with respect to the various institutions comprising our culture, this category is formally close to the one of horses as it can be inferred from a mere study of their names! Therefore, my hypothesis is that in the circus acts which have been described earlier, this cultural "truth" about horses (and possibly also about chorus girls) is redundantly displayed. As it was noted by Lévi-Strauss (1962:273), it is now difficult to assess the exact position of the horse because technological changes have upset the symbolic structure. This is why he refers exclusively to racing horses which form a rather well-defined set, adding that a part of the horse population could be classified with the dogs – incidentally as Leach (1964) does – and another part with the cattle. From a historical point of view, it would seem that the particular cognitive relation that I endeavored to set forth in this chapter appeared in Europe during the nineteenth century precisely at the time when the type of circus acts described here were developed as a novelty. There are many literary pointers to the metaphoric drive we have identified. The nineteenth-century novelist Honoré de Balzac, for instance, alludes to the tendency of men to talk about attractive women in terms usually applied to horses (see *Le père Goriot*, 1976 [1835]), and, almost a century later, Jean Cocteau notes in an article published in the newspaper *Paris-Midi* of June 2, 1919 that the dancing girls of the *Bal Tabarin* – the genre of entertainment which would later be illustrated and Americanized under the brand name *Crazy Horse* – had stage names that evoked the names of racing horses. More evidence of this semiotic slippage is found in the visual arts such as the Max Ernst's collage of a coquette with a horse head in *La femme 100 têtes* or the scene in the Marx Brothers film *Animal Crackers* in which Harpo shows the picture of a horse when he is asked whether he is in love with any girl.

However, the "military drill" is another, more ancient model that also serves as a reference for Liberty Horse Acts. This model, rooted in history and still perpetuated in the nostalgic mode in some circus presentations, appears sometimes to fuse with the ballet and vaudeville models which inspire the decoration and composition of circus horse acts. But the latter remained more productive for a much longer time.

The dancing girls' feathers, in addition to the music as well as the patterned movements performed by the horses, actualize in the "text" of such circus acts a set of selective cognitive features which subsume or neutralize the other ones, in a way reminiscent of Greimas's *classemes,* that is, a sign that signals a particular level of consistency and activates only one of the various meanings that a lexical unit can receive in a range of contexts (Greimas 1966: 50–54). For instance, if the movements of the horses in the ring replicate military drills, the mere presence of colorful plumes re-categorizes these movements as dance. The same effect is achieved by the selection of the musical score that accompanies a Liberty Horse Act.

If the interpretation developed in this chapter is correct, one might wonder why liberty horses are often introduced as "stallions" (whether they are geldings or mares). In fact this supplementary verbal sign, which can override any contrary visual information because the audience cannot really scan the horses which are fast moving in circle, constitutes an important fact in the decoding of the complex semiotic operations involved in a circus act. Paradoxically, this is congruent with the general hypothesis which has been developed above. Indeed, the quality of "stallion" represents the maximum possible of "horsiness" – remember that we are in the context of a traditional male-dominated society – and signifies both freedom and hypersexuality; the stallion stands at the very limit of the scale of domestic animals, as close to wilderness as a domestic animal can be in contrast to the bull which, in western cultures, except in the Hispanic sphere, is a breeder well kept under control by a ring in the nose. Therefore, those features, combined with the rest of the act, redundantly express the presumed status of chorus girls in the collective representations of the (male) audience. Let us not forget that the gentrification of the circus is a relatively recent phenomenon and that it was traditionally not as respectable as it has become nowadays.

4.4. Circus horses in times of cultural changes

The view expressed in the previous sections of this chapter is confirmed by many literary exploitations of the tacit knowledge whose dense network of systematic relationships is an inexhaustible provider of "true" metaphors. The pertinent opposition *horse* vs. *cow* is exemplified by comparing Victor Hugo's *La vache* [the cow], which is portrayed as a generous icon of mother nature, and Balzac's assessment of desirable women in terms borrowed from horsemanship terminology as we noted above. The tendency to fuse horses and women in a single image had become so prominent in the mid-nineteenth century that it triggered some protests such as the one documented in a critical edition of Balzac's works: in 1845, Francis Mey, a commentator of contemporary events, pointed out that it was shameful to write about a woman as if she were a horse, referring to her in terms of breed, gait, and using the vocabulary of horse anatomy to describe her physical qualities. More recently Francis Ponge's *Le cheval* [the horse], a text considered by its author as an "*eugénie*" (that is, a felicitous event according to the Greek etymology of this word), contains incidental depictions of a horse as a *courtisane* with "woman's eyes", " fine legs", "high heels", or as a "tall poultry which lays golden eggs". Similar phenomena can be noted in art. Dali's example, in the following quotation from *The object as revealed in surrealist experiments* (1932), is symptomatic:

> It is through a clearly paranoiac process that it has been possible to obtain a double image, that is to say the representation of an object which, without the least figurative or anatomical medication, is at the same time the representation of another object that is absolutely different, one that also is free of any type of deformation or abnormality that would reveal some sort of artificial arrangement... The double image (*for example, the image of a horse that is at the same time the image of a woman*) can be prolonged.... (Breton 1972: 274; emphasis mine)

It is also relevant to point out another symbolic treatment of horses in a context totally different from both circus performances and literary texts: the *Palio*, a ritualistic horse race which for centuries has been taking place twice a year in Sienna (Italy). It has been thoroughly described and interpreted in great details by Alan Dundes and Alessandro Falassi in a book titled *La Terra in Piazza* (1975). It would seem that, in this case also, a cognitive interference similar to the one analyzed above plays a decisive part and provides a key for the understanding of this puzzling phenomenon: there is historical evidence that in the past whenever for some reasons horses were not available, prostitutes were forced to substitute for them and race around the city square.

Do the circus horses' feathers still make sense in contemporary culture, after the feminist revolution? The conditions which determined the horses' position with respect to the other domestic animals had become similar to the position of the same category of women with respect to the others, and what was congruent to those women was also congruent to the horses. In the cultural context where they were observed, the horses' feathers made sense. Nowadays, horses are less and less often presented with plume ornaments in circuses. Female equestrians who ride high school horses usually use a male dancer in the position where dancing girls were made to accompany the horse's steps in the previous century. A vivid turning point occurred in the 1970s when Circus Lumière, a British avant-garde theatrical troupe, produced an extraordinary spectacle which was meant to transgress all the stereotypes of the traditional circus. There were systematic inversions such as a magician who was dramatically extracting a top hat from a rabbit. The Liberty Horse Act was rendered by a female trainer in dominatrix attire who was controlling eight men, harnessed like circus horses, who were made to cavort around the ring and mimic whatever circus horses do. It is symptomatic that *inverting* a horse act consisted of replacing the horses with men.

Until the Internet became a reliable repository of visual documents, it was difficult to prove a point such as the one which has been made in this chapter. Doing research on the circus consisted of actually going to the circus in order to observe performances and to describe them in detail. Many circuses were reluctant to grant permission to photograph or otherwise record the acts they presented in their programs. Nowadays, even if the semiotics of the circus still requires that researchers engage in actual "fieldwork", data concerning the decoration and staging of circus horses, for instance, are readily available online. Some circuses maintain visually rich websites in which they provide glimpses of their displays. Circus fan associations create illustrated archives. Even some performers put videos of their acts online as a way of advertising them. Readers interested in exploring further the destiny of horses's feathers can visit, among many other possibilities, the French website http://www.aucirque.com or the German website of the European Circus Association (http://www.europeancircus.info).

They will note that the majority of the Liberty Horse Acts do not any longer use plumes as an equine decoration of choice and feature women in the role of presenter. It thus tends to show that not only the political economy of gender is articulated in the visual discourse of the circus, but also that this discourse is attuned to the cultural transformations occurring in its societal context.

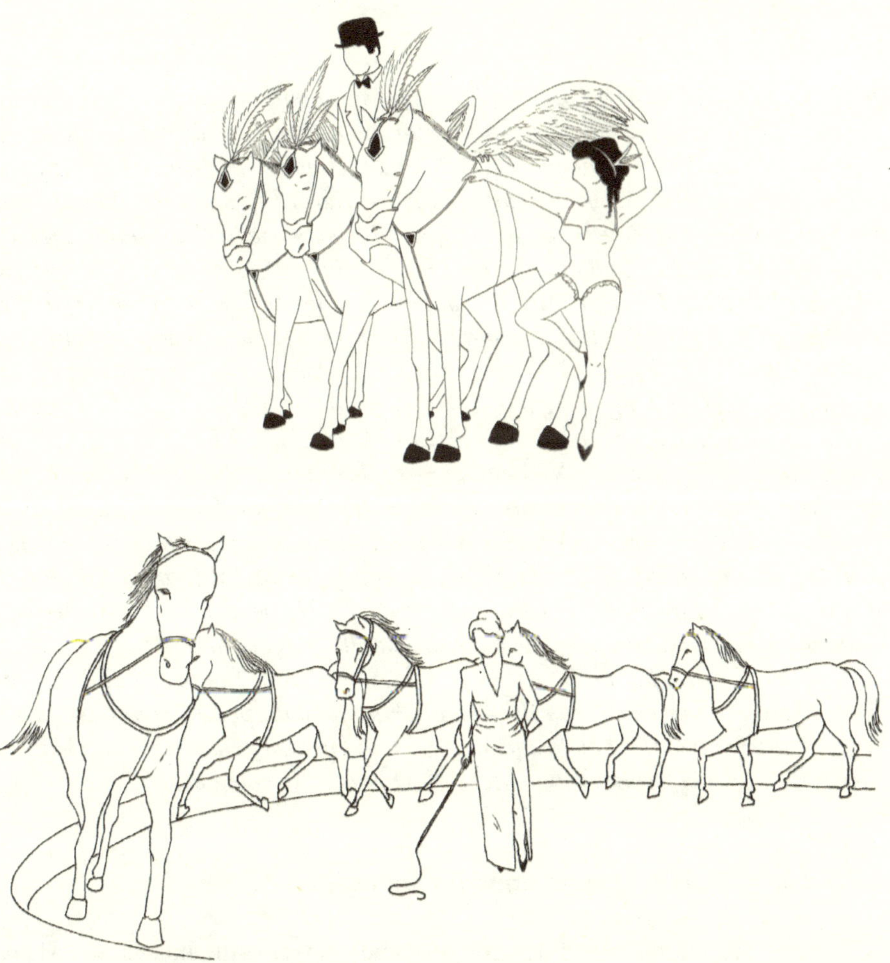

Figure 3. Between bare "liberty horses" and emphatically be-plumed or winged animals, the circus equine paradigm displays a range of visual metaphors which are relevant to gender politics. The horse, the rider, and the dancer compose a trio that may undergo significant gender-sensitive permutations.

Chapter 5
Circus and cycles

It is two in the morning. The telephone rings. I jump on my feet. It is Gérard, my circus business partner who stays with the animals in our winter quarters, outside the city. I expect the worst. "What happened?" – "He made it! He made it!". "He" was Mylord, the Himalayan bear. Gérard had been trying to teach him how to ride the bicycle for some time. This was tricky. You cannot coerce a bear to sit on a saddle and push on the pedals. You have to create a situation. The animal itself must discover the relation between the pushing and the speed. The balance comes naturally, like for humans. The body of a bear is not very different. Riding a bicycle is a mental process. Mylord had mastered already most of the ursine routines: walking upright, drinking from a bottle that looks like a trumpet while the band plays the march of Verdi's Aida, *making a few fast steps toward the trainer on Tchaikovsky's* Nutcracker *ballet music, climbing a ladder and tumbling down a kindergarten slide. This was like play for this young animal and there was always a sweet carrot for reward. But the tricycle, which was the first step before graduating to the real thing, was an issue. Mylord would willingly sit down on the saddle that had been custom-made. His feet would spontaneously rest on the pedals. Then, whatever Gérard could imagine to prompt him to push brought no result. That night, the trainer had persisted. The bear had been kept seated longer than usual and the carrots had been dipped in honey. Suddenly, Mylord started pedaling as fast as he could and the tricycle almost crashed into Gérard. After this breakthrough, everything would become easier.*

5.1. Horse and bicycle: preliminary analogies

In the last chapter, the 'enculturation' of nature, specifically horses, was shown to be an uncommonly rich process demonstrating the complex ways in which the circus employs, amplifies, and make into spectacle those resources available to it. Indeed, it should not be forgotten that the 19th-century circus was primarily focused on horses and horsemanship, not only as a means of transportation for traveling circuses but, more importantly, as the very substance of the spectacles themselves, to such an extend that the circus can be viewed, in its modern form, as a ritualistic celebration of the domestication of the *Equidae* and of their integration into a culture to the creation of which they have greatly contributed.

We have focused so far on a particular symbolic use of horses in a limited period of cultural history which bears witness to the horse's semiotic versatility. In fact, circus type spectacles involving horsemanship are documented over the whole Euro-Asian area that is characterized by steppe cultures and their branching out through conquests achieved mainly thanks to the domestication of the horse. The Chinese word for circus can be translated literally as 'horse theatre'.

Before considering the circus's incorporation of cultural evolution in the guise of technology, a brief review of the circus equestrian paradigm, closely related to, but in revealing ways distinct from the cycle paradigm, is now in order. In general, equestrian acts display various forms of control of *Equidae* by humans who use both technological aides and semiotic means to make them perform tricks. Most of the tricks consist of eliciting particular forms of behavior which convey the illusion that the horses have reached some degree of humanization. There are two categories of presentation which are based upon the modalities of the controlling process: *riding* acts and *liberty* acts. In the former the horses are mounted by human riders; in the latter they are directed and cued from a distance. The two modalities combine to form coordinates, each act being defined by the distance of the controlling agency and the degree of sophistication of the movements performed by the horses: the more remote the control, the more difficult it is to obtain the patterned behavior which is the goal of the training. The special long whip used in liberty acts is actually a sort of prosthetic device which extends the trainers' arm and puts the animals within his/her reach. Riding acts comprise trick riding, bareback riding and *haute-école* [high school] in which the horse allegedly performs dance steps; liberty acts involve the more or less complex movements of one or several animals confined in the circular space of the arena; the standard act in this category includes twelve horses moving freely but in coordination. In a sub-category, often called "comedy horse", an animal is trained to respond to cues which elicit a variety of interactive behavior which the trainer frames within a socio-semiotic context. For such acts to produce the intended effect, the horse must be controlled in a subtle way so that it does not appear to act under constraint but spontaneously, something it does to a degree since the behavioral segments which are elicited all belong to the ethological and biosemiotic repertory of the horse.

Keeping this system in mind, it is obvious that bicycle riding cannot generate such a dichotomy as mounted vs. un-mounted vehicles. Secondly, a bicycle rider must at the same time both propel the machine by pedaling and perform some other actions if the performance is to trigger interest and excitement. By using the force of inertia to its very limit an acrobat can alternatively provide the energy needed to keep the bicycle running and engage in some feats of balance, strength or dexterity. Team-work can combine the efforts of several persons. The only category of circus horsemanship which can reasonably smoothly be transferred to the category of bicycling is bareback riding, in which the horse plays the role of an unstable moving platform whose uneven surface is often fitted with a padded cover and whose patterns of instability are sufficiently predictable for acrobats to learn how to control their balance while performing their particular skill (e.g., jumping, juggling, balancing an object or another person) while the horse is in motion, a tempo that the acrobat must espouse. A trainer need to monitor from the center of the arena the gait of the horse and to correct any deviation from its optimal rhythm is somewhat analogous to the way in which a bicycle acrobat must ensure a constant and well-controlled speed for the machine if it is to remain stable under the variations of weight and the shifting of load caused by the additional movements and/or bodies which are introduced in the dynamic system of the act. However, a crucial difference is that in bareback riding the horse is controlled mostly through the liberty act modality, since the rider negotiates the instability of the support surface without having the means of regulating it, the latter task falling upon the trainer who monitors the gait from the center of the ring. Moreover, most bareback riding specialties are based upon ground acrobatic skills which have been transposed to the more difficult and dangerous context provided by the broad back of a moving horse. Therefore, it is quite conceivable that even in the hypothetical absence of the bareback riding model, ground acrobatics would have been combined with bicycle riding according to the same logic which combined them with horsemanship.

A metaphorical use of the bicycle in the circus which seems to be directly derived from horsemanship is the one patterned on the comedy horse model. Naturally, it is considerably constrained by the fact that the bicycle is not endowed with an ethological program of interaction of its own but simply follows the laws of physics – even though, as it will be indicated below, it is not entirely clear how these laws apply in this case. However, through skillful manipulation of its movements and parts, a bicycle can be construed as an apparent agency which is prone to thwart the cyclist's plans or even attempt to implement a counter-program of action. A significant portion of such tricks is based upon mimicking horse behavior, such as refusing to proceed, rearing, bucking, jumping, kicking, and unseating the rider, and generally being uncooperative. Like in the comedy horse act, such motions are framed in an interpretive context which transforms them into signs of mischievous or humorous intentions. However, the equine analogy does not account for all tricks involved in such art; the structure and principle of the bicycle itself offer a *sui generis* potential for original gags and transformations.

5.2. History, cultural evolution, and the circus

The ascent of the circus in 19th-century Western societies and its continuation through the 20th and 21st century can be explained to a great extent by the urge to synthesize, or at least collocate within the ritual space of an organized perspective, the semiotic diversity produced by a period of intense explorations and discoveries. Very early, this harbinger of globalization brought exoticism home and accommodated novelties to its ancestral skills. At a time when traditional European cultures were confronted by otherness as colonial empires and technological innovations kept expanding, there was a need for a template able to produce cosmological representations. Such an interpretation does not, however, necessarily imply a functionalist perspective: suffice it to note that an institutional *locus* where novelty could be assimilated at a glance by the masses, in a manner such that its potential disruptiveness could be ritualistically controlled, would naturally tend to compete with other institutional *loci* such as, for example, the church or the traditional theatre which mostly were past-oriented and introverted. The nomadic mountebanks which had previously been repressed, and even, at times, fiercely persecuted, expanded their activities in the form of traveling and stable circuses, and many prospered in a relatively short period of time.

The circus came to occupy a sizeable economic niche, generating cultural signs that soon started overflowing into painting, fiction, poetry and theater, and later into the cinema art and other media. The circus reinvented itself as an educational institution in Victorian England (Assael 2005) and competed with natural history museums and zoos. Selection pressure at the cultural level can alone account for the rise and decline of symbolic commodities. As a semiotic industry that catered to urban societies hungry for dreams and fantasy of otherness, the circus was and remains competitive as its selling arguments are authenticity, truth, and genuine risk and the form of its performances straddles ritual and entertainment. A comparable phenomenon occurred at the peak of the Roman Empire's expansion and, in the same vein, 16th-century Europeans witnessed the development of both princely collections of *exotica* (adumbrating the modern museums, zoos and circus sideshows) and "Triumphs" which were remarkably similar to the great circus parades in 19th- and 20th-century Europe and North America. The orderly display of exoticism in the circus – both as institution and performance – constrains and regulates the temptation to yield to the dissipative seduction of otherness and novelty. The rhetoric, both visual and verbal, of the displays can be understood as a discursive device through which a conservative balance is achieved between cultural accommodation and assimilation, if one may thus extrapolate to the social domain Piaget's psychological terms (1974: 397). Indeed, the circus at the same time underlines pure information ("unheard of", "first time ever", etc.) and normalizes it by developing its own stereotypes. From this point of view the cultural assimilation of alien elements can be considered to be a form of cognitive "predation": wild animals and often even human "savages" in its heydays were displayed and brought into focus as symbolic parts of a world that Western culture was able to condense in a template which coincided with its own center.

But, this is not all. The modern art of the circus can be conceived as a bundle of cultural units – the acrobatic and animal-training techniques – which are transmitted across generations by oral tradition and observational learning in the restricted context of families or castes. Brought together as they were in the 19th-century circus, they form a representative array of special behaviors which encompasses – as we will see later – the complete human repertory of survival competencies under stress, a characteristic highly compatible with the handling by the circus of the cognitive stress caused by the unavoidable confrontation with exoticism. Moreover, the successful expansion of the Western culture of the period is symbolically ascribed to the heroic behavior – similarly action under stress – of the colonizers who, like the circus acrobats or animal trainers, are supposed to be able to overcome formidable resistance and thus to prove their exceptional fitness. The ideological context was indeed provided then by social Darwinism.

The success of the circus "meme" (Dawkins 1989), that is, its extensive replication within the cultural space of Western nations and beyond, its power of appropriation of others' cultural forms and its eventual dissemination in all cultures, can undoubtedly be attributed to its idiosyncratic capacity for symbolic condensation of an ethos and a cosmology, and to its structural resistance within the milieu in which it developed. From the mid-twentieth century on, the circus has proved to be one of the most marketable symbolic commodities worldwide as if it were pre-adapted, so to speak, to cultural globalization and adaptation to universal novelty, as *Cirque du Soleil* has demonstrated by reaching the status of a global brand name.

5.3. The introduction of the bicycle in circus spectacles

The background and conceptual framework outlined above is crucial in the examination of a well documented cultural change: the technological innovation which, after some terminological hesitation, came to be called the bicycle, and its introduction into the circus as a productive acrobatic paradigm. This phenomenon is all the more interesting since the bicycle seems to be the only object, among the cornucopia of novelties produced by the industrial era, which was almost instantly appropriated by the circus and soon became a standard acrobatic specialty in a great variety of forms.

Naturally, over the last two centuries, the circus has assimilated a large number of other technological innovations which modified its infrastructure: for instance, canvasses supported by metallic poles provided space for a larger audience; the circus' mobility was considerably improved by switching from horse-drawn to motor vehicles and trains; its marketing became more efficient when it adopted modern commercial advertising; electric generators were introduced as an essential part of its basic equipment; microphones and amplifiers transformed the presentation of its spectacles, laser lighting enhanced and dramatized its displays, and so on. But, in spite of all these technological changes, the content of circus performances remained remarkably stable and traditional, to the degree that the circus came to be explicitly construed as anti-technological and even nowadays often promotes itself through its nostalgic appeal, even while being at the same time encapsulated, so to speak, in a well developed technological shell.

Before examining the apparently paradoxical introduction of the bicycle in the circus, consider the treatment of other novelties by the circus. For instance, the automobile has given rise to two specialty acts: a *casse-cou* [risky] stunt and a comedy theme. The former consists of suddenly releasing a wheeled vehicle, which has the appearance of a racing car, at the top of a high structure, on a steep artificial slope and of using the force of inertia to accelerate along the suspended track until a sharp up-turn or a spring projects the vehicle in space, causing it to perform a loop before landing upon another curved track which brings it up-hill and thus to a standstill. Sometimes the "car" is simply made to "fly" over a gap and end up in a net. Several apparatuses have been constructed for various sorts of performance. Although this is a purely mechanical trick, the presence of a "driver" in the vehicle, the introduction of the act as a "salto mortale" in an automobile, and the dramatization of the staging put this act – somewhat improperly – in the category of acrobats. Naturally it forms, within this paradigm, a fringe group which includes "human cannon-balls", "divers into a narrow bucket or a sponge" and the like, and which is only occasionally productive. These stunts take more daring than skill and the "acts" themselves are completed in a matter of seconds.

The comedy use of the automobile generally involves a driver whose vehicle behaves erratically or gives signs of mischievous intent. A variety of contrivances convey the impression that the car acts of its own will in order to ridicule its owner. This type of act is derived, *mutatis mutandis*, from a subspecialty of horsemanship, the comedy-horse, which has a long tradition in the circus as was mentioned at the beginning of this chapter.

It is worth noting that both kinds of act – the car stunt and the comic act – were first performed with bicycles at the turn of the 20th century and that the introduction of the automobile into circus spectacles followed the patterns first set by the bicycle but was definitely not as productive. Later, diminutive planes and rockets also appeared in circus spectacles, but exclusively in a decorative capacity. They may be important for determining the theme of a display, but they do not serve any technical function exploiting their technologies. In this context, the quick appropriation of the bicycle by the circus and the development of an abundant and diversified acrobatic paradigm based upon this innovation constitute an interesting cultural phenomenon which requires explanation.

The first question which comes to mind concerns the possible relationship between the bicycle and the traditional circus acts which might suggest some essential compatibility which could account for this instantaneous and successful adoption.

The building blocks of circus spectacles are typical behavioral patterns of survival, more precisely of the immediate survival of organisms (humans or animals) which are challenged by life-threatening situations. These situations have the particularity of being artificially constructed rather than directly borrowed from the natural environment. As we have seen in Chapter 2, circus artifacts are devised with a view to isolating a particular variable of the environment and to model an extreme situation that individual humans or animals have been trained to negotiate. The necessity for specialization – based both on individual physical or psychological predispositions and technical knowledge often kept secret by families or castes – resulted in a set of acrobatic and animal-training specialties. Fundamentally, a circus spectacle is a representative sampling of the whole gamut of these specialties.

Since motility and mobility are prerequisites for human survival – for instance, collecting food, catching prey, avoiding predators, and mating – anything that can demonstrate agility at the limit points of these prerequisites may form the basic for a circus specialty. Thus *keeping one's balance* in spite of drastic variations of the surface upon which mobility is required, *grasping and holding the grip* in order to prevent a fall when the ground is failing beneath one's feet, *clearing obstacles* that may be gaps or large objects which introduce discontinuities or extreme variations of level into the environment, *throwing and catching implements* and, finally, *controlling predators* form the five basic competencies of our primate heritage upon which all subsequent developments are built. All acrobatic and animal circus arts can be shown to exemplify one of these competencies or a combination of several as we will see in greater details in the following chapters of this book.

Thus, the circus gives its audience an object of contemplation which is all the more involving as it implements, in real-life if not in everyday life situations, those essential behavioral capacities which define humankind. The principle at the root of the circus differs greatly from the one which governs sporting events of all kinds – including, for instance, the Olympics – because it does not rest upon competition with respect to a scale of "more or less", but upon an "all or none" outcome in which success means life and failure means death, or at least a crippling condition which in primitive or natural situations soon would result in death. From an evolutionary point of view the survival of the fittest implies a large number of casualties, and it is not average challenges but extreme ones which set the criteria.

Naturally, it should be kept in mind that circus displays are of a symbolic nature. Individual acrobats or animal tamers are not necessarily the fittest in all aspects of human capacities. Their hyper-specialization can be a serious liability, and also they often rely on tricks of the trade which deceptively create a mere appearance of superior physical or psychological power. Nevertheless, whatever the techniques of representation may be – and most of them are based on exacting training and truly exceptional physical fitness – the spectacles are experienced by their audience as credible feats of outstanding abilities performed at the limit of the humanly feasible, at the interface between the possible and the impossible. Ultimately it is the cutting edge of the evolutionary process which is represented in the circus arena.

The hypothesis which will now be introduced concerning the bicycle is that the reason why this innovation was smoothly and productively appropriated by the circus is that the bicycle pertains to a biological evolutionary paradigm rather than to a purely technological one. In the remainder of this chapter, the following aspects of the bicycle will be examined to support this hypothesis: (1) the circumstances of its creation, (2) its structure and function, (3) its symbolic treatment in the cultural domain.

5.4. Pondering the strange history of the bicycle

The bicycle is a new kind of object which burst into existence in mid-nineteenth century, was soon mass-produced, and greatly transformed society by increasing individual mobility at little cost in the context of the period's intense urbanization. Although the history of this revolutionary artifact is well documented (e.g., Baudry de Saunier 1891; Palmer 1965; Woodforde 1977; Alderson 1972; Ritchie 1975; Wilson 2004), its presence in our everyday environment is now so much taken for granted that it is worth recalling the particularities of its origins.

Variously combining the power of the wheel with cranks, levers and steering controls, early prototypes of the bicycle which appeared during the first part of the 19th century, were clearly related to a long-standing technological heritage. Attempts to design vehicles whose propulsive force would come not from horses but from the passengers themselves actually go back at least two centuries earlier. Jean Theson, for instance, had conceived in mid-17th century a four-wheel machine that was set in motion by two seated men operating a system of levers. Other similar vehicles were conceived and even built but remained mere curiosities. The *"vélocifère"*, a French neologism that juxtaposes the Latin words for "transportation" and "speed", invented in 1690 by Count de Sivrac, is thought to be the first recorded device with two aligned wheels whose axes were joined by a beam supporting a wooden structure on which a person could sit astride and strike the ground with his feet alternately so as to propel the wheeled device forward. About a century later, a German engineer, Baron Karl de Drais de Sauerbron improved the "*vélocifère*" by adding a steering system to the front wheel and in 1818 he took his invention, soon to be called the "*draisienne*" ("draisine" in English), to Paris. For a while, riding it became a fashionable pastime, but with no practical applications. However, copies were made in England and in America where they enjoyed some popularity. In 1839, MacMillan, a Scottish blacksmith, made a self-propelling version of the "draisienne" by combining two swinging cranks linked to two levers fixed on each side of the rear wheel. This is generally considered to be the first successful attempt to generate the propulsive force by applying muscular energy to a mediating mechanism built as a part of a two-wheeled vehicle rather than merely improving the output of walking or running by channeling to the wheels a part of the force thus produced. After raising considerable interest, this device, however, did not enjoy great popularity probably because of its heavy weight and relative clumsiness.

The creation of the bicycle proper is attributed to Pierre Michaux, the owner of a workshop in Paris who, in 1861, while repairing an old "draisienne", got the idea of adapting the crank handles of a vertical grindstone to the front wheel of such a vehicle. With his son Ernest, he constructed a wood and iron frame that could be propelled in this manner. Called "velocipedes" these new machines were copied and disseminated in several European cities and within a few years they were industrially produced in both Europe and America.

The basic features characterizing the bicycle – and with respect to which subsequent improvements of Michaux's device have not introduced any real variety – are truly remarkable. Both its morphology and its functionality have been hailed as a most felicitous achievement on a par with the best results obtained by the fine-tuning of biological evolution. It is still considered to be the most efficient means yet devised to convert human energy into propulsion (Whitt and Wilson 1989). The average gain yielded by the bicycle is about four times a walking pace. However, despite its ubiquity and familiarity, the principles upon which this device rests remain a scientific puzzle. Thus, its simplicity and elegance are associated with mystery, and if the serendipity of its creation is kept in mind, the analogy of the bicycle with biological forms is indeed striking.

The complexity of the problem arises from the fact that the bicycle and its rider do not constitute a rigid body but combine at least nine degrees of freedom with the parameters of the various dimensions of the actual bicycles and the particular properties of the ground. The successful negotiation of the laws of gravity appears as a fine line between stability and chaos; equations which have been proposed so far apply to simplified problems such as assuming "that the wheels should be on the ground, while – at least on level ground – neither the absolute degree of rotation of the two wheels nor the absolute position and direction of the frame can be relevant to stability" (Maddox 1990: 407), or defining the problem to be solved in terms of a rigid body subject to some selected constraints. Franke et al. (1990: 116), for instance, reduces the numbers of variables that they wish to take into consideration.

This longstanding controversy (e.g., Whipple 1899) at least demonstrates the unique status of the bicycle among all other human artifacts and is indispensable for understanding both its place in the circus and how the circus incorporates new features of society at large. Actually, the bicycle should be considered a sort of *prosthesis* rather than a tool, but one which adds an idiosyncratic physical competence to the repertory of human behavior rather than merely palliating accidental deficiencies and impairments. False teeth, glass eyes, artificial limbs and the like can model with sufficient approximation the appearance or functional structure of missing organs and become a part of previously established programs of action geared toward survival. But, when in use, the bicycle does become fully integrated into a biological program of general action – maintaining stability during locomotion – and not focusing on the transformation, exploitation or neutralization of some aspect of the environment. The relationship between artifacts and humans has various degrees of immediacy, or intimacy. The bicycle achieves a maximal interactive involvement to such an extent that, as an adaptation to gender differences both biological and cultural, the bicycle evolved two distinct morphologies, a male one and a female one, thus mirroring sexual dimorphism. The shape of the saddle, the pattern of the frame, and the curvature of the handlebar came to differ markedly in each case. Only later did a unisex model appear under the pressure of specific contemporary cultural changes. A mere morphological compromise between the two extremes, this new design has not caused the disappearance of the others.

Except for this differentiated adaptation to the human body, the bicycle does not attempt to directly model any "natural" forms; it is nevertheless based upon the most fundamental design features and economy of biological morphology: the selection of axis and circumference as an overall structural principle. Assessed from the point of view of mechanical advantage, which provides basic insights into the selective architecture of all organisms with respect to the kind of constraints afforded by their environments, the bicycle possesses features which are analogous to the most common biological ones. After all, as Wainwright (1988: 38) notes, not all the parts of an organism are made of living materials. If "[m]any biomaterials are living, for example, wood, tendon, skin and bone, some are not, for example, coral, shell, scales, claws, hair and the cuticles of plants, insects, and other arthropods".

As a mechanical support system, the bicycle can be viewed as an extension of the primate skeleton (monkeys and apes can become expert cyclists with appropriate training and as long as the frame is proportionate to the size of their own skeleton, as is the case with children), and the properties of this morphology and structure seem to have been constrained by the same principles of selection. And, as we have seen in the introductory anecdote to this chapter, a bicycle can also nicely fit into the body plan of a bear.

5.5. The semiotics of the bicycle

The socio-cultural impact of the bicycle has been investigated from several points of view. Once it was industrially produced and readily affordable – the average cost of an American bicycle went from $ 120 in 1893 to $ 10 in 1902 – it radically transformed the relation of the masses to their living space, expanding individual territories and creating new social networks and interfaces. It was soon characterized as a social leveler "that bridged social space and made travel over longer distances accessible to the middle and lower classes who could not afford a carriage or automobile (Kern 1983: 317).

Observers of bicycle use in its early years monitored its effect and assessed its further potential. In fact, it quickly became a political symbol (Pivato 1990) as well as a sign of modernity and civilization. As early as 1869, optimism and idealism marked in France the celebration of this "sign of the time".

Notwithstanding the vituperations of clergymen – who still in 1896 were denouncing the bicycles as "diabolical devices of the demon of darkness" (quoted in Smith 1972: 1) – the bicycle steadily spread with the expansion of industrialism and entered into a quasi-symbiosis with humans all over the world. First bicyclists expressed their elation at experiencing this new device noting that it gives humans the impression of having grown wings or – for the more educated – of riding Pegasus, a feeling that Maurice Leblanc, a French popular writer at the turn of the 20th century, encapsulated in the title of a novel devoted to the emancipating power of the bicycle: *Voici des ailes!* [Here come the wings!] (1898). Naturally this was after the early "boneshaker" of Michaux was fitted with pneumatic tires around 1888.

As the bicycle became a cultural focus and an institution, a rich semantic field developed, producing a terminological explosion; not only did the object itself and its parts have to be named, but its place in culture and society needed to be symbolically assimilated. This semantic process has been fully explored and documented by R.W. Jeanes (1949) in an unpublished doctoral dissertation on the origins of French bicycle vocabulary. Jeanes' sources include a vast array of publications which show that, within a few years, Michaux' invention not only had become a common topic in the general press but had also sustained sufficient popular interest to justify the launching of commercial periodicals as *Le vélocipède* and *Le vélocipède illustré*. In another fascinating account of the terminological impact of the bicycle, B.R. Diez has documented the special language which was created about it in Spanish (1981). In books primarily concerned with the social history of the bicycle, Smith (1972) and Ritchie (1975) incidentally document the semantic innovations in the British and American linguistic domains respectively.

Very early, horsemanship provided a powerful metaphor for the description and denomination of a device which seemed destined to replace the horse in its capacity as facilitator of locomotion. "Steel horses" and "silent steed" became common metaphors in the press; the pedals were perceived as "spurs"; the saddle soon lost its metaphorical value; cyclists formed clubs modeled after the "Jockey Club", and organized competitions which were patterned on horse races.

However, except for the remote analogy that may exist between a symbiotic relationship and a *prosthesis*, which both improve human mobility, few things could be more different than a horse and a bicycle. On every ground imaginable the bicycle appears, on the contrary, as an anti-horse. Even though early two-wheeled devices were commonly fitted with wooden equine heads on the pattern of familiar hobby-horses used in folk dances and children's games, this visual metaphor is grounded on the superficial similarity of the "riding" positions without considering the vastly different neuromotor behavior which allows both kinds of "riders" to increase the speed of their locomotion while maintaining their balance. Structurally, horses and bicycles are both definitely longer than higher but this feature which, incidentally, they share with benches, caterpillars and other numerous objects, can hardly be considered a sufficient definitional property.

For the rest, they consistently belong to markedly contrasting categories from the point of view of their locomotor, ergonomic and economic principles as well as of their evolutionary status. True, both domestication and technological innovation are forms of human adaptive behavior, but from this point of view shepherd dogs and barbed wire, which both control the movement of cattle, could also be placed in a similar category. It is nevertheless a fact that before the bicycle itself became the organizing focus of its own semantic field and symbolic domain, its meaning was spontaneously processed through the metaphor of the horse, as if this new object which was bringing about deep cultural and social changes could be semiotically assimilated through the only familiar object with which it shared a single biological advantage for the human species. It should, however, be noted that the bicycle soon gained its symbolic autonomy, was celebrated as "the little queen" or a "scientific angel", and that whatever reminders of the horse persist in its terminology are now dead metaphors for the most part.

5.6. The bicycle enters the kingdom of the horse

Now returning to the circus, let us examine the modalities of its quickly adopting the bicycle. In view of the hypothesis which has been developed in this chapter regarding, on the one hand, the nature of circus acts in general and, on the other hand, the particular status of the bicycle among the other technological innovations of the time, it should be clear that the creation of a circus specialty based upon the potentialities of this new device was a predictable event. After all the mere riding of a bicycle is an acrobatic feat which needs to be learned from an experienced rider. That the affinity of the rising art of bicycle riding with circus acrobatics was perceived by contemporaries is demonstrated by a documentary drawing published in the Paris magazine *L'illustration* (September 25, 1875) which shows a benefit race in the Tuileries Garden. Each rider, mounting a penny-farthing which was the then current model, is shown performing an additional acrobatic feat while pedaling: jumping over a man lying on the ground, playing the violin, juggling four balls, balancing a plate at the tip of a rod, making a handstand on the handlebar (Ritchie 1975: 87).

It took less than a decade – the first professional bicyclist acrobats appeared between 1869 and 1876 (Cervelatti 1961: 190; Strehly 1903: 309; Fréjaville 1922: 160) – for Michaux's invention to become an original circus specialty, but as in the linguistic domain, the horse metaphor outlined at the beginning of this chapter lingered for some time in the use of the bicycle in performances. Yet, clearly, the art of bicycling developed its own acrobatic paradigm with only minimal influence from circus horsemanship. Since speed and balance are narrowly correlated in the successful riding of a bicycle, the circus' search for limit situations led to acts based on both ends of the spectrum of speed. Bicycle acts are basically of two kinds: those which involve a static bicycle and those in which the bicycle is in motion. In the former, the challenge to survival is how to keep one's balance on a motionless bicycle; the latter consists of introducing a variety of perturbing factors and ensuring that, by the production of an appropriate speed, the outcome remains in perfect balance.

Static bicycle acts are performed by one or two persons on the ground, or more frequently, on a small elevated platform either at the top of a tall pedestal or suspended high above the circus arena by a system of rigging. There, the acrobat(s) maintain(s) their balance on a free-standing bicycle, even at times on a single wheel, while achieving acrobatic movements such as handstands on various parts of the frame or the wheels.

Bicycles in motion are used by single performers and by groups combining a variety of exercises. If the bicycle is propelled at maximum speed the rider can maintain both balance and adherence to the surface of the steep wall of a circular enclosure and appears to ride the bicycle parallel to the ground level. High speed, combined with specially designed curved tracks, can also produce jumps and somersaults. Comedy bicyclists may draw from both static and moving techniques of balancing. Beside speed, the other parameter that can be varied for acrobatic purposes is the dimension of the whole bicycle or of some of its parts, or indeed its reduction to a single wheel. Finally monkeys, apes and bears, as it has been indicated in the opening anecdote to this chapter, can be trained to ride bicycles and to perform some tricks on them. Bicycle acts demand close attention in a semiotic investigation of the circus. We will describe in the next chapter a bicycle act that was observed in an Indian circus, in which the potential of this technological innovation is exploited both for acrobatics and comedy.

Chapter 6
The pyramid and the wheel: the visual discourse of circus acrobatics

The hired car which drives us back to Mysore through the jungle from a visit to a settled forest tribe, in Southern India, suddenly stops. The road is blocked by a rogue elephant. Kikeri Narayan, an anthropologist from the Central Institute of Indian Languages had offered to take me with my research assistant Jajang Gunawijaya, a student at Universitas Indonesia, to the wildlife reserve of Nagarahole. On the way back, we had paid a visit to a settlement of Jenu Koruba, the "honey people" with whom he had spent a decade studying their language, narratives and customs. We had just left their village. It had been a very pleasant, instructive trip. But now the atmosphere is tense. Rogue elephants are unpredictable. Fatal accidents are reported almost daily in the local press. We keep silent. The animal does not budge. Some youngsters from the village stealthily appear on the side of the road and make signs to be cautious. The worst would be to try and force our way by attempting to pass the elephant. More youngsters emerge from the backdrop and intensely observe the beast who stomps the ground with its trunk. They assess the situation. Then, unexpectedly, they form a half circle and all converge toward the elephant making gestures and uttering shrieking sounds. They had decided that the mobbing tactic would probably pay off. Otherwise, they would have run away in all directions and climbed trees. This time, the elephant slowly moved away. We breathe deeply in relief and start talking again.

Now Kikeri tells us how these people had saved his life some years ago as he was chased by a rogue elephant near a settlement. The usual strategy, running in large circle, getting rid of one's shirt to distract the animal, was not working, and there were no trees he could climb fast enough. The elephant won't quit. Sensing the seriousness of the situation the Yenu Korubas rushed on the path of the coming animal and instantly formed a high human pyramid, extending their arms and shouting loudly. The elephant gave up and went away. In confrontations, size matters and a smart, well coordinated pack can tip the balance of fear... most the time.

These two anecdotes suggest that moving in circles and building human pyramids are not merely formal games but are, indeed, grounded in basic survival strategies.

6.1. The representation of law and anarchy

Order and chaos are ever present themes in circus performances. Both are displayed in a redundant manner in most spectacles. Order is manifested by the parades which often open or conclude a show, the etiquette that governs the interactions of the artists among themselves inside the ring and their behavior toward the audience, the studied solemnity that is the rule for certain dangerous acts, and the usual *gravitas* and formal attire of the Master of Ceremony who is assisted by uniformed helpers and ushers. Order is also obvious in the pre-established structure of the program, and in the circus apparatus itself that assigns each one to his or her proper space. As we have seen in Chapter 1, both the public and the circus population are distributed according to socio-economic categories over distinct areas within the precinct of the circus. Whenever boundaries are crossed by accident or by design, the transgressor is put back in its place, whether a trained dog jumps over the ring curb or a spectator tries to move to a better seating without having paid the corresponding price. Extreme cases such as people attempting to gain unlawful access to the circus ground or, for an animal, escaping from its cage or stable, usually require the intervention of the city police. In some countries, uniformed representatives of the civil order and firemen may be assigned to attend the spectacles as a part of their official duties.

The organization of a circus is by necessity based on a strong hierarchy often grounded in constraining family structures. The occasional emergence of communal circuses creates short-lived adventures unless a charismatic or ruthless leader eventually takes the commands for a while. Like in any closed groups of a certain magnitude, either familial or professional, tensions and conflicts abound in the inner society of a circus that is usually recomposed year after year as the program changes at least in part. Daily circus life is rife with personal antagonisms, artistic jealousies and conflicting interests which have to be controlled if the institution is to survive and prosper. But most of the time the interface with the public offers an image of harmony and well-ordered diversity that is displayed quite often at the end of the show when the smiling owner and the happy-looking artists come to take a final bow. In family circuses, there is no hint, at that moment, of any kind of dysfunction. This ideology of order and social harmony is occasionally made quite explicit. It was particularly manifest in the welcoming announcement of the lady owner of a German circus who used to conclude her brief speech by these words: "Circus is a well-ordered microcosm that reflects a harmonious society in which everybody works at a place that has been assigned by God."

However, this is only one aspect of the circus. It is indeed no less obvious that countless figures of disorder and chaos are closely associated with the circus. Popular expressions such as "It is a real circus!" do not mean to refer to law and order but to disorganization and chaos. Some traditional acts convey an impression of undisciplined behavior like, for instance, the charivari, a fast succession of apparently unsynchronized acrobatic jumps and other antics by a multitude of clowns and other artists accompanied by a noisy and cacophonic music. In the long history of the circus, there was a standard introductory display in which all the artists who were to take part in the spectacle were performing in turn or at the same time brief fragments of their acts. This used to be done in front of the circus enclosure in order to entice the public inside. It is still done now in the ring as a sort of introductory homage to the past and a reminder of an enduring tradition. In the main of the performance, the quick pace with which the acts follow each other or are simultaneously presented in three-ring circuses, creates a sensorial saturation that makes it difficult not to be submerged by an impression of anarchy. The spectators' attention is divided. Even with a single ring, it is not always easy to process the information in an orderly fashion. A skillful performance conveys a sense of unexpected turns of event although it has usually been carefully staged. The spectators are often surprised and find it difficult to anticipate what will come next as a circus act unfolds.

The anarchic image of the circus is reinforced by the anti-social behavior of some of the clowns while some of their partners embody the opposite. But the former is the marked one, the one that gives its peculiar carnival flavor to the circus. It involves inappropriate conducts and a general confusion of genres and genders that seem to be the rule, or rather there seems to be no rule at all, as we will see in the next two chapters. From this point of view, the very substance of circus spectacles combines with the properties of circus space, which were noted earlier, to create a unique collective experience in which order and chaos achieve an exhilarating albeit paradoxical synthesis.

Both are dynamically represented in the ring through a variety of visual metaphors that articulate fundamental social and cultural contents, using the rich repertory of the circus's multimodal signs and its creative syntax and rhetoric.

6.2. The language of the pyramid

The term "pyramid" belongs to the technical vocabulary of the circus. It designates a spatial disposition of humans or animals that is actually closer to a triangle than a pyramidal volume but which probably owes its name to the fact that such vertical arrangements are stable in spite of the natural instability of their components. The bases of these pyramids are either pedestals of various heights on which animals are trained to stand so as to form a triangular config-

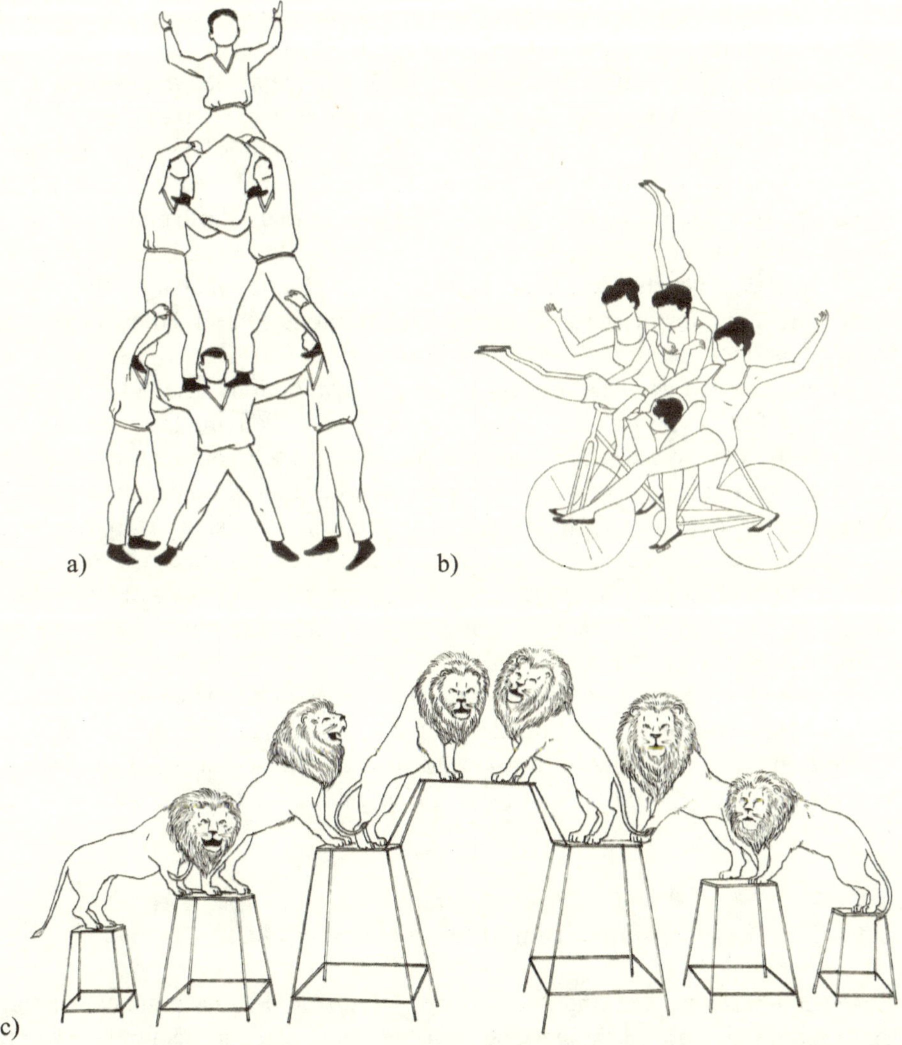

Figure 4. (a) The construction of human "pyramids" of various forms requires flawless cooperation and embodies harmonious social structures. They are usually performed in contrast with anarchical jumps by individual acrobats. (b) Like in natural languages, the syntax of the circus's visual language shows creativity by combining techniques to form novel acts such as a human pyramid on wheels. (c) The symmetrical figure of the pyramid can also be implemented by wild animals such as lions which are trained to stand on pedestals of various heights after having been engaged in individual exercises.

uration, or acrobats who balance on their shoulders other acrobats and so on in decreasing number until there is only one person standing at the top. The word also has currency in gymnastics where it applies to the same kind of figure.

In wild animal acts, a metallic apparatus is constructed across the center of the steel arena and tigers, lions, or other felines, sometimes bears, are driven to the particular platform each one has been trained to occupy. For instance, a lion is made to seat on the highest pedestal. Then two animals climb on lower lateral stools, putting their front paws on the level above. There can be several more thus displayed on each side depending of the total number of charges the trainer can command in his or her act. The resulting figure is what is called a pyramid in circus jargon.

At the root of this visual metaphor are the twin notions of equilibrium and symmetry. But "pyramid" is also a graphic way of visualizing hierarchy. In the ritual of the Olympic Games, the three winners in each competition stand on platforms that embody the pyramidal pattern with the gold medalist in the elevated center, and the two lesser prizes located on each side. Moreover, any geometric figure can be virtually rotated, inverted, or combined with other figures, and thus can generate a variety of configurations. As we will see below, human pyramids can be made to stand on their tip, so to speak with striking semiotic effects.

Both wild cat acts and acrobatic acts often are built on the contrast between order and chaos through the realization of stable pyramids and anarchic rotations. Three examples will now be introduced in order to demonstrate the formal organization in space and time of the signifying material that produces meaning in the circus ring.

6.3. The Tangier troupe: from order to chaos and back

Seven acrobats enter the ring in a dynamic, almost impetuous manner, running and fanning out toward the periphery of the circle so as to occupy the whole space. Each one performs a somersault while shouting and lands on the ground facing the audience which they salute. They then move to the center of the ring where they build six different pyramidal patterns in succession:

(1) Five acrobats form a straight line. They are all equally spaced. The two remaining men climb and stand on the shoulders of number two and four. They grasp the hands of the one who is in the central position and lift him with the help of his two neighbors who grab him at the hips. At the same time, the two men in the top position lift with their free hand acrobats one

and five who stand at both extremities of the line and whose feet on the inner side secure a lateral anchor point on the thighs of the two remaining on the ground. These two now support five men. They start walking in a circle, each in the opposite direction, so that the whole construction rotates until it returns to its initial position.

(2) Three acrobats now form the base. A fourth one climbs on the shoulders of the middle one, and a fifth one ascends to stand on the shoulders of the latter to create a three men high central column. Number six and seven take position on each side raising their bodies laterally with supports from the legs of the second man in the column and a push from the two side acrobats at the base.

(3) The same base of three men is repeated but now two columns of two men stand in balance side by side on their shoulders.

(4) Now two men form the base and support two others on their shoulders. Number three climbs to the top and keeps his balance standing with one foot on each acrobat's shoulders. The remaining two anchor themselves to the legs and arms of the bearers and lift up their own bodies until they are upside down on the sides of the pyramid.

(5) Three acrobats form a circle firmly holding each other's upper arms. Two stand on top of them. The sixth one climbs and set himself up on top of them. Finally, the last one swiftly ascends this three-height human column and keeps his balance at the summit.

(6) In the last segment of this routine, a single man, obviously the strongest one, supports his six partners by himself. He forms the base of a three-man column with the two on his shoulders while the remaining four hang laterally on each side.

An examination of the combinatory variations shows that this act involves two factors: the ratio between how many people form the base and how many are supported by this base, and the number of people that are comprised in the height of the construction. In this particular act, the progression went from a base of five to a base of one, and from a height of two to a height of four. It is obvious that "pyramid" is a generic technical term that only loosely describes the configurations achieved by these acrobats. We can notice, however, that the typical pattern is maintained across the variations, going from a maximal length of the base to a minimal one, when, so to speak, the pyramid is inverted and stands on its tip. Each one of the configurations which have been described is in itself a challenge of strength and balance for all the members of the troupe, and the poise and fastness with which they are built and undone require a flawless technique. As it was suggested in the opening anecdote of this chapter, this technique is not as gratuitous as it may seem. It is not a purely formalistic exercise of team gymnastics. It is the basis for overcoming dangers not only by impressing a predator from which one cannot flee, but also for watching at a distance when neither trees nor other natural or artificial facilities are available for this purpose.

Let us return now to the staging of this act whose theme is how a team of men can maintain balance and stability under challenging conditions thanks to the perfect coordination of complementary actions. The act is rhetorically constructed from relatively manageable situations to the overcoming of increasingly risky ones ending with two configurations which respectively involve maximal height and minimal base. It is significant that the youngest and smallest member of the troupe who reaches the top is given a hero status when he climbs down as the Master of Ceremony then introduces him by name to the audience. The same thing happens in the following and final pyramid toward the stronger and apparently older acrobat who has supported all the other members of the troupe. But this is not the end of the act.

The second part, after a brief pause to acknowledge the applause, displays twelve individual jumping feats in succession. Except for the first one which performed right in the center of the ring, all the others are executed either following a circular path along the ring curb or crossing the arena on the diametric axis from the ring entrance. Each acrobat excels in his specialty and receives signs of appreciation from the public. Technically, these jumps spell out the complete paradigm of the art of propelling oneself in the air and regaining a vertical balance after turning and twisting the body in various manners. (1) "*rondades*" that consist of turning around laterally on the spot using the support of both hands; (2) somersaults in fast sequence along a line; (3) "wheels" around the ring; (4) "lion jumps" involving a particular dynamic pattern; (5) somersaulting across the ring with the projecting of the two hands in front; (6) "rondades" on the spot in the center like for the first one but with the support of only one hand. Interestingly, this trick is performed by the strong acrobat who carried all the others in the pyramid part of the act, and it is punctuated by a brief comical demeanor. Note also that it is at the middle point of the series of jumps. (7) "double wheel" made by two men grabbing each other by the waist upside down and turning laterally on a circular path; (8) varied somersaults across the ring on a syncopated rhythm; (9) "Arabic jumps", that is, lateral somersaults in a crouching position; (10) comical somersaults across the ring with the acrobat "losing his pants" at the end; (11) still faster somersaults around the ring; (12) collective activity with three jumping men who are soon joined by the rest of the troupe, and conclusion with all the acrobats performing their own particular kind of jumps at the same time with no attempt to achieve synchronicity.

However, they all stop at the same time when the leader imperatively blows his whistle. They leave the ring walking backward and waving their hands toward the audience.

6.4. The staging of acrobatics as social metaphors

This cursory description of the second part of the Tangier Troupe act clearly shows that it is as deliberately constructed as the first part. But the means and the effects are different. The first part proceeds as a gradual and disciplined elaboration of figures of symmetry and stability, every time adding new challenges in height, scope, and area of support, to end up with a pyramid standing on its tip. Each configuration results from the actions of a team oriented toward a single goal. The second part is the exact opposite as it displays figures of movement and instability, dominated by individual self-centered acrobatic behavior. Some of the jumps are called "wheels" in gymnastic jargon, others are "rondades". Many progressions are circular. The whole is characterized by fluid, apparently chaotic activities that succeed each other and in which each acrobat claims his own share of triumph. The theme is competitiveness rather than complementariness as the latter is the case in the construction of human pyramids. The ending of the second part is a glimpse of visual chaos that saturates the space of the circus ring.

There is a remarkable binary opposition between the two parts of the act. The distinctive features that define the structure of the human group in the pyramid part are inverted in the jumps part: "all for one and one for all" versus "everyone on his own". The group is composed exclusively of males as it is most often the case in this type of act which is a North-African specialty. The only visible differences are indicative of age and stature, both being related to acrobatic functions (younger and lighter body for the upper positions, older and sturdier individuals for those who constitute the basis of the pyramids and columns). Their complementary properties converge toward the completion of the collective tasks. But the compositions also evoke social hierarchies: maturity and seniority are the basis of the system while the swifter and slender youngsters have to negotiate a delicate balance. The bearers who give the signals project very serious facial expressions and demeanors. A male adolescent who was interviewed after watching this act referred to the last segment in which a single strong individual supports his six partners remarked, using a German term, that this was real "Männlichkeit" (manliness). He had perceived this episode in a way that was involving a quality that was more than mere physical strength. This suggests that this act as a whole is connoted with patriarchal values, an ever present authority commanding discipline and coordination. The second part is an explosion of individualities during which the only two brief comical episodes affect the acrobats who had embodied leadership values in the first part. This subtle touch of carnival transgression that made the leaders behave in a ridiculous manner: dancing like a woman and losing one's pant, is congruent with the temporary loosening of hierarchical constraints. Let us note however that it is the lead acrobat who blows the whistle which instantly stops the charivari and that the troupe leaves the ring in good order.

The semiotic logic of this twofold act is not a mere gratuitous contrast for the sake of symmetry. It performs a political economy algorithm that is embodied in an implicit dramatic representation. The first pyramid is grounded on a large base, a form of democratic harmony that persists in the following constructions with a progressive reduction of the basis until the whole group is supported by a single individual. It is significant that it is at this precise moment that the act tips into the second part that produces anarchic and chaotic displays until the strong man symbolically restores order and stability.

6.5. Revolution(s) on a trampoline

The conceptual oppositions that are used to produce the deep meaning of a circus act can be expressed in a great variety of forms. Circus selectively uses cultural codes to create supplementary layers of signification and to embody structural transformations into narratives familiar to popular cultures. For instance, acts can be characterized by ethnic or historical signs conveyed to the audience through the choice of costumes, demeanors, staging, and music. We will now examine a trampoline act that is based on acrobatic skills close to the ones displayed in the Tangier Troupe performance. This act is generated by the same oppositional matrix formed by social order and chaos but it is implemented in a very different manner.

It was observed in a program presented by the Russian State Circus before the end of the Cold War, a circumstance that must be kept in mind when analyzing its semiotics. Trampolines provide elastic bases upon which acrobats can perform the same jumps as they do on the ground. However, they can achieve more complex dynamic patterns such as twisted double somersaults since they are mechanically projected higher and are given more time before gravity drags them down. In many trampoline acts, the acrobatic skills of the acrobats are fore-grounded. The design of the apparatus is functional as are the gymnastic style of their costume. There is usually a clown acrobat who punctuates the performance with a few antics in order to bring some comic interludes that allow the other members of the team to catch their breath between their exercises.

In the staging of the Russian Soviet Circus, a historical theme was established at the onset of the trampoline act. The apparatus was decorated with historical motifs, all symbolizing the "Old Regime" in the traditional Europe of kings, tsars, and princes. An elevated platform was added at one end of the trampoline. A royal throne was fixed to it. All the acrobats wear stereotyped court garments that indicate their ranks and functions: a king, a duke and a duchess, two marchionesses and a musketeer, an officer with a saber, a guard, a buffoon and some servants. The king enters first followed by a uniformed servant who ceremoniously presents him with a glass of wine. The king is short and the servant is very tall. They ascend to the trampoline where the wine serving continues repeatedly while they perform some elementary acrobatics. The king starts jumping higher and higher, and propels himself toward the platform where he lands sitting in the throne with the servant at his side. The aristocrats with their attendants arrive and take their place on the sides of the trampoline. They perform in turn diverse jumps in front of the king who gives signs of being increasingly inebriated. All display in succession ever more spectacular jumps as if they were competing for the king's attention in a frivolous court-like fashion. They adorn their acrobatic prowess with affected gestures and facial expressions. The two marchionesses who first accompanied the musketeer switch their romantic attention to the officer after he had performed a stunning series of jumps holding his saber in his hand. Suddenly the drunken king collapses and his servant takes him away in his arms. Instantly, the acrobats change their behavior and aim their jumps to the vacant throne. One after the other, they propel themselves toward the platform bumping out whomever they find seated there. Each one uses a different acrobatic jump. Eventually, they all pile up on the throne forming a momentary pyramid. The music is interrupted by a loud gun shot. The human column falls down. There is a black out and a brief silence while all the acrobats leave the ring in complete darkness and the circus hands hastily remove the apparatus to make way for the next act.

"Dance of the fools on the trampoline" was the title under which this acrobatic performance by the Vladimitowy was listed in the program. Its semiotic structure was based on the same fundamental oppositions that sustained the act by the Tangier Troupe. However, the transformation of order into chaos was expressed in a different cultural idiom: the aristocratic icons of historical Europe plunging into obscurity after a chaotic period of time marked by selfishness and frivolity. The circuses of the Soviet Union usually featured at least a few acts that indirectly conveyed some ideological contents. The socio-political message of the staging of this trampoline act was not that a social order that has reached its extreme limit tips over into chaos, but that extreme, unregulated competition in the context of a failing hierarchy leads to anomy. This act was taking a shot, literally, both at the abuses of monarchic power and the nefarious effects of free enterprise as opposed to rational planning and collectivism.

Building up human pyramids and columns as well as performing somersaults are physical exercises that require natural dispositions and demanding training. They are displayed in the circus not only for themselves but also as elements of a more complex semiotic discourse. Their compositions articulate social metaphors and implicit narratives grounded in the context of the political economy of their time.

6.6. Triumph and tragedy: the semiotics of fear and danger

The general hypothesis that purports to explain the cultural semiotic relevance of circus acts such as the ones that were described in the first sections of this chapter can be formulated as follows: as these acts involve the collaboration of several persons they can model various types of human relations and modes of interaction on the symbolic level. These acts can represent cooperation, solidarity, competition, and conflict; oppose single versus collective achievements; and either blur or emphasize gender differences. They can be construed as political and gender economy visual metaphors conveyed through appropriate acrobatic techniques and staging.

But circus displays are not simple reflections of states of affairs concerning social structures and gender specializations. They apply semiotic operations upon these metaphors to transform them through duplication, inversion, negation, or deconstruction. These transformations are not purely formal but bear upon socio-cultural contents, thus producing deeply meaningful effects that pertain to the tacit rules that sustain social norms and expectations.

The Burger Sisters act exemplifies this sort of semiotic complexity. It was repeatedly observed at the Blackpool Tower Circus as well as in several other European circuses between 1978 and 1988. Two young women scantily dressed alike in colorful leotards enter the ring, with huge chorus girl plumed headgear. They gracefully walk to the center of the ring where two attendants take their feathers and assist them by holding the rope ladders which they climb to reach two parallel bars at the very top of the circus. On the side of each bar are two trapezes. From the bar hang twelve leather loops about fifty centimeters apart. For the spectators it is obvious that these young women who are ascending the rope ladders will perform some dangerous acrobatic feats at great height without the protection of a net should they happen to fall. An older man and two attendants keep holding their rope ladders tight from the center of the ring and follow attentively all their moves as each woman reaches her goal at the end of one of the bars and grasps the trapeze that hangs lower beside it.

They perform on their trapezes six classical acrobatic tricks in perfect synchrony such as hanging by their hands, feet, revolving around the trapeze bars, taking esthetic poses, and so on. Once this part of their act is completed, they reach the parallel bars to which the loops are attached. They face each other from opposite ends. They lower their bodies so as to hang upside down from their insteps which are placed in the first two loops. Then, giving an impulse to their hanging bodies which start oscillating back and forth like two pendulums, each one releases her foot grip on the first loop and reaches for the third one. Then, once this foot's instep is securely held in the third loop, they move their other foot from the second toward the fourth one. They progress in this manner toward each other from their opposite points of departure and eventually pass each other on their parallel paths. This "walk on the ceiling" – as this type of act is called by circus folks who also feature it some times as "the human fly" – is staged in a tense atmosphere with the attendants in the ring below showing signs of being anxiously focused on each of their movements high above. The music is grave. The audience keeps silent and some spectators lower their head in order not to watch an exercise that causes empathetic anguish. This is quite justified indeed. The first time I saw the act, I almost witnessed a tragic accident. As one of the girls reached the ninth loop of the bar along which she was proceeding, the loop suddenly snapped and she screamed in fright. The public stopped breathing while the helpless acrobat dangled from the eighth loop by only one instep. Her body oscillated dangerously while she made efforts to reach the tenth loop over the broken support. Her sister froze. She was too far apart, hanging from the other bar, to save her. The attendants in the ring had immediately rushed to the spot below her as if they were expecting her to fall at any moment. Eventually, after long-lasting seconds, she regained her control and both acrobats resumed their progression toward the opposite ends of the parallel bars. Then they came down to the ground sliding along the two ropes that had been lowered and were now hanging within their grasp. They took their bow while the relieved audience loudly clapped their hands. As the girl who had experienced the near-miss accident was leaving the ring, I noticed that she was making toward her sister a hand gesture that signified that she had been really scared. Although I knew that circus artists sometimes introduce a staged failure at a given point in their act in order to stress the difficulty and danger of their stunt, this latter piece of behavior seemed so spontaneous that I was convinced that a freak technical incident had happened under my eyes.

6.7. Under the semiotic magnifying lens

This "after the fact" and "matter of fact" account attempted to summarize in the "objective mode" the episodes and events that constituted the perception of this act. But recollecting my reactions in the real time of experiencing its performance – reactions I felt were fully shared by the whole audience – I can retrace the cognitive and emotional stages through which the unfolding of this act had taken me.

First: pleasure at watching shapely, healthy young bodies attractively molded in their colorful leotards; also, feeling that the extremely large chorus-girl plumes of their headgears were not in the best taste and would have been more appropriate in a cabaret; but the attendants were already removing them as the acrobats were taking position in front of their respective ladders. As they started their ascent, I had a glimpse of their personalities, noticing their smiles, decisiveness, and graceful movements; a question came to my mind: were they really sisters? Could they be twins? Or simply partners? Or, what else? At the same time, I was scanning the space and assessing the altitude, evaluating the difficulty and danger of what they were going to do; I could see the actions implied by the form of the apparatus; I had seen before these hanging loops and could expect what would follow but, in my previous experience of this type of act, it had always been performed by a single acrobat; it was normally rather safe albeit somewhat nerve wrecking; featuring two in parallel was indeed innovative; reconstructing my stream of consciousness as the act unfolded, I remember having been sensitive to the skills and grace they were displaying on their trapezes in harmony with the music and in perfect synchronization with each other, waiting for what would come next: the walk on the ceiling; as they positioned themselves upside down, I had the ambiguous feeling that doubling such a risky exercise tended to play down its difficulty but seeing these young women in danger triggered a deep-seated anxiety that was reinforced by the dramatic sounding music as they started to proceed from loop to loop; I reflected that their technique was crisp and impeccable but they must also trust their apparatus one hundred percent; At least they were now close to the end; I was preparing myself to relax although I was still perspiring and tense; no! a scream; the music stops; the unthinkable has happened; the dreaded accident which I have seen in the past staged in circus films; but this time it is real; I feel helpless, angry at not seeing a protective net below; my heart beats twice as fast; I hold tight the arms of my seat; there is an empty feeling in my stomach; she is still holding by one foot; will this loop stand the weight? Can she regain her momentum and reach the next loop available? At long last, she has managed; tears come to my eyes; my breathing and my heartbeat calm down as both girls slide along their ropes toward the ground as graceful as ever. I do not suspect that the gesture she quickly makes to her sister is a part of the staging. It is so spontaneous, almost a breach of etiquette. But all is well that ends well. Six zebras are now cavorting in the ring. The next act has started.

Let us now briefly reflect on a methodological issue which will be discussed in more detail in Chapter 10. How can the experience of a circus performance be transformed into a text? The first account of the Burger Sisters above was a factual, albeit sketchy description of the successive events that formed the performance which I had observed at a certain location and date. It was based on a few notes written as the act unfolded and on the recollection of some components, for instance the number of loops which I had counted. But I had stopped taking notes when the act seemed to go awry. This summary description was actually a challenge because it was not possible to rely on stereotyped expressions to render these unusual acrobatics. The behavior to be described was indeed out of the norm. At the beginning of this section, the second attempt at communicating my experience as a *bona fide* spectator called upon the recollection of my thoughts and feelings, and the way in which this act had played on my emotions. It tried to explain how I had come to the decision that this was indeed a genuine mishap not a staged episode destined to precisely create this emotional response. My knowledge of circus acrobatic acts had told me both that such failures are often purposefully included in an act and that fatal accidents do also occur sometimes. Actually, I had previously witnessed two such falls that had happened during a performance.

I returned to see the show the next day. Once again, when the acrobat girl reached the ninth loop, it snapped and she screamed. The circus hands rushed to the center with anxious looks, and she made the same sign of relief to her sister when they left the ring. I went once again. The same thing happened as the perfect implementation of a musical score. However, surprisingly, this knowledge did not prevent the triggering of the emotions I had experienced during the first performance. It was as if this evocation of a tragic outcome was built into the meaning of this act, as if failure, even death, had a symbolic role in the premise of this particular act. It seemed that chaos was threatening the good order of the act from within.

6.8. Gender economy and tacit rules: norms and transgressions in the air

The Burger Sisters act, as it has been described here, has a peculiar status in the paradigm of aerial acrobatic acts. An aerial act always includes an apparatus hanging from the top of the circus, usually at a height that would make a fall extremely dangerous. The acrobat reaches this apparatus by ascending a rope or a rope ladder, and performs several exercises on it involving strength, balance and speed of movement. His/her safety is ensured through the human capacity of grasping an object primarily with the hands but also with the teeth or even by an appropriate use of the more limited repertory of the foot and leg muscles, and supporting one's own weight. The key to survival is to maintain a constant and firm grip with a part of the body on a part of the apparatus, or, if the contact is lost – accidentally or as a part of the trick – to re-establish it instantly before gravity takes its toll.

Aerial acts can be divided into two sub-classes: acts involving only one person and acts in which two or more acrobats work as a team. The single trapeze, comprising several specialties, is most of the time used by only one individual, male or female, who displays his or her skill in isolation. In general there is only one act of this kind in a program. This is also true of the acrobatic act called "walk on the ceiling" which was described earlier and which normally is a solo act. In contrast with the performer's solitude that characterizes such acts, the other category of aerial acts involves the cooperation of two or more people who engage in complementary movements on aerial apparatuses. The survival of each individual depends on the solidarity of the team and implies an absolute mutual trust, mainly on the part of those who release their grasp only to be caught an instant later by those who maintain theirs to stay aloft. In this latter category, pairs have a special status because the mutual dependency, harmony, and trust they display, create a striking metaphor for a love relationship all the more striking since their routines require very close body contacts. In some way, it takes the absolute love commitment that may exist between two human beings to the extreme limit of the confrontation with danger and death. In addition, the musical scores that usually accompany such acts include popular romantic songs. The great majority of the pairs usually performing in circus programs are formed by a male and a female. Whether or not they are actually lovers is irrelevant, like in a ballet. They symbolically embody heterosexual love. In societies which do not discriminate against homosexual relationships, these acts can feature same sex couples. Otherwise, if two males or two females engage in this sort of aerial act, they are usually introduced as brothers or sisters whether or not they actually are siblings. The family framework that is thus created shifts the perspective to another type of solidarity and somewhat lifts the ambiguity produced by the closeness of the bodily contacts that aerial acrobatics make necessary.

This is not a moot point because there is a psycho-social compulsion to establish at once the status of two persons exhibiting physical closeness with respect to kinship. Every member of a culture uses a few indicators to reach a decision and classify the group or the couple as family, siblings, lovers, or artistic partners. The audience's fantasies and prejudices form an important input for the eventual decoding of the circus acts. The staging of an acrobatic act may remain within the limits of social acceptability in the context of the culture in which the performance takes place, or it may choose to shock the community standards at the risk of provoking adverse reactions. There is indeed a fine line between the gymnastic and erotic modes when two bodies slide against each other along an aerial apparatus that reveals the details of their anatomy under glaring spotlights.

It is symptomatic that the announcements of circus acts very often include some information concerning the kinship status of the performers. For instance, "The Yong Brothers" or "The Burger Sisters" set up the sibling frame of mind and imply the presence of parents, mainly if mature people are present in the ring, overseeing the performance and watching over the performers. A single patronymic title such as "The Salvadors" or "The Geraldos", whether it is a stage name or not, signals in western cultures a "legitimate" couple, while "Luis and Gloria" or "Erik and Marco" suggest a less institutional coupling. In family circuses which foreground kinship as a part of their display (Carmeli 2007) both first and family names are given and the printed program provides ample details about genealogies and filiations, distinguishing senior and junior rank whenever there is some ambiguity about who is who.

Let us return now to the Burger Sisters act. The preceding remarks allow us to assess more precisely the peculiar characteristics of the acrobatic substance and staging of this act. When circus acts are analyzed from the point of view of their reception as it is the purpose of this book, it is important to keep in mind that the audience as a whole perceives and understands a particular performance against the background of previous experiences. As in sport or literature where respectively the spectators or the readers process the information within a template that has been constructed over many years, the circus audience has a set of expectations. Except for the cases in which a visit to the circus is a first time event – something which has necessarily happened once to everybody – the audience holds a repertory of remembered acts. Novelty bears upon details of conception or implementation within the range of a limited number of genres. With respect to the aerial acrobatics paradigm the Burger Sisters apparatus seems at first an anomaly because the walk on the ceiling trick is usually a solo act. The trapeze routine that forms the first part of the act is also at odds with the norm because the exercises are merely duplicated in synchrony. When two acrobats perform a trapeze act together they are expected to combine their routine on a single trapeze with complementary roles such as flyer and catcher. Here, there are two performers of the same sex doing exactly the same thing in parallel. The mirror effect emphasizes symmetrical harmony and the acrobats do not depend on each other to accomplish their daring feats of strength and balance. This acts displays a double transgression with respect to the norms of the paradigm: on the one hand, the dramatic effect of a solo trapeze act is noticeably lessened by the impression that if two people can do the same thing with such apparent ease, the exercises are probably not as difficult and death defying as they are supposed to be. Duplication leads to trivialization. In fact a sense of security progressively builds up as the act unfolds and esthetics is fore-grounded until drama takes over when the "accident" occurs.

But there is more. The image of two sisters involved in an activity marked by an obvious absence of cooperation inverts the definition of the family cell held by traditional European societies and beyond. The two young ladies who first appeared in the ring scantily dressed as chorus girls are obviously mature and assumed to be unmarried, a status reinforced by the fact that they dress alike, as young twins often do, and that they are introduced as sisters still having the same name, it can be inferred, by their father. Traditional circuses display conservative values even though somewhat stretched at times toward the margins. From the kinship point of view, the Burger Sisters can be classified as "spinster sisters" [unmarried female siblings], a traditionally undesirable status as it is equated with sterility and lack of productivity in many cultures. This symbolic profile is congruent with the structure of their act since each one performs in front of the other as if it were in front of a mirror with a narcissistic flavor, without any body contact that would indicate some measure of cooperation. Their assumed status, combined with their a-social behavior, is connoted, directly or indirectly by death, as anthropologists have repeatedly shown (Lévi-Strauss 1962: 267–270; Goody 1976: 56–61). Moreover, in the circus code, with respect to both specialties – the solo trapeze act and the couple or team act – these two acrobats are guilty of a sin at the level of the system because, for the former, they duplicate what should be unique and, for the latter, they split into two isolated entities what should be a single functional unit formed by two cooperating members whose actions are complementary and are aimed at the survival of the team.

If acrobatic acts can be construed as metaphors for social conditions and solidarities expressed in terms of kinship systems with respect to the contextual culture, The Burger Sisters present a negative image of the principle of exogamy since being of the same sex and being united like an object and its mirror image their activity within the family cell is introverted to the extreme and yields neither goods nor services. They display with the clarity of an abstract formula a logical possibility that can never be fully implemented in real life: the total closure of a social group, a mode of existence that stands in a binary opposition with exogamy, endogamy representing a mediating solution between these two poles rather than the opposite pole itself. This is quite different from the case of the solo trapeze in which an acrobat, male or female, stands alone in his/her confrontation with death, The solitude is anti-social but in a positive sense: the vicarious capacity of a hero to go beyond the limits that restrict ordinary people.

If this analysis is correct, the Burger Sisters act visually conceptualizes a logical sequence of implications which is a part of a wider system and the effect their act causes on the audience can be understood only with reference to this system that is a part of the tacit cultural knowledge of the audience. This would explain why, on the level of the process, the whole design of the act seems to lead to the "close call with death" which is all the more effective for the audience as it is congruent with unconscious expectations. The dramatic emergence of chaos in the form of a technical failure can be seen as both feared and predictable as the result of a major transgression of the social order.

An act such as this one can be accounted for on several levels from the point of view of its meaning. It plays, so to speak, on several semiotic registers. The aerial apparatus and the successive stages of the development of this act are not easily described in words because they are at odds with the artifacts and behaviors of ordinary life. But in the Burger Sisters act they even deviate from the circus norms. This act's conception was obviously based on the idea of creatively duplicating in parallel two identical acrobatic routines but it must have been quickly obvious that duplicating what is introduced as exceptional tends to trivialize and defuse the suspense created by the "walk on the ceiling". Too much of the same thing can cause boredom, hence the reinsertion of information in the form of a potentially fatal mishap which is not a failure of the acrobat but of the equipment, a kind of "act of god". But this rhetorical strategy articulates deeper cultural contents. As we have seen, there is a subtext that involves kinship and, by extension, social order. Breaking the tacit rules which sustain this order threatens chaos. Order must be repaired either by the virtual suppression of the transgressor or the restoration of the balance and complementariness of the processes. Most circus acts resonate in the audience by activating deep layers of meaning, thus creating emotions that transcend our capacities for articulate expression. Whatever contradictions or subversions are symbolically implemented in the circus ring, the acts always come to their ends in a manner that resolves the problems. Individual acts and circus shows as a whole always conclude in good order, unless of course a truly tragic accident brings havoc into this symphony of well controlled signs, like when the male elephant "Teak" trampled to death his trainer, Eloïze Bertchold, in front of the audience as her act had just started.

It is not necessary to assume that circus artists possess an explicit knowledge of tacit cultural rules when they elaborate the structure and staging of an act. They work with traditional patterns which they adapt and modify, striving for excellence and originality. But whether an act brings them success or falters ultimately depends on the feedback they receive from their audience. They proceed by trial and errors. Acts evolve through a process of cultural selection. When artists hit a formula that deeply resonates in the public, a great act is born. For many years the Burger Sisters act has been definitely sought for by directors of major circuses. The ground for its remarkable cultural pertinence, its deep semiotic substance, was probably a fluke of tinkering: a father devising an act for two acrobat daughters but realizing that something dramatic had to be added in order to spice up a routine that lacked excitement if there was a mere duplication of the routine. In so doing, he struck a rich anthropological vein.

6.9. The predictive power of semiotics

Naturally, the tentative interpretation of the intense meaning produced by an acrobatic act like the one which was described and discussed in the last two sections of this chapter is in the form of a hypothesis. Is it possible to generalize the semiotic theory of acrobatics that has been sketched above, namely that these acts are social metaphors and that kinship structures form the subtext of some of them? In order to find out, let us look at other acts belonging to the same paradigm: female aerial acts involving more than one individual in the apparent same class of age, and let us restrict the sample to cases in which identical routines are performed in parallel and synchrony by two individuals.

The first example is an act that was performed by two young women who were members of the French "Ecole Nationale du Cirque". The act was observed in the program of *Cirque Alexis Gruss*. The apparatus was a "three-place trapeze": the bar was of a length equal to three times the length of a regular trapeze and was hung by four ropes that delimited three sections on the bar. The two acrobats climbed a rope ladder from the ring to the apparatus and took place on the two opposite segments of the bar, leaving the central portion free. They performed simultaneously the same acrobatic routine at both ends of the bar. Then, one of them moved to the middle section and the other one reached out for her hands which she grasped and from which she soon was hanging above the ring below. They combined several movements in which they alternated the roles of flyer and catcher. After this, each of them returned to her end section of the bar and resumed identical exercises in parallel. The whole act consisted of three simultaneous solitary routines and three combined routines in which they cooperated to achieve increasingly difficult tricks. The act began in the solitary mood and concluded by a collaborative display. This pattern is congruent with our hypothesis since the initially asocial connotation of the act is immediately corrected by a display of functional collaboration. The same sequence is repeated three times ending on a strong sign of solidarity as the last routine involves more risk than the previous ones.

A similar pattern was observed in India (Cannanore, Kerala) at the *Venus Circus*. The apparatus was the same as above but included three acrobats who first accomplished a series of six routines in perfect synchrony. Then, the girl who was hanging from the central section of the trapeze bar was caught by the other two girls. Holding their hands except for brief moments when she somersaulted in the air, she performed a series of daring aerial acrobatics that owed their success to the fastness and firmness of the catching of her two partners. Another relevant Indian example recorded at the *Great Jai Bharat Circus* concerns two young female contortionists who were displaying side by side identical figures of body bending but punctuated their performance with episodes of joint displays with their bodies combined to form complex, unexpected patterns of contortions.

While one should be cautious about generalizing patterns based on only a few observed instances, it seems that it is epistemologically sound at least to tentatively state the hypothesis that in the paradigm of aerial acrobatics sociality is fore-grounded in the extreme form of mutual assistance in life-threatening situations such as attempting to control or overcome gravity. Flying trapeze troupes orchestrate this theme with particular clarity. By contrast, a solo aerialist relies only on his/her own physical resources, thus demonstrating a kind of extreme individualism that borders the negation of sociality. Merging the two in an act like the Burger Sisters creates a dangerous paradox which violates fundamental rules and spells out virtual death and chaos.

6.10. Order and chaos on wheels

It is tempting at this point of the inquiry to check whether this semiotic matrix generates comparable visual discourses in other circus specialties. Let us now focus on a bicycle act that appears to implement the same oppositions and transformations in a register different from aerial acrobatics.

The following act was observed in 1984 at the *Apollo Circus* in Mumbai. This act belongs to the rich paradigm of bicycle acrobatics which was discussed in Chapter 5. It starts with the display of two female cyclists who execute identical routines along the periphery of the circus ring, each one being located at the maximal distance from the other, that is, at both ends of a diameter since they maintain a constant speed. While pedaling intermittently to keep their bicycles moving, they balance in various positions such as standing on the frames or reclining on the saddle. After having completed six different tricks in perfect synchrony and in a kind of mobile mirror symmetry, they exit just as a succession of disruptive, unexpected events make noisy irruptions in the ring: first, a dwarf on a giant monocycle, then a bear on a motorcycle with a flashing headlight which drives several time around in darkness, finally the dwarf returns with a miniature bicycle. Suddenly a group of boisterous clowns invade the ring and seize the dwarf's bicycle which they take apart, pretending to play music with the components of the machine. Two use the wheels as if they were guitars, while the others play flute with the pipes of the frame. Eventually, they put the parts together but in reverse order with the pedals positioned where the saddle should be. The dwarf leaves the ring pedaling in an grotesque position that keeps his backside high above his head. This disruptive and monstrous interlude is succeeded by a group of ten young women who perform several routines which all involve some form of cooperation such as forming a small circle while holding hands as they pedal, or using two bicycles moving side by side to give support to a bar upon which one of the acrobats keeps her balance in an erect position. In the final displays, all the girls form moving pyramids on wheels, ending with the bicycle equivalent of the last construction that was described in the Tangier troupe act: they all join, climb, and keep their balance on top of a single bicycle that is powered by the strongest woman of the group. As they leave the ring, they extend their arms so as to increase the volume of the pyramid and salute the audience.

The comparison of this act with those which have been reviewed in this chapter seems to indicate that there is indeed a degree of consistency across the visual discourses generated by circus acrobatics. The opposition between order and chaos is not purely esthetic but results from a symbolic transgression. It is structured by an elementary narrative that is sometimes made explicit by specific cultural signs like in the Russian trampoline act, and other times remains virtual as it was the case in the acts of the Burger Sisters and the Apollo Circus cyclists. In the latter, the first section displays a situation similar to the Burger Sisters that is suddenly sanctioned by the irruption of chaos. Then, good order is restored through the powerful metaphor of the pyramid on wheels implementing a vision of social cooperation and harmony. Perhaps these acts resonate so deeply in their audience because they visually articulate the dilemma between the social imperative and the claim of the self to an individual destiny. This destiny can be tragic as we will see in Chapter 8 in which we will evoke accidents either real or staged. But enough drama for the time being! All circus programs bring in the clowns – as the next chapter will do – whenever a serious act has elevated the level of tension and anxiety in the audience.

Chapter 7
The logic of clown faces

As I am waiting in line to purchase my ticket for a circus that has set up its tent in the Belgium city of Ghent, I notice the banners which advertise the program. Acrobats in blue leotards, a dog standing on its hind legs, two white horses rearing in front of their female trainer, a tiger jumping through a hoop of fire, and a stern face that is billed as the star of the show "as seen on television". This must be the "post-modern" clown who was mentioned in the press release I read in yesterday's evening paper. At the other end of the array of banners, two traditional European clown faces beam their smiles toward the crowd, a way for the circus to say: we also have real clowns!

Like many circus goers I dread this new brand of clown who originated from the street performers of the 1970s and specializes in preying on the audience to make the public laugh at the expense of a few randomly chosen spectators. Although I know that the individuals the "clown" brings to the center of the ring to make them do stupid things are sometimes stooges who have been planted among the audience, this is not always the case. Some of my friends feel so uncomfortable at the thought of being ridiculed in this manner that they stopped going to the circus when this type of act became a regular item in reputable circus programs.

As the circus gates open, I proceed with my ticket toward the highest row of benches, hopefully out of reach of the "post-modern" clown. It happens that I have already seen this one perform. His expressionless face and aggressive manners always make some young children cry. He is certainly good at ridiculing people who, incidentally, have paid their admission to be entertained rather than the reverse. The rest of the audience laughs all the more heartily as they are relieved not to have been unwittingly assigned the role of the scapegoat.

The show starts. Soon after some fast-paced acrobatics on horses, the traditional clowns enter the ring and engage in worn-out gags. Their make-up makes it easy to recognize who is who: an elegant but authoritarian white-face character attempts to repress the musical talents of his partner, a shaggy, sloppily dressed insolent individual who does not take "no" for an answer. The public feels sympathy for the under-dog who at times looks pathetically at the audience for moral support. At the end, he will triumph by playing on a bicycle pump the "Carnival of Venice" to everybody's delight, including his early oppressor's. The crowd has been involved in the action through this one-to-many-face encounter.

The colorful and contrasted make-up of the shaggy clown, the "august", projected up to the last row of benches his innocent insolence and deep humanity.

7.1. The structure of European clowns' make-up

In an earlier study of clowns that was inspired by the principles of structuralism (Bouissac 1976), I showed how the two basic characters which performed comic circus acts implemented a complex binary opposition involving behavior, costume and make-up. A tradition that goes back at least to the beginning of the nineteenth century in continental Europe features an elegant, articulate, and authoritarian white-face clown and an awkward, sloppily dressed, and foul-mouthed partner who displays a heavily colored make-up. The latter became known through the generic name of "august", a name that probably originated in a sarcastic term of address since his persona evokes anything but imperial distinction and poise. Historically, this contrasted couple seems to be rooted in ancient folk cultures that thus represented the tension between earthy peasantry and abusive aristocracy or urban smugness. However, this consideration was irrelevant for a structuralist approach that exclusively focused on the way in which the semiotics of the performance could be explained by the functional oppositions of the signs which were displayed contemporaneously to the observer. A clown act was construed as a multimodal text that had to be analyzed from the point of view of its system or its "langue" according to Saussure's linguistic terminology.

Using a limited set of examples, it was possible to demonstrate that the two characters who performed gags and short dramas in the circus ring were the embodiments of "culture" versus "nature". This could be shown to hold across the whole range of signs they were projecting to the audience but it appeared particularly obvious if one concentrated one's analytical attention upon the facial features the two clowns displayed. Each was indeed a symmetric inverse of the other: the white-face clown was thus designated because of the prominent absence of natural color on most of his face that was uniformly painted in white with the exception of a thin red line underlying the contours of his mouth, nose, and ears. His eyebrows were visually erased by the white make-up and a stylized black eyebrow was drawn only on one side of his forehead. Each white-face performer was identified by a particular eyebrow design which he called his "signature". His hair was carefully combed or, most of the time, entirely covered by a conical white hat.

In the august's make-up, all the white-face's signs were inverted: it emphasized the natural colors that the human face displays through the variety of skin pigmentations and the range of emotions it signals (red, brown, black, and the white of the teeth and the eyes). The mouth, the nose, the eyebrows and the hair were exaggerated by the make-up, and the color contrasts were expressed redundantly. A perfect symmetry of natural features was opposed to the artificial dissymmetry of the white-face clown. The hair was usually unkempt and reddish.

Such a systematic set of oppositions led to the hypothesis that the make-up of these two clowns was governed by a Saussurean algorithm which posited signs whose meanings depended on their mutual negative values: natural symmetry versus un-natural (cultural) dissymmetry; spectrum of natural colors versus absence of transitions between overwhelmingly un-natural white and minimal red; undisciplined hairiness versus hyper-disciplined or negated hairiness; enlargement of the natural orifices and protuberances of the face versus their visual reduction to the cultural organs of speech and music (thin outlining of the mouth that make articulation clear and underlining of the ears which are the cultural correlates of both verbal and musical productions).

Such an algorithm – that is, the set of instructions that a clown-to-be would follow in order to create make-up which would both conform to the genre and be distinctly original – also generated stereotyped social behaviors: the white-face clown was always elegantly dressed in glittering costumes that fit his body perfectly, emphasizing the poise and distinction of his gestures; he was wearing ballet dancer's shoes and stockings; he could speak eloquently with an upper-class accent; he was an expert musician and could dance artistically; he was knowledgeable and prompt to put his partner to shame. The latter was indeed shabbily dressed with ill-fitting gaudy garments, either too large or too tight; he mangled his words; he behaved like a child or an uneducated lower-class individual; he was prone to transgressing the rules of basic etiquette.

But the clown acts which were observed did not consist simply of the redundant displaying of these systematic binary oppositions: they were performing short dramas through which the initial semiotic equation was transformed since, at the end, the august outsmarted the white-face and proved to be endowed with superior talents. However, this was not meant to be a crushing defeat for the white-face since the two protagonists eventually managed to overcome their initial opposition and left the ring displaying signs of being the best friends in the world, ready to start again their bickering in the next show. A clown act could be shown to encapsulate in the limited time of a performance a systematic transformation of great socio-cultural relevance. The tension resulting from an abusive repression of nature by an aggressively normative culture was resolved through the integration of the former into the latter. This conclusion was reached through a reading of the clusters of signs that posited at first the two clowns as diametrical antagonists, one representing an extreme form of culture which negated as much as possible the natural features of the human face, the other embodying the naturalness of humans by emphasizing their animal characteristics: hairiness, colors, inarticulate sounds, large mouth, and instinctual reactions. The eventual triumph of the august was ambiguous since it usually turned out to be a kind of integration through cultural assimilation rather than a "naturalization" of the white-face. These clowns were not radical anarchists; rather, they exposed and commented through their actions the tacit rules of the culture that prevailed in the society for which they performed. In this respect, they engaged in meta-semiotics. If the white-face would say: "We are to play cricket. Bring me a bat", and the august would bring a stuffed bat (animal) and a model of a cricket (insect), the clowns would foreground the arbitrariness of linguistic signs and the fundamental ambiguity of language, thus exposing ultimately the fragility of cultural conventions by showing how easily they can be transgressed.

7.2. From structuralism to biosemiotics

This theoretical view had been elaborated from the observation of a limited set of examples, a dozen or so couples each of which exhibited similar contrasts in their make-up and the dramatic structures of their acts. The variants were within the range of the relevant oppositions: the dissymmetrical eyebrow of the white-face could be on either side of the forehead and its design was markedly different from all the others; the august could display red noses of various forms and the enlarged patterns of his lips and natural eyebrows varied in forms, hues, and intensity as did the color of his shaggy wig.

However, further research revealed data that were well beyond the pale of this structural model such as white-face clowns with symmetrical eyebrows and ears painted in red, and augusts who were bald and whose eyebrows had been totally erased by their make-up. This expanded corpus required a different, more encompassing model that could adequately describe and interpret from a semiotic – but not necessarily structuralist – point of view both the data presented in the first section of this chapter and the new evidence accruing from an inquiry that went beyond a few stereotypic examples and covered a variety of cultural areas including North America, India, and Indonesia.

The method shifted from an a priori search for distinctive features in cultural artifacts toward a more general investigation of the biosemiotics of the human face of which the make-up of clowns was a subset since they were necessarily grounded in the natural repertory of facially expressed emotions that had evolved in the context of social interactions. The heuristic strategy consisted of examining how the natural expressive features of the face were treated in the make-up process. Although faces form integrative wholes that are interpreted in social interactions as global patterns, it was methodologically sound to first isolate the parts of the face whose modifications under the actions of muscles and blood circulation contribute to the signaling of different meanings with respect to emotions and social attitudes. This approach proved to be all the more productive since the semiotics of facial expressions has been for several decades scrutinized by psychologists (e.g., Ekman and Friesen 1978; Ekman et al. 1982) and human ethologists (e.g., Eibl-Eibesfeldt 2007 [1989]: 438–480).

The eyebrows in particular have been the focus of research because they are both visually distinct and moveable within the range of complex muscular controls. Their physiological function that shields the eyes from perspiration running from the forehead, and possibly from rain, seems to have been "exapted" for at least two signaling purposes: they grow heavy and bushy in older males, thus indicating seniority and, assumedly, authority; they can display various patterns and movements which are all the more visible as they are located in the periocular area which is the focus of attention in human interactions because this is where the attitudes and intentions of the interacting individuals can be most reliably read. The "eyebrow flash", an instant raising and lowering of the eyebrows in synchrony that lasts only a few microseconds, has been shown to spontaneously convey greetings signaling a positive attitude toward the individual to whom it is directed. By contrast, the sustained raising of the eyebrows, mainly if it creates a dissymmetrical pattern which includes a vertical furrow in the center of the forehead (frowning), conveys the opposite: dominance, repression, or rejection. Cross-cultural studies have demonstrated the great generality of this human behavior which appears to be hard-wired. However, it has been shown that various cultures differently manage the natural semiotic repertory of the face. The cosmetic treatments of the eyebrows bear witness to this. The fact that the natural signaling of the eyebrows is spontaneous and unconscious, and only partially under voluntary control, has compelled some cultures to develop drastic cosmetic rules such as the shaving of natural eyebrows and the redrawing of stylized eyebrow lines well above the muscles that make possible the dispatching of signals through muscular contractions. In the Japanese aristocratic tradition, for instance, as it is documented in the masks of Noh drama, ladies wear such light symmetrical and horizontal eyebrow lines high on the forehead. It can be assumed that it would not be proper for them to disclose their emotions in such a natural (or "animal") manner as eyebrow flashes do. The interested reader can be referred to the early work of Ekman and Friesen (1978), Ekman (1973, 1979), Fridlund (1994) and Eibl-Eibesfeldt (2007 [1989]: 438–480) for ample documentations regarding this natural phenomenon and its cultural management. Let us now apply the body of research on the biosemiotics of eyebrows to an understanding of their treatment in the traditional make-up of European circus clowns.

We have seen above that the formal opposition between symmetry and dissymmetry that was the basis of the structuralist interpretation was not adequate to account for all the data provided by an exhaustive documentation of European clowns make-up. The biosemiotics approach does not invalidate the relevance of this opposition but can integrate it into a more comprehensive explanation. Indeed, it is not so much the dissymmetry that is the marked cultural feature but rather it is whether the natural eyebrows are emphasized in the make-up or not. The eyebrows of the white-face are always erased by the white paint that covers the face and are redrawn well above the area of the forehead that is under muscular control. There may be a unique eyebrow on one side or there may be two symmetrical eyebrows, the semiotic effect of dominance and repression is equally achieved through the resulting freezing on the face of a "raised eyebrow" configuration, a facial pattern that fits the role of the white-face.

The august's make-up most of the times displays emphasized natural eyebrows either through artificial dark coloring or the addition of a wig. This makes the eyebrow movements very visible at a distance when the clown interacts with the audience or with his partner. It also qualifies the august face as "natural". However, the data show that some augusts have completely erased their eyebrows under their pink and reddish make-up. The next best thing to not raising eyebrows is to have no eyebrows at all. Such augusts, deprived of eyebrows, may not be able to display eyebrow flashes but, more importantly, their face is totally devoid of means of expressing negative attitudes. Moreover, they implement another powerful biosemiotic pattern: the "neotenic" face, a technical term that refers to the typical face of neonates that usually triggers positive feelings in their social environment.

7.3. Icons of biomorphology

Systematic observations of neonates whose survival depends on the care provided to them by adults, including the mother and other related individuals, have revealed a consistent set of facial morphological features that hold across a great range of species. Lorenz (1981) and Tinbergen (1989) for instance, documented:

their relatively large head and eyes with respect to the body;
their much smaller nasal and chin protuberances compared to those of adults;
their protruding forehead;

and the fact that their eyes are located at mid distance between the top of their skull and the tip of their chin.

Photos of puppies, kittens, chicks, and babies provide easily observable examples. It is believed that these features trigger protective behavior on the part not only of adult members of the same species, but also on the part of other species which share in common some kind of hard-wired reflex when they encounter these morphological traits. This phenomenon has been called upon to explain the protective attitude of modern humans toward species such as pandas and seals which happened to have preserved some of these neonate features in adulthood. This seems to run counter to well-documented infanticides among some social species, but such killings of the young are usually done by adult males competing to reproduce their own genes. The neonates of social mammal species are defenseless and these species would have quickly gone extinct if they had not evolved some powerful signaling system that semiotically constrains adults to ensure their survival.

Mature adult facial morphologies vary with species but some consistent features have also been identified: nasal and chin protuberances are more pronounced, often markedly so; the eyes are located higher and closer to each other; ears tend to be larger; and the face is generally less round and more elongated, sometimes evoking a rectangle with sharp edges. In all species, dominant males display morphological features that strongly contrast with the neonate facial morphology, such as, in humans, heavy and bushy eyebrows whereas babies have hardly any visible ones.

This latter remark brings us back to the differing facial make-up of the clowns which was introduced above. Dominance and aggressiveness obviously can be expressed by redundant signals that naturally belong to the mature male face, and the opposite can be achieved by artificially reproducing features that are typical of the neonate facial morphology. This is indeed what is observed when the great variety of European clown make-up is analyzed along these lines of inquiry. Such a biosemiotic approach explains both the oppositions that were elucidated through a structuralist analysis of the data and what appeared at first as unexplainable exceptions.

The genesis of the two algorithms which underlie the great variety of make-up in each category does not assume a deliberate design that would have been conceived in view of ethological knowledge. The traditional European clown make-up considerably predates the research of Tinbergen and Lorenz. Their work has simply made explicit the intuitive knowledge that prompts humans to relate differently to faces which preserve some neonate features in adulthood and to faces that naturally exhibit exaggerated signs of mature aggressiveness and dominance. Clown make-up as it can be observed in the circus tradition has been generated by cultural evolution: the response of the audience is a powerful selecting force. The august is endowed with an endearing persona and the white-face is a character that the public loves to hate when he oppresses his partner. The contrast is all the more efficient since both "masks" are grounded in biosemiotics and redundantly express relevant features in the iconic mode. In some instances, the role of the white-face is performed without special make-up by the master of ceremony, the ring director or the chief equestrian, who all embody authority within the circus context.

7.4. White faces and white patches: the management of leucosignals in clown make-up

But there is more. In the preceding sections of this chapter, little attention has been paid to the use of white paint in the production of clown make-up. We will now examine the role of white signals in the biosemiotics of the human face and investigate their treatment in the two categories of make-up that have been described above.

It has often been noted that the face can be compared to a display board on which the moods, intentions, and emotions of interacting individuals can be instantly read. Psychologists have shown that even in faces that deliberately lie there are some detectable tell-tale semiotic leaks (e.g., Ekman 2001).

Irrespectively of skin pigmentation, the natural transformations of the human face in social interactions comprise at least three types:

(a) Contractions of the superficial skeletal muscles that create patterns through the interplay of skin folds and shadows. These contractions are mostly but not entirely under voluntary control. We saw earlier, for instance, that the eyebrow flash is a spontaneous signal which cannot be perfectly faked.
(b) Circulatory variations which modify the shapes of erectile vascular tissues, such as the lower eyelids and the lips, and change the color of the facial skin, for instance, the cheeks and the lips.
(c) Neuro-automatisms that are under the control of the autonomic nervous system, such as the enlargement of the pupils at the center of the eyes when the person is in a state of arousal. These modifications totally escape voluntary control and can be created only through artificial means in the absence of actual arousal.

Between the transformations which are spontaneous and unconscious, and those which can be willfully produced in order to achieve a deliberate effect, there is a grey area in which some changes can be obtained at will through training and with the help of artifices. In the case of clown make-up it is these latter techniques that will now be the focus of our attention with respect to the addition of white patterns on the face.

Among the numerous transformations and variations that are displayed on the primate face, as well as some other mammal species, there are two particular areas of contrasts which are the locus of effective signal productions irrespective of the color of the skin because they involve white which ensures maximal reflectance and therefore visibility even at a distance and in low luminosity: the sclera of the eyes (most visible in humans) and the teeth. Both can be shaped into a variety of patterns through muscular contractions such as squinting and smiling. The contrast is optimally perceptible if the eyes are wide open and if the lips are pulled back or up so as to reveal the teeth. The contrast is hardly visible if the eyes are half-closed and it completely disappears if the mouth is closed and the jaws are clenched. These two contrasts are extremely important from a biosemiotic point of view because they indicate the social disposition of the signalers who thus advertise their friendliness or hostility, dominance or submissiveness, and their readiness to interact according to the moods that are conveyed not only by the quantity of white but above all by the patterns of the white patches that are created by muscular contractions. Such leuco-signals (from the ancient Greek *leukos* = bright white) have evolved through different means in other species. Tigers, for instance, flash warning signs by turning forward the back of their ears which sport tuffs of white hairs, a message that can be translated as “watch out! I have detected your presence and you had better to stay away from me!” (McDougal 1977).

To what extent are leuco-signals in the human face reliable indicators of the status and attitude of interacting individuals? Is it possible to infer from a relatively safe distance whether someone is friend or foe, whether the information available from the face can be trusted or not? It seems that this depends on how much white is visible. If the eyes are open so as to clearly show the sclera, precious information is provided regarding the direction of the gaze. But if the periorbital muscles are contracted, the actual focus of attention is concealed as well as the degree of aperture of the pupil. Whether an individual is relaxed or not during an encounter is signaled by how and how much the mouth is open. The well-documented half-open mouth of chimpanzee which shows the upper teeth signals a playful mood. This is the opposite of the baring of the teeth as a preparation for biting. Genuine human smiles combine the showing of the upper teeth with some swelling of the lower eyelids which markedly modifies the contour of the sclera. Specialists of the face who developed an anatomically based coding system that allows for the identification of muscular contractions

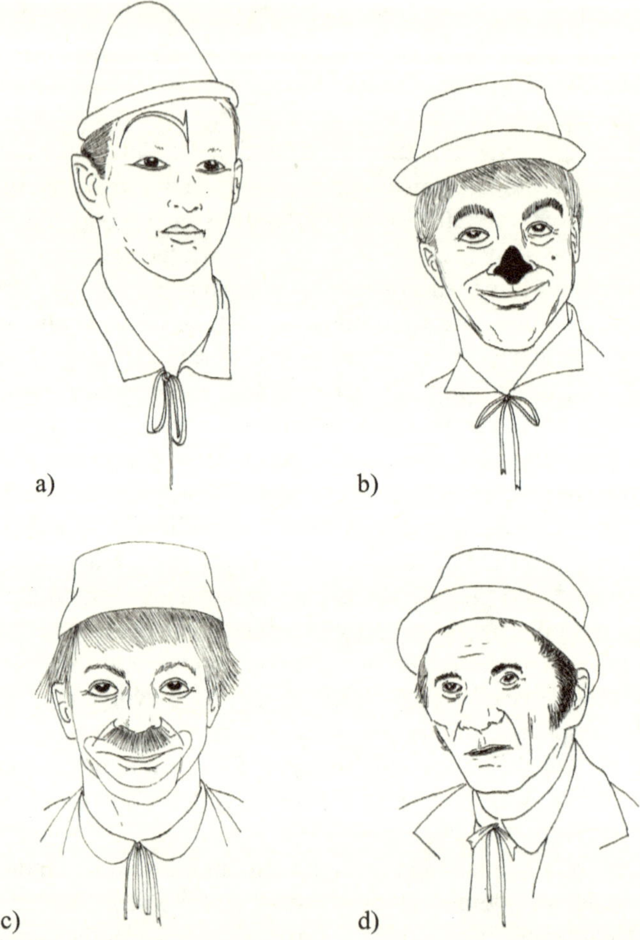

Figure 5. The variety of facial patterns in the make-up of clowns follows some basic rules in the traditional European circus to create two types of contrasted characters: the authoritarian "white-face" (a) and the transgressor "August" (b and c). Rules, of course, can be transgressed to produce special effects like in the case of George Carl (d) who reached fame by trampling the codes of performance, including not using clown make-up on his uncharismatic face (see Chapter 8).

have identified the smiling configuration which conveys the most positive feeling. Dubbed the "Duchesne smile" (from the name of its early descriptor) or true smile, this signal involves the raising of both the lip-corners and the cheeks (Ekman and Friesen 1978; Messinger et al. 1998). It expresses friendliness and submission or seduction. On the other hand, a clenched mouth or the displaying of the lower teeth through the pulling back of the lower lip indicates dominance or aggression. Such crucial information concerning the mood of the interacting individuals is conveyed by leuco-signals, the signs that are the most readily decipherable at a distance. Of course, supplementary relevant information might come from other sources such as gestures and sounds; but in encounters whose outcome could be a matter of life and death, it pays to be able to rely on fast and frugal signals which leak from the face, so to speak, and not to waste time on analyzing a complex array of signs.

If we turn now to re-examining the two contrasting types of clown make-up, we understand how their use of white paint is grounded upon a deep-rooted biosemiotic signaling behavior. The white-face eliminates all possibilities of showing variations of skin coloration and muscular contractions that would convey information on his emotions. A dark line is usually drawn along his lower eyelid, thus neutralizing the sign of any genuine smile that is produced by these erectile tissues. In addition, the contrast between the sclera, the teeth and the skin of the face is greatly reduced because they are of the same color. This mask practically eliminates the possibility of emitting clear leuco-signals since the contrast with the skin color is greatly reduced.

In opposition to the white-face, the august makes ample use of white patches. Each august clown has his own patterns of white that identify him from a distance but the white marks are not distributed at random on the face. They are exclusively found both in the eyes and mouth areas where they pick up and artificially increase the white of the sclera and the teeth. Seen from close, these patches can be found to be of somewhat rough design but, seen from a distance in the performance situation, they broadcast wide and large the leuco-signals which proclaim the innocence and trustworthiness of this character.

7.5. A cross-cultural probe of clown make-up and its transformations

The human face is endowed with the capacity to broadcast signals which are of utmost relevance to a social species. In encounters between strangers, identities, moods, and intentions are first read on this biosemiotic display board. Many of the signs emitted by the face depend on hard-wired circuits: intimidation, fear, disgust, arousal, and curiosity, for instance, are caused by information coming from the environment in which other humans are of prime interest. However, some of these signs can be modified to some extent through voluntary contractions of the rich muscular structure which underlies the facial skin. Some of these contractions can be made selectively for various purposes such as appearing to be shocked, angry, or pleased in order to conform to social expectations or to change the behavior of other people. Cultures have exploited this relative flexibility by developing particular normative managements of the face in social interactions. Whether children are encouraged to honestly disclose all their moods and intents, or whether they are trained to refrain from expressing their emotions in general or some specific emotions which are deemed improper in some contexts, depends on the complex rules that social groups have elaborated to regulate the mutual interactions of their members. Cultures and sub-cultures generate idiosyncratic sets of constraints among which those pertaining to the face are prominent. As a consequence, the observation of face-to-face interactions must take into consideration both the biosemiotic systems that govern facial expressions and the cultural constraints that interfere with them. A third layer must be added in order to have a complete picture of the situation: the cosmetic transformations which further determine the reading of faces. Some signaling parts such as the eyebrows can be artificially emphasized or neutralized; cheeks and lips can be made more colorful so as to create the impression of a permanent state of arousal; hair style and facial hairs can be manage with various semiotic effects.

Humans, like many other social species which principally rely on the visual medium, receive from the new faces they encounter a set of vital information: sex, age, status, in brief, the identity kit of the individuals with whom they come into contact. It is also there that changes of attitude in known faces can be discovered. It is therefore predictable that the face will always be the first part of the body which is scanned in encounters. Therefore, it is not surprising that the faces of performers attract a disproportionate amount of attention on the part of the audience, even in ballet and in acrobatic circus acts in which it would seem that the focus should be on the whole dynamic actions which are displayed.

As we have seen so far in this chapter, the make-up of the two types of European traditional clowns can be read immediately at a performing distance which is the only point of view from which they must be described since they are designed not for close up examinations but for the benefit of a large circus audience. Consequently, the most relevant feature of their respective characters must be redundantly expressed while, at the same time, their identities as individual performers must be recognizable. Although these clowns apply a single general algorithm when they devise their own make-up in the category of their role, each one has a unique make-up due to deliberate variations within the range permitted by the algorithm. In this respect, many forms of make-up that have been preserved by painters of circus subjects and by professional photographers are true works of art. They show how the natural features of the performers' faces were subtly enhanced or modified so as to create either an endearing charismatic persona or an imperious and sophisticated character that lasted a life-time and became icons of the circus lore.

When the popular British clown Charlie Cairoli had his miniature concertina snatched from his hands by his abusive white-face partner who was determined not to let him play music in the ring, the public was spontaneously taking side. When the enraged white-face was throwing the "baby" concertina into a garbage can, the audience booed in earnest. Then, when Charlie was carrying away the garbage can with a pathetic expression of sadness, true hatred on the part of children and adults alike was targeting the oppressor. And when Charlie, before leaving the ring, lifted the lid of the can to reveal that the concertina was playing by itself inside, there was a wave of joy and triumph that stirred the whole circus audience. This brief glance at clowns in action show that the make-up expresses deep-rooted values both on biosemiotic and sociosemiotic levels that function as operators in the production of the acts. A gag is not so much what is being done but who does what to whom.

This example is borrowed from the European tradition and its score, so to speak, can be, and has been played by many clowns. Like for the implementation of their personal make-up, European clowns have been performing with more or less virtuosity a set of scenarios whose origin is lost in the deep time of folklore and popular comedy. Each clown may add a touch of innovation which, if successful, is picked up by other clowns and further generations.

But this chapter would not be complete if some other traditions of clowning were not probed, at least tentatively, in an effort to show that the principles which regulate the genesis of clown make-up as it has been described here are not limited to the cultural codes of the area in which they have been observed. If a theory of clown make-up is grounded in biosemiotics, it should be relevant cross-culturally. However, it would take at least a full volume to address this problem thoroughly. Let us simply probe a few domains in the cultural periphery of the European circus tradition.

In North America, an idiosyncratic circus has developed under the influence of the European institutions. But this new context has transformed the art of clowning first by presenting spectacles for much larger audiences in three-ring tents and in sport arenas with the consequence that the distance between the performers and the public was greatly increased. Make-up had to be considerably modified with the result of creating a typical august that displays much expanded white patches and darker chromatic contrasts. Democratic ideologies also played a part in the disappearance of the authority figure embodied in the white-face clown. Whenever traditional European clowns have been hired to perform for American popular audiences, the make-up, garments, and behavior of the white-face did not make sense to the public who had not been exposed to this cultural code and its stereotypes. In American circuses august type characters are playing visual tricks on each other or perform gags which do not involve interacting verbally with a dominant figure. A new type of clown has emerged: the tramp or "hobo", who symbolizes cultural marginality and transgression. This type picked up in his make-up some of the features of the traditional European august. But it usually foregrounds a sign that would be inconsistent with the neonate features of the august: he is ill-shaved, not bearded though, thus displaying disdain for cosmetic conventions rather than sporting seniority and authority. His garments are ill-fitted, worn out and torn in places, and squarely put him outside the civil norm. In the ring, he has to deal with the "straight man", the culturally updated version of the white-face, who tries to give him a hard time.

A second factor of transformation has been the silent cinema and its early link with circus and vaudeville which provided some popular types of entertainers who relied on visual effects rather than dialogues. The archetypes of this new genre of clowning are Charlie Chaplin, Stan Laurel, and Buster Keaton who have been imitated by numerous European clowns when their films became popular globally, and whose characteristics fit rather closely the august type, except that the close-ups allowed by the film medium do not require the redundant signs made necessary by the context of a circus ring.

The American street entertainers of the 1970s usually attracted attention by performing some acrobatic or juggling tricks in order to prompt pedestrians to stop and form a circle. Then, they often acted as a white-face using carefully chosen members of their audience to unwittingly play the part of augusts. This was a challenging and high-risk behavior but it would pay off if the improvised partners took it as a playful experience and the audience laughed. Some of these street entertainers reached fame through being highlighted by television and became stars of European circus programs. They could indeed fit well in a one-ring context because their "act" involved dialogues. As a rule they do not wear a clown make-up and display the "straight man" demeanor because their performance requires that they show authority in manipulating the behavior of often unsuspecting spectators who are first asked if they agree to lend their help for some task and are thus enticed to step into the spotlight. It should be noted that the dimension of a circus ring is such that performing artists have to learn how to walk within this space with shorter steps than usual. Any outsider who walks across a ring for the first time is bound to look awkward, somewhat like an august.

But in the circus as in any other cultural institutions nothing is ever consistently stable. Innovations and accidental changes keep transforming the state of play. Any novelty that happens to be met with popular success sooner or later becomes the norm at least for a while. Some august types have imitated the street performer's formula. Protected by their august's make-up, they are less offensive as they can manipulate their audience without foregrounding excessive authority. Who would resist helping such a charismatic face? The result is the same. The joke is on a few spectators and the clown saves the costs of buying and carrying props, and hiring a partner.

7.6. Expanding the scope: toward a global semiotic theory of clown make-up

Probing the make-up of the American clowns is not straying far from the European cultural domain because there is historical continuity between the two circus cultures and their semiotic transformations can be rather precisely retraced. The situation is much more complex if we venture beyond western cultures.

The Indian circus offers examples of clown make-up which somewhat parallel the pattern of evolution that was observed in the previous section. Although the history of the circus in India has not been the object of serious research, it is generally considered that the tent circuses that have prospered in great number during the last centuries were influenced by early British traveling shows. There is ample evidence that most of the circus arts including acrobatics, animal training, and clowning, have very ancient roots in the Asian subcontinent. After all, the gypsies who traditionally made a living by entertaining European crowds since the Middle Ages originated in nomadic tribes from Northern India and Pakistan. But the massive urbanization of modern India has prompted the development of a circus culture which owes more to the western institution than the traditional traveling performers who still visit villages. In large circuses, Indian clowns, which are referred to as "jokers", display exclusively august type make-up. The consistent adding of white patches in the eye and mouth areas of the face seems to indicate that there is a similar use of the biosemiotic functionality of leuco-signals. Their natural complexion does not require the addition of extra coloring. Whether this practice predates the European clowns or results from cultural imitation is a moot point. Indian jokers perform in a ring that is very distant from most of the audience because of the huge dimensions of the tents that are set up in sprawling Indian cities. The most relevant signs must be clearly visible for the whole spectrum of spectators, and these signs obviously fulfill their biosemiotic function.

During several years of research on Indian circuses, I never saw what could be considered the equivalent of the white-face because the jokers, like the American clowns, play visual tricks on each other and any outside authority is usually represented by the ring master.

However, it should be noted that in the ancient tradition of the Sanskrit dramas there existed a stereotyped comic character, the Vidushaka (simplified spelling) whose face was apparently painted in white and whose costume evokes the much more recent European white-face. Unfortunately, there does not seem to be any reliable iconography except for a very few early photographs which documented the last performances of these dramas before they became culturally extinct. Whether such a similarity is of strictly historical significance or pertains to a deeper semiotics is difficult to ascertain. Deciding between influence and convergence in order to explain a marked morphology remains a thorny issue in semiotics. It addresses the problem of the relative parts played by biosemiotics and history in the emergence and development of cultures. However, it is worth noting that the revival of the Hindu dramatic traditions in the Koodiyattam of Kerala (South India) bears witness to the resilience of the Vidushaka, under any other name. These performances indeed include a jester who is prone to eliciting laughter by his explanations of the Sanskrit dramas and his comments in vernacular languages, and whose elaborate make-up features black designs drawn on his whitened face. His extravagant costumes evoke the glittering garments of the European white-face.

But this tentative exploration into the domain of comic performers' make-up would not be complete without including the Javanese Punakawans. We have traveled so far along culturally contiguous areas along which it is not always clear in which direction cultural models have spread and how they have negotiated biosemiotic constraints. The Indonesian archipelago was colonized by Hindu kings early in the first millennium before it was conquered by Islamic rulers. Hinduism and its various cultural traditions which had blended with the folk cultures persisted in the form of cultural syncretism. Episodes of the great Hindu epics such as the *Ramayana* and the *Mahabharata* are still being performed in various media: puppet show, dance, and theater. The intense dramas excerpted from Hindu epics are interspersed with interludes by the Punakawans (sort of clowns) who provide comic relief by commenting on the lofty actions of the gods and heroes from a down-to-earth perspective. They are four, a father (Somar) and his three sons (Petruk, Gareng, and Bagong). They are dressed like peasants but they are said to be actually representing the ancient, pre-colonization Javanese deities. Their proper names have the same kind of status as "august" in the European circus. These parts are performed by many specialized actors but each actor has devised an original version of the stereotypic make-up of the character he embodies. However, all the versions of the make-up of Somar, for instance, are clearly identifiable as a Somar make-up which includes a completely whitened face upon which distinctive black patterns are drawn. These patterns are not identical to, but they are congruent with those of the

Vidushaka as well as the white-face clown. Petruk and Gareng wear individual make-up that implement the same principles as their father's albeit in a way that allows them to be individually identified. Bagong, however, whose role is very similar to the circus august, displays a make-up which emphasizes reddish colors around the mouth and eyes with white patches that enhance the contrasts of the teeth and the sclera. It seems that the same biosemiotic constraints are at work, irrespective of whether these contrasted types of make-up have emerged independently or have spread through cultural contacts.

These reflections lead us to raise, once again in the context of this volume, the issue of the interplay of nature and culture in the framework of the circus, even perhaps in relation to all artistic forms. Biosemiotics affords a raw material upon which artists apply transformative techniques to create a second order of perceptions and meanings. This process is particularly obvious in the semiotic engineering which produces make-up and masks. Clowns selectively use both the biosemiotic constraints of their evolutionary heritage and the social rules of their culture in order to achieve what could be considered to be "hypersigns", that is, signs from which any information irrelevant to their purpose has been eliminated.

Chapter 8
Incident, accident, failure: life and death at the circus

As I wait in line to buy a ticket to the circus that the Shriners have brought to town this summer, I observe Daniel Suskow, the elephant trainer, who leads one of his charges around the lot with a load of children on the howdah. This is a part of the experience that brave children expect from their yearly visit to a circus show. Riding an elephant is like being in a boat on a rather rough sea. Some giggle and some cry for their mommies but most are deadly serious. The trainer walks calmly on the side of the placid animal's left shoulder, impervious to the children's agitation but intensely focused on the mood of the pachyderm which he addresses from time to time with brief orders. He does not use his hook but holds it firmly in his right hand. I am close enough to see the piercing eye of the elephant which keeps scanning its surroundings without losing sight of the man and his hook. At one turn, the man inadvertently drops the hook. He does not pick it up. In one instant, he blocks it with his foot, throws it back up from his instep and deftly catches it in the manner of a juggler. This is the rule of thumb: never lower your body close to your elephants. They are unpredictable and most lethal accidents occur when the trainer trips and falls down. This quick reaction brings back to my mind the memory of Eloise Berchtold who was trampled to death by the tusker "Teak" after she tripped in the ring in front of him during her act (Bordez and Juliani 2002).

I am now in my seat and half of the program has unfolded. Tarzan Zerbini's tigers open the second part. Then come some clowns and learned dogs, a Korean contortionist, and three seals catching and balancing balloons on their wet noses. The next act is a young couple who gracefully enter the ring. It looks as if they were on their honey moon. The man climbs the rope to a trapeze and firmly takes the position of the catcher. While he rubs his hands with talc to dry them, the woman ascends toward him. She reaches him and grasps his hands. The act starts on a soft, romantic music accompaniment. Several aerial exercises are successfully performed. Then, it is solemnly announced that she will somersault and be caught by the feet. The drums are rolling. Then, silence. We hear the voice of the man: "Go!...Oh no!". She has fallen to the ground. A brief moment of confusion ensues. Quickly, the music starts again as the horses which were kept waiting behind the curtain cavort in the ring. Only a few spectators realize what happened. It was so fast. Tomorrow, this act will not be a part of the show.

8.1. The representation of negative experience in performance

The focus of this chapter will be circus acts that represent failures or evoke the possibility of accidental death as an essential dimension of their meaning. Accidents are extremely rare but they do occur. This aspect of circus performances will be approached through a detour in the work of sociologist Erving Goffman (1922–1982) who developed the notion of "negative experience" in everyday life and explored its application to the characterization of some social events in the realm of public entertainments. We will return to this topic in Chapter 10 when we discuss the factors which make a bad performance bad. But, here, we are more concerned by the challenge of understanding what makes an apparently bad performance good.

Goffman addressed this issue in chapter eleven of *Frame Analysis* (1974) in which he observed that the occasional disorganization of experience ('breaking of a frame', 'flooding out', 'capsizing') is also the object of careful staging in a range of public entertainments such as sports, theatre, radio, film and circus. Goffman's consideration of 'the manufacture of negative experience' or in other words, 'the organization of negative experience in pure performance' (that is, institutionalized performance as opposed to the dramaturgic structure of everyday life) led him to hint at the generality of this phenomenon but stopped short of formulating an explanatory hypothesis. Goffman's characterization of this notion proceeds through phenomenological descriptions of familiar instances and through an accumulation of examples which fit the category of social experience that has been thus evoked. As a result, it appears that there are indeed sufficient phenomenological grounds for justifying the intuitive construction of such a category but some important questions remain unanswered. Is it possible to give a better conceptual delineation to the notion of 'negative experience'?

This expression obviously does not refer to an experience which would be modified by the logical sign of the negation but rather to the experience of something or some situation which is accompanied by an unpleasant feeling of a particular kind; the negativity involved here is qualitative rather than quantitative. But if this unpleasantness is marked by a sense of failure or by the presence of an urge for redress through repairing or redeeming, one may wonder why social institutions such as public entertainments should foster such an interest in 'manufacturing' or rather 'staging' negative experiences? Moreover, when they do so, how do they implement such representations and in which context, and how are these representations of negative experiences construed as positive experiences by their audience? These are the sort of questions that will be tackled by scrutinizing Goffman's concept of 'frame' in relation to the central issues of this chapter: the general concept of situation from a non-phenomenological point of view; the categories of 'incident', 'accident' and 'failure' as typical instances of negative experience and their problematic representations in circus performances. The staging of two circus acts in which negative experiences are 'manufactured' will be described and analyzed at strategic moments in the course of the demonstration. In so doing, particular attention will be paid to the broad contextualization of the examples provided. A relevant clown act will be introduced once a basic model of negative experience is proposed, and, after further elaborating the notion of situation, an acrobatic act will be examined.

8.2. A science of the individual

Anybody, it seems, could immediately give a series of examples of negative experiences if presented with this term. It would include, for instance, being denied a favor; missing a flight; witnessing a traumatic event; losing something; making a bad impression on someone whose opinion is considered important; failing to meet a commitment. The list could be indefinitely expanded. Indeed, this tentative definition in extension initiates an open repertory of situations which could cover a large portion of everyday experience but which appears of little theoretical value until an examination of a more or less random set of examples reveals two important aspects; first, each one of these instances of negative experience presupposes a cultural construct, a social structure and context, and, secondly, it implies a value system; this acknowledgement brings into focus the relative nature of most of the experiences listed above, their culture-sensitivity, while raising, at the same time, the issue of a possible scale going from strictly individual circumstances to biological universals. Even if occurrences of the two extreme categories are considered highly improbable – in as much as they are theoretically situated outside the cultural spectrum – the existence of some variation along the scale seems unquestionable. Being late or having to negotiate a joke on a sensitive topic may involve more cultural constructs than failing to make an impression on a potential mate or withdrawing in front of a stronger competitor. Secondly, the diversity of all these instances raises the problem of their conceptual definition: do they simply have in common the same kind of affect, or can they be understood as effects resulting from systematic variations of parameters amenable to a theoretical formulation? It is toward the latter hypothesis that Goffman's use of the notion of frame has led us in spite of his first-person approach to the notion of situation. While a personal experiencing of circus shows is at the core of our inquiry, the semiotic understanding of such performances and their appreciative reception by audiences requires the heuristic elaboration of the frame provided by the code of the spectacles and the constitutive rules of the institution that produces them.

In his introduction to *Frame Analysis*, Goffman situates his inquiry in the context of phenomenology, communication theory and semiotics, indicating the origin of the notions he uses in his book. In particular he specifies: 'it is Bateson's paper ('A Theory of Play and Phantasy') that the term *frame* was proposed in roughly the sense in which I want to employ it' (1974: 7). However he distances himself from the grand projects more or less explicitly fostered by phenomenologists, communication theorists and semioticians of discovering the system of constitutive rules which would account for the diversity of patterned social behavior. It is in this context that he indirectly mentions semiotics and the 'scientific' notion of code which forms the problematic backbone of these approaches: [. . .] the modern effort in linguistically oriented disciplines to employ the notion of code as a device which informs and patterns all events that fall within the boundaries of its application' (1974: 7–8). In contradistinction with these 'scientific' endeavors from which he admittedly borrowed some of his most fertile concepts, he sets for himself a less ambitious goal: 'my perspective is situational, meaning here a concern for what one individual can be alive to at a particular moment, this often involving a few other particular individuals, and not necessarily restricted to the mutually monitored arena of a face-to-face gathering [. . .] I assume that when individuals attend to any current situation they face the question: 'What is it that is going on here'? [...] "(1974: 7–8). Such an approach may provide an interesting framework for exploring the reception of circus acts by audiences which are made of individuals who constantly need to answer this question, but this can only be a first step.

Goffman's aim can indeed be defined paradoxically as a science of the individual in the form of a repertory of examples with which particular instances can be matched in the same manner as when someone looks up a word in a dictionary. This could inspire a research that would consist of collecting a large number of individual reactions on the part of circus spectators. This always conveys the secure feeling of dealing with tangible entities or, as Goffman puts it, 'to speak of something happening before the eyes of observers is to be on firmer ground than usual in the social sciences' (1974: 9). However, Goffman is conscious of the illusory nature of this secure feeling as he qualifies the above statement as follows: 'but the ground is still shaky, and the crucial question of how a seeming agreement was reached concerning the identity of the 'something' and the inclusiveness of 'before the eyes' still remains' (1974: 9).

'What sort of an instance of the type the particular undertaking was' is the key sentence that describes the dictionary-like nature of a would-be science of the individual. Goffman states later: 'My aim is to try and isolate some of the basic frameworks of understanding available in our society for making sense out of events, and to analyze the special vulnerabilities to which these frames of reference are subject' (1974: 10). All dictionaries must indeed come to grips with the problems of polysemy and homonymy – a word occurrence can always be a pun or a metaphor. Significantly, he justifies his use of press reports and popular books in the same way as the lexicographer picks up a sentence which typifies the use of a lexeme. 'The design of these reported events is fully responsive to our demands – which are not for facts but for typifications' (1974: 14).

However this should not be taken in too absolute a sense. When Goffman talks about the 'definition of a situation' he means the way in which the situation at hand is matched with its entry in the dictionary and not in the sense that one would say 'what is a situation' or 'what is a word'. For instance: 'I assume that definitions of a situation are built up in accordance with principles of organization which govern events – at least social ones – and our subjective involvement in them; frame is the word I use to refer to such of those basic elements as I am able to identify. That is my definition of frame' (1974: 11) or 'This book is about the organization of experience – something that an individual actor can take into his mind – and not the organization of society. I make no claim to be talking about the core matters of sociology – social organization and social structure' (1974: 13). He insists that he addresses 'the structure of experience individuals have at any moment of their social life' (1974: 13). But he nevertheless adds: 'I personally hold society to be first in every way and any individual's current involvements to be second; this report deals only with matters that are second' (1974: 13). A semiotic inquiry of the sort that is developed in this chapter precisely attempts to go beyond individual experiences and elucidate the frames which account for the very possibility of such experiences.

Therefore attempting to frame Goffman's concept of situation in a more general, detached, or, if one prefers, objective manner is not so much taking a theoretically opposite stand as developing or completing Goffman's project beyond the voluntarily restricted domain of his analyses. After all, 'frame' can refer metaphorically to the closure of a situation as well as to its inner structure. It evokes the fact that the subject apprehends the situation as a whole, as an opposition between an inside – which is formed by the subject attending the situation – and an outside which is a mere outer limit, a sort of fencing off of irrelevance, but it is also a trap: in the slang of criminals, framing someone means to superimpose a situation upon another situation which loses its autonomy and becomes contaminated, so to speak, by the engineered or fabricated situation; in other words situation A is framed by situation B and becomes ambiguous as it is congruent with both frames, with the difference that situation B is usually more pregnant (or more deviant) than situation A and entails a legal sanction.

In a socially different register, circus acts always frame a "safer" routine within a wider narrative marked by uncertainty and high risk. We will encounter two such strategies later in this chapter.

Obviously the image of 'frame', which designates both a conceptual delineation and a unified and integrated experience, also implies an inner structure. Synonyms offered in English dictionaries include 'construction', 'structure', 'order', 'plan', 'scheme', system', 'definition form', 'regular procedure', 'shape', 'building', 'skeleton' (e.g., Murray and Bradley 1901). All situations may have in common that they are 'frames' both in the limiting sense and in the structural sense, but they are not all identical and their differences are also relevant parts of the picture. One of the main assumptions of this chapter is that 'negative experiences' cannot be fully described without explicit references to the complex systems of rules which constitute the frame of Goffman's 'frames', not in absolute terms but within a given society. The celebrated clown George Carl (1916–2000) became famous for an act in which he systematically produced negative experiences that were grounded in his skillful play with frames as we will see later in this chapter.

8.3. Toward a model of negative experience

From the point of view of a conscious organism, the business of everyday life can be described as a patchwork of plans, some encompassing others, some overlapping, some even conflicting at times with one another; from the point of view of a society of such organisms, individuals' plans can be perceived with some measure of objectivity as compatible, converging or competing. Overall notions like strategies and tactics, routines and sub-routines, policies and counter-policies, attempt to bring some rational order among the intertwined flows of goal-directed actions. In human terms, plans can be as short as the temporal integration of a sentence, or as extended as the implementation of a lifetime ambition. This is evidenced by the phenomenon of 'repairing', i.e., taking appropriate measures to correct an error in the course of an action. This behavior can be observed in animals, in particular in primates. For instance, when gibbons produce their solos or duets, any deviation occurring in the production – whatever the cause may be – has an impact on the performance which is corrected, interrupted or started anew, or simply abandoned (Haimoff 1988); this phenomenon has also been studied in great detail in human conversations (Schegloff et al. 1977). Goffman had a keen interest in the way in which external disruptions of scripts are negotiated in social interaction, to the extent that he often himself caused such disruptions in order to observe from within the working out of this process. The repairing phenomenon is probably the best objective evidence that planning and monitoring are definitional characteristics of social action, and necessary conditions of negative experience, which can thus be constructed as a failure to repair or redeem a disrupted or interrupted plan. In the staged failure we have examined in the case of the Burger Sisters act in Chapter 6, the apparent technical failure and the repairing action give extraordinary saliency to the overall plan and its eventual success.

However, plans are not purely abstract representations of hierarchized moves in a tree form with optional and substitutive strategies at some nodes of the schemata: they are motivated behavior. Indeed, they are not usually implemented for their own sake but with a view to some form of gratification whose failure to achieve generates frustration. Any experience which results in a situation that may be qualified as negative implies both a plan (a structure of actions) and a desire (a structure of motivations). The latter is particularly important and requires some clarification. It is indeed usually taken for granted that any goal-directed activity – as opposed to mere reflexes or pathological agitation – is structured in the sense that a plan is a mental representation of a non-random sequence of tasks and sub-tasks (Miles 1977), but that motivations are un-analyzable primal drives such as sex, hunger, survival and the like. As we saw in Chapter 2, acrobats display such plans' implementations as forms of achievements that are acknowledged by their audiences.

Trivial homeostatic models, more or less implicitly conceived as hydraulic systems which metaphorically relate depletion and satiation have been shown to be definitely insufficient for accounting for human motivations (Toates 1986). Models and theories of motivation form a rich domain of contemporary psychological inquiry which cannot be glossed over when addressing the issue of negative experience in a social context. Therefore, the complexity of motivations, which to a large extent are culture dependent, should translate into a great structural diversity of negative experiences. The deliberate, and perhaps desperate decision of Goffman to remain at the level of what 'one individual can be alive to at a particular moment' (1974: 8) is probably what precluded him from going beyond a purely phenomenological description of what an individual can verbally express with respect to his/her experience of the outcome of an action or the conscious monitoring of a plan. These verbal accounts are doubly constrained first by the limitations of the conceptual repertory encapsulated in the language of description or by the dynamic of the root metaphor that may be creatively chosen (for instance, drama); secondly by the fact that all cognitive processes are not necessarily conscious, and that an individual can be cognitively alive to more information than he/she is conscious of and therefore can report directly (Lewicki 1986). This is a point we have raised in the introductory chapter of this book when we retraced the experience of attending a circus show and on which we elaborated in Chapter 4. The definition of a situation in strictly phenomenological terms puts a tremendous pressure on the verbal expressivity and conceptual creativity of the semiotician as a social scientist and may result, as in the case of Goffman, in subtle and novel texts of literary stature, but it entails an unjustifiable renouncing of accessing abstract, comprehensive knowledge through the various strategies of scientific inquiry (Elias 1987). The latter alone can yield an understanding of what 'being alive to' means. A consistent metaphor has the merit of pre-figuring a metalanguage, but its predictive value can only remain within the realm of self-fulfilling prophecies. Such is the suggestive image of 'frame', with its tantalizing ambiguities and conceptual fuzziness.

8.4. When failure means success: the staging of a negative experience

The French surrealists of the nineteen-twenties created a society game which consisted of inventing analogical identities such as: if so and so were a flower, what flower would be/she be? If one were to ask: if Goffman had been a circus performer which one would he have been? The answer then might be: George Carl, a popular comedian who produced his own act in vaudeville, night clubs and circuses during the second half of the twentieth century. Indeed his script amounted to consistently testing how far it was possible to push the limits of an anti-performance, and still qualify as a performer, that is, being successful with an audience and securing long-term contracts. Not only did George Carl's 'manufacturing of negative experience' seem to perfectly illustrate Goffman's take on this topic, but also his *dramatis persona* – both physical and psychological – was not without some resemblance to the famous sociologist who, as it has often been mentioned, enjoyed straining social interactions by obnoxious behavior in order to gain some insights into the 'frames' at stake. In a fascinating account of his own research career, the psychologist Paul Ekman (1987) recounted an episode from the time when he was involved in joint research with Goffman at the University of California, San Francisco. The study consisted of asking two students from opposing political persuasions to discuss their differences while the debate was filmed: 'As this interaction proceeded,' – Ekman writes –

> I pointed to Erving some of the more interesting expressions which we would be able to dissect later when reviewing the videotape. He however was taken with the fact that serious people were willing to engage in such conversations in a laboratory setting, and decided to test how much interference they would tolerate. Dressed in his usual casual style, he posed (quite credibly) as a janitor. He walked

> into their room, saying that he had to remove some piece of furniture. He removed one piece of furniture after another while they continued their argument, until finally he took away the chairs in which they were sitting. They continued their argument standing up! For Erving, the videotape demonstrated that someone who was not a player – Erving – could not really interfere with the scripted interaction. (Ekman 1987: 31–32)

Having taken a glance at Goffman the comedian-experimenter, let us now turn to Carl the experimenter-comedian and let us follow in detail his fifteen-minute act before attempting to analyze it from the theoretical perspective of this chapter.

This act was a part of the 1983 show of the National Swiss Circus Knie. It was observed in Luzern (July 1983). The printed program announced Carl as a genius of comedy, and the ring master introduced him without comment but in a tone of voice which indicates star status. By contrast, his entry was undistinguished and unassertive. He was wearing a drab, not too well fitted tuxedo and a black, floppy hat. He looked uninterested and slightly worried; he was paying little attention to the audience, walking toward the right, then the left, aiming at the exit, coming back toward the centre where a microphone was standing; he whistled as when one walks leisurely or is somewhat embarrassed, in order just to do something or break the silence.

He did a few dance steps, nodded at the audience informally, walked a bit, nodded again twice, came to the microphone, stepped on the tangled wires, pulled one wire, got his feet caught in a mess of wires, said 'allo' in the mike, as if he were testing the sound; he looked pleased, but kept glancing toward the exit as if ready to leave the ring at any moment. Finally he settled in front of the microphone, buttoned and unbuttoned his jacket, fiddled with his hat and fixed his hair. He put his thumbs in his suspenders, moved his fingers and got them caught in the suspenders, disentangled them with an angry look. He wanted to put his left hand in his pocket but could not find the pocket. Not knowing what to do with his hands, he crossed his arms. He appeared awkward, self-conscious. He looked again for his pocket, searching along his thigh, down to his knee. He tried to button up his jacket but got his finger caught in the buttonhole. Now and then he looked back anxiously toward the exit. He noticed someone taking a photo, made a sign toward this person, winked, then, knocked his hat against the microphone which was standing in front of him. He took off his jacket, fixed the pleat of his trousers, put his jacket back on; his hat fell down, he caught it and tried to make a few ordinary tricks with his hat. He attempted to keep it in balance with the edge standing on his forehead, but failed, and threw it so that it would land on the microphone; he bowed to the audience. He grasped the microphone stand and moved it a bit, his hands got entangled in the wire; the stand and the hat got tied up together by the wire. He managed to free his hands but the stand fell apart and one of his fingers was now stuck in one of the stand's pieces. He used the microphone as a hammer to push his finger out, but another finger got caught. The microphone was hanging; the wires were more entangled than ever. He did not know where to put his hat so that he could use his other hand; he put his hat back on his head, tried again to button up his jacket, stuck again a finger in the buttonhole; his hat fell on the floor. He looked agitated and was overwhelmed by the situation, losing control, looking toward the exit; he tried to move backward but his suspenders had now become tied-up to the microphone stand; he could not free himself; he scratched his nose, his ear; his fingers got stuck under his hat; he pulled his hand out; he picked his nose; his finger got stuck in his nose; he pulled some dry mucus from his nose, looked at it, threw it on the floor and kicked it away. He seized the microphone as if he were going to do something but noticed that one of his sleeves seemed longer than the other; he tried to fix them, could not succeed, jumped: now they looked the same length.

He suddenly rushed toward a small metallic table, which was standing beside the ring curb, with a tray which appeared to be full of harmonicas of various sizes. He carried the whole thing with a lot of noise and, when in front of the microphone, the table, which was a collapsible one, fell flat on the ground. He picked up the frame, snapped it back into position and behaved as if his testicles had been caught in the frame; he mimicked pain, then, showed that it was his fingers that were pinched. He walked around the mess and started putting things back into place with a lot of banging noise. At long last he was ready to play the harmonica in front of the microphone but the stand slid down. He put it back into position and gestured as if he were using a bicycle pump to push the stand up. He fixed the stand at the right level, bowed to the audience, but knocked his head on the microphone; actually, it soon became clear that the microphone had penetrated into his mouth. Some inarticulate sounds were broadcast by the amplifiers. He extracted the microphone from his mouth. He pulled his tongue, and put back the microphone and started playing, but at the same time he tried to button up his jacket, got his finger caught in the buttonhole, used the other hand with the harmonica which got entangled in his suspenders with the stand and the wire. He looked helpless, struggled and got out of the mess, again putting everything into position, and resumed playing the harmonica, but something interfered; there was a noise coming from his nose; he grossly blew his nose, using his fingers, then did not know what to do with the wet mucus on his fingers; he rubbed it on the microphone stand as if there were plenty of mucus, and threw the rest toward the public as inadvertently. But he suddenly seemed to notice that people were watching him and he looked hostile.

He played the harmonica again, producing a cacophonic version of a typical American western tune. One of his legs tapped in rhythm, but his foot started behaving abnormally. The music stopped; the leg kept moving frantically as if the foot were stuck on the floor. He pulled his leg with his hands and found a piece of chewing gum which was stuck to his sole. He took it out but could not get rid of it because it adheres to his fingers; he tried to put it in his pocket; then put it back on the sole; but the foot got stuck again. Finally he put the chewing gum in his mouth, and resumed his music playing, but the harmonica got glued to his mouth and his tongue got glued to the microphone. He managed to pull himself out of this situation.

With his left hand he then gave the beat to the orchestra which started playing an American Indian musical rhythm which took over his own rhythm and overpowered his music; he started a mock Indian dance with the microphone in his hand like a hatchet, and uttered 'Indian' war cries.

He suddenly stopped and produced some fake language, then laughed as if he had told a joke; he bowed to the audience but got the microphone stuck in his mouth again. He resumed his music, but hardly audibly, then pulled an antenna from the harmonica and talked toward it, and placed it against his ear as if it were a walkie-talkie. He then played seriously with orchestra accompaniment, but the orchestra changed the tune and played a French cancan. After a few seconds of cacophony, he stopped, protested to no effect, and while the orchestra continued its piece threw the harmonica on the ground, took another one, tried to play but the same situation persisted. He broke the harmonica in small pieces, threw it on the tray; making lots of noise, and agitated the tray on which there were several forks and spoons which scattered on the ground. He started dancing for a few seconds to a rapid rhythm and left the ring. As he exited, he progressively flexed his legs, keeping his torso straight so that he gave the impression that his height decreased a little at each step and he appeared to be reduced to half of his size when he disappeared behind the curtain. He came back to bow to the audience, which usually applauded with enthusiasm. He seemed pleased at first, but soon started looking at his watch as if in a hurry or if annoyed because of the time he is wasting now in the ring, being obliged to acknowledge the public's appreciation. He occasionally made gestures of exasperation or boredom. His behavior was at times frankly insulting. He exited while the audience was still clapping their hands, some rising on their feet as a sign of utmost appreciation.

At first, one may wonder why for several decades – George Carl had been indeed for years a fixture of the famous *Crazy Horse Saloon* in Paris – this succession of stage mishaps, casual attitudes, and failed plans had triggered such a consistently appreciative reaction in the audience. In order to attempt to understand this phenomenon, and at the same time the cultural significance of staged negative experience, an examination of the nature of the performance is in order. As we will see in more detail in the last chapter when we address the question of what constitutes a bad performance, five principles underlie the frame of the social events which counts as performance in western cultures; maxims of the sort which were proposed by Grice (1975) with respect to felicitous conversation can be derived from these principles and the violation of any of these rules results in some degree of dissatisfaction in the audience. The first principle concerns the accountability of the performer, i.e., the contractual nature of the relation between performers and audience. It involves a complex institutional process including advertising, marketing, selling, delivery, acknowledging, and concluding. A successful performer is one who meets the expectations created by the terms which have been spelled out, or suggested in the promise which lures the audience into the premises in which the performance is to take place. This promise defines a particular order of competence (singing, acting, balancing, juggling, etc.) and is ascertained to be worth the money and time spent for witnessing its demonstrations. The second principle has to do with the semantics of the performance's contents; in order to be relevant it must refer to cognitive categories, social structures or cultural issues with which the audience is intimately familiar. There are, of course, various levels of relevance, from the very general anxiety linked with physical danger to the particular concern of a local social issue such as the rivalry existing between neighboring cities or between sport teams. Thirdly, the principle of rhetoric applies to the articulation and patterning of the performance, the ordering of the successive phases toward a climax, the clarity of the demonstrations of the competence concerned; as it was made clear in Chapter 2, the audience must always perceive which plan is being implemented, or which plan is designed to create a particular expectation, even if this expectation is eventually frustrated by the surprise implementation of an unexpected plan which effectively supersedes the initial one. The fourth principle is the respect of social congruency; it involves the way in which the performer socially behaves toward the audience; a general code of behavior prescribes how the performer should present himself/herself, acknowledge the public's reactions and take leave of the audience. This etiquette allows for variations depending on the style and genre of performance, but it is far from being a dispensable aspect because it symbolically regulates the insertion of the performers in the interactive network of the society in which they occupy a marginal eccentric position, and enjoy an ambiguous status, both idealized and stigmatized. Finally, the time principle, undoubtedly the most complex and elusive, pertains not only to the appropriateness of the scheduling and the length of the performance, but also and above all to the necessity to take control, so to speak, of the audience's temporal experience; it involves beat, tempo, rhythm; it causes the audience to abandon its multiple and heterogeneous short and long term plans and their related worries, and to surrender to the performers' momentum, goal and strategy;

the psycho-biological implications of this principle set it apart from the other four, which are more amenable to purely socio-cultural definitions.

8.5. The semiotic dissection of George Carl's comic act

If we turn now to George Carl's performance and examine each of its segments with respect to the first four principles, we can make the following observations. The most obvious systematic violations apply to the social congruency principle. Indeed, it takes a while until he acknowledges the presence of the audience by giving casual, brief, perfunctory nods but while keeping his hat on his head. Actually, during all that can be considered as the first installment of his act, he does exactly as if he were alone, being engaged in seemingly endless preparations (grooming himself, adjusting his garments, sorting out technical problems). In the second part, in which some form of performance in the usual sense (music, dance) is attempted, the audience is the butt of the performer's derision or contempt: no bow is properly executed; he makes fun of members of the audience who take photographs; he engages in offensive behavior such as uninhibited manipulation of nasal secretions, or repulsive manners with the recycling of the discarded piece of chewing gum. During all the performance not only does he rarely smile, but occasionally glances at people with a hostile facial expression. Finally, he reacts to the public's appreciative response in an insulting way, producing signs of boredom, looking at his watch in order to signal his impatience with the length of their applause, treating his own performance as a worthless chore and therefore questioning the audience's judgment.

The latter is a very strong transgression because it goes beyond the bracketing of the performance *per se* and denies the distinction between the *dramatis persona* and the actor. It foregrounds the contempt of the performer for his audience beyond the conventions of his acted performance in a way which could shatter the fragile suspension of the rules of civility that those conventions entail. It seems indeed that he could not go much further without triggering some form of counter-aggression, as he treads the fine line between play and non-play.

The accountability principle is also transgressed to some extreme extent – although, as we will see, in a more ambiguous manner. George Carl does not demonstrate any artistic competence of particular merit. His tentative juggling with his hat is a failure, his musical talent is on the level of an ordinary child, his dancing is trivial; moreover, he exhibits his inability to control his equipment, to exercise any authority on the accompanying orchestra. Even the dwarfing illusion of his exit is not acrobatically significant. To sum up, the completion of each of the tasks he explicitly assigned to himself is ordinary or even substandard. It seems that plain mediocrity is cultivated for its own sake without even a hint of a parody.

It could be claimed that the semantic principle is taken less casually in his performance; the categories of objects that are present or evoked, the patterned behavior that is enacted or suggested, the specialties which define a variety artist, the tunes that are played, are all familiar components of the cultural environment of the audience and their experience of the entertainment world. However, all these cognitive dimensions are brought into play in a low profile manner, characterized by a flat, low-information, redundant mood. Western cowboy music and French cancan are worn out musical themes in circus and variety shows; the plain harmonica is certainly the most unspectacular instrument that can be imagined in a circus setting. None of the gags performed by Carl are original; they have been seen again and again (the collapsing microphone stand, the miming of the air pump, the sticking of the finger in a hole, the impossibility of getting rid of a sticky object, etc.); they belong to the repertory of any beginner in the trade; and they are accomplished as such, in a low key, uninterested way by George Carl who makes no effort to show inventiveness and to cultivate unpredictability. If the semantic principle yields maxims such as: 'be relevant', 'be interesting', 'be informative', George Carl's performance implements a minimal semantic level.

The same observation can be made with respect to the rhetorical organization of this act. At the outset, the presence of the microphone assigns the performer to the broad category of vocal or instrumental artist, but seemingly erratic complications delay the beginning of the performance whatever it may be within the range defined by the setting. The table, with its implements, is not prominently located in the ring. It is a low undecorated, functional collapsible table. From the hesitations and confusion of the first phase of the act, the expectation of a musical performance emerges; at this point plans, counter-plans and their complications become more perceptible but nevertheless remain immersed in some fuzziness which places the act on the verge of randomness and disorganization. The only clear articulation is the passage from the supposedly preparatory to the implementation phase of the act although the second part constantly threatens to fall back into the first one.

We are thus confronted with the case of an artist who does very little and does it in a rather confused manner. Moreover, he is ostentatiously uninterested and impolite, even at times insulting toward his audience. His act is a succession of failures, and construes a global negative experience whose consequence is to belittle his artistic status, a result that is symbolized by the dwarfing of his stature when he leaves the ring. The contrast with the usual triumphal exit which concludes all circus acts is striking because of its explicitness and literality. It was nevertheless a huge success as George Carl consistently 'brought the house down', that is, caused in his audience an intense feeling of gratification indicated by their lengthy and sustained applause. His act was considered both by the public and by his peers a masterful achievement.

How was all this engineered? How could success be built upon a series of failures? And why did such a systematically negative transformation of the most basic elements of a circus act become the source of both intellectual and emotional delights? In order to account for this, three factors will be successively taken into consideration: the framing, timing and systematic properties of George Carl's act. It should be noted, though, that this remarkable example belongs of a rich paradigm which includes dog acts in which the animals are trained not to do what they are ordered to accomplish and magic acts which feature deliberately failed tricks. These acts could be analyzed along the same lines.

8.6. Anatomy of a negative masterpiece

First, the act was categorized at the outset as a comic one. Carl was introduced as a "genius of comedy". This created a frame, a set of expectations among which the knowledge that whatever would be shown could not, actually should not be taken at face value. Whatever the performer will do is therefore bracketed and raised to a level which implies some form of intellectual challenge in as much as sophisticated clowning implies jokes, riddles, puns, wit, gags which require mental alertness for being understood. The appearance of George Carl immediately indicated that his act would not involve the standard clowning as he did not wear the regular costume and make-up of circus clowns. The series of violations of the accountability principle, which was pointed out above, constituted one of the contents of this act rather than its form. The expression "genius of comedy" implies the promise that the performer will make the audience laugh, not that he will sing or play music with distinction. Ultimately, the accountability principle was not transgressed, but the question remains of how this was possible given the actual contents of the performance.

The second factor considered provided a part of the answer. In George Carl's performance it was the principle of timing which was not transgressed and it is highly probable that given the nature of the rest, he could not have afforded to alter it. A micro-analysis of the performance shows that it consisted of a succession of short-term plans integrated in a temporal structure whose beat coincided both with the outcome of each plan and the initiation of the next one. There was no dead time until George Carl disappeared from the ring. Further study of his act, which was integrally recorded for a television channel, might try to determine the exact periodicity involved, but it can be hypothesized that it was a constant value. During the first part of the act, before some musical performance was involved, the orchestra provided a discreet rhythmical percussion background. It should also be noted that the very beginning of the act included walking, changing directions, whistling and dancing, all actions which are good time-setting devices, thus creating the temporal frame which could take over the attentional structure of the audience's perception. My verbal description of the act, which was made during the performance, indirectly bears witness to the sustained rhythm of the succession of the actions. As the recorded verbal description goes on, no time is indeed available for elaborated syntax or correction of errors in the word selection. On the other hand, the description can unfold relatively smoothly because actions succeed one another without interference. The observer's attention – and it can be safely assumed the spectator's as well – could focus on a plan at a time without being distracted and was led with the help of the beat from one to the other without any slackening in the performer's dynamic. But this phenomenon is not sufficient to explain the profound gratification of the audience. By itself, applied to empty or random gestures, this temporal form could do little more than fascinate or even hypnotize the audience. The intellectual and emotional involvements of the audience reveal that the cognitive contents of the performance were highly relevant.

The third factor concerns the meaning of the act which addressed with a high degree of systematic consistency the very nature of performance. As was shown earlier, all the actions comprising this act represented violations of the rules related to the principles which combine to generate felicitous performances. In other words, each action denoted the rule as a rule by representing it in its negative form rather than subverting the performance's principles themselves; it was indeed the principles of performance themselves that were the objects whose successful representation was the act for which the performer was held accountable. The challenge was such that George Carl was introduced as nothing less than a 'genius' of the comic world. His success in making a performance out of a systematic violation of the rules of performance indeed amounted to achieving an impossible task. The negative experience which was manufactured as the substance of the act was not so much the experience of the negative feelings associated with failure as it was an experimentation with the negative – in the photographic sense – of the very system which makes this experience possible. There are obvious limits to this systematic transgression because of the institutional constraints which regulate performances in our culture. Only Dada, in its time, applied the systematic inversion of the rules, including timing and structure, to its ultimate consequences, that is, the impossibility of performance. But George Carl seemed to go as far as possible in the representation of a non-performance within a performance frame. As previously emphasized, the violation of the timing principle would have in all likelihood disqualified this act as an acceptable performance, but it is worth noting that even in this sensitive area Carl was taking some chances by creating a cacophonic sequence when he had the orchestra play a different tune than the one he was himself playing. The superposition of two incompatible musical timings had as a result the jamming of the dynamic which kept the act afloat. It was a brief but tense moment, a brush with catastrophe, during which the performance momentarily 'capsized', that is to say that the five principles of performance were all violated at once.

To return to the issue of Goffman's phenomenological notion of a situation as defined by the conscious immediacy of what those involved are "alive to", it seems difficult to reconcile the participants' direct awareness with the above abstract construct, obtained through logical reasoning in a step by step process from phenomena to the structure or system of rules which account for them.

Reflecting upon this example, we can infer that a formal, universal description of performance must proceed through a succession of moves such as the examination of truly failed performances, detailed comparisons between these instances, construction of provisory models, tentative predictions, opportunistic explorations of "natural" experimentations such as the chance witnessing of an accident, heuristic generalizations, and so on. These epistemological strategies lead to a theoretical point of view which considerably exceeds the possibility of direct conscious experience of a particular situation in the midst of which the analytical or structural understanding of the events is usually overpowered by inarticulate enthusiasm or frustration. This is not to say that semiotic processes are inhibited or annihilated by these emotional outbursts, which are after all the direct results of their cognitive relevance, but that, even when emotional states are quiescent, awareness usually focuses on only a particular aspect of these processes whose comprehensive, intellectual contemplation can be reached through the sole scientific method, under any other name. Spontaneous, even reflexive verbal accounts of the performance experience by those involved either as performers or as audience can yield relatively little knowledge. This information will always be necessarily both partial and redundant because, on the one hand, too much will be taken for granted and, on the other hand, it will enrich but not explain the phenomenon. Even metaphorical modeling like 'breaking the frame' or 'capsizing' form a part of the problem rather than of the solution.

8.7. Subjective vs. objective situations

The definition of situations is understandably an obsessive concern for humans. The difference between adequate and faulty assessments can be a matter of life or death. Success involves either mere chance or appropriate cognitive processing of all relevant information and efficient computation of the data at hands. This obviously requires either a strong tradition which has produced reliable rules of thumb or the ability to generate innovative strategies; in both cases a sound capacity for abstraction is a prerequisite as situations can be properly handled only with respect to some general models. A large number of models which are too concrete would be uneconomical for long-term survival. Plans are psychological realities which are conditioned by the representation and evaluation of situations.

To further explore the concept of negative experience and its problematic representation in public performance, let us attempt to set forth some third-person definitions of the notion of situation. A first approach will be to consider a situation as a certain state of a set of interacting elements, which can be stable or unstable. If we take as an arbitrary point of departure a stable situation defined for example by the homeostatic control of its environment by an organism, any event which puts this control in jeopardy creates a new situation. This organism may either give up the control and disappear or attempt to retain it by identifying and assessing the nature of the disruptive event and by implementing an appropriate strategy in order to neutralize it either by suppressing it or by adjusting to it, and then reaching again a state of equilibrium with its environment. For the time being, the role of the innate mechanisms and the degree of learning required for the adaptive behavior of the organism will be ignored. The magnitude of the disruption with respect to the controlling capacity of the organism is a measurable variable as well as the appropriateness of the controlling strategy whose output indicates whether or not the identification and assessment of the disruption by the organism was correct. This is a common cybernetic model which isolates the relations existing between an organism and some independent variables within its milieu. This model is largely a theoretical fiction because it assumes a stable state as a point of departure, and because it implies that parameters can vary independently from one another. This exemplary scenario could be implemented only in laboratory conditions with an artificially impoverished context. Nevertheless, it takes into account, albeit in a simplistic manner, the fundamental structure of the notion of situation, even if in the form of an ideal, impossible extreme case. When the disruptive element is the intrusion of another organism, the basic scenario is not simply duplicated but its nature changes. The study of ecosystems, ecological niches, predation, competition, and so on has amply documented the complexity of the notion of situation both globally and from each organism's vantage point (e.g., Rubenstein et al. 1986). Goffman was aware of this sort of research, but his deep rooted conviction that all social facts were accountable exclusively in terms of cultural relativism (see Ekman 1987:

32) seems to have isolated his theoretical horizon from the advances which were made during his lifetime in animal and human ethology, and in neuro-ethology.

Once an elementary model has been constructed, a look at the successive stages of the scenario makes it easier to locate the points at which the control process can fail. Naturally, there is first the possibility that the disruption is uncontrollable: a sudden, disproportionate, catastrophic modification of the environment, physical or social; or a slow, deceptive, irreversible change; or, still worse, an unidentifiable and lethal alteration such as odorless gas, radioactivity, some viruses and the like. But if the disruption is within the range of the evolutionary adaptive competence of the organism, the correct assessment of the disruption and of the new situation it creates is a prerequisite for its control. If it fails to meet these conditions, the organism will engage in an inappropriate strategy which will result in its demise. Obviously, the definition of the situation has degrees of adequacy. It always implies the selection and combination of features in order to represent a state of play with respect to which a strategy is implemented. In dealing with a new social encounter which requires some form of negotiation each member of the dyad must decide whether the other person is sane or insane, drunk or sober, endowed with a lower or higher IQ, armed or unarmed, friendly or hostile; depending on whether the encounter occurs in a public or isolated place, in an institutional or marginal setting, at home or in a foreign country, etc., the outcome might be either withdrawal or confrontation or compromise.

Experiencing a situation takes first the form of simple rules: if *a*, then flee; if *b*, then attack; if *c*, then negotiate; and so on. The selection of the wrong features (such as interpreting the flattened position of the ears of horses as a submissive sign, as is the case for dogs, whereas the interpretation should be exactly the reverse) or the construction of a faulty configuration of features (such as confusing genuine interest and deceptive behavior) entails the failure of the organism to the advantage of its competitors. Mimicry, deception, and lying belong to the realm of situation engineering as do the moral or juridical constraints which attempt to correct or counter these strategies in the wider context of the social contract. Failure to negotiate a situation which has been otherwise correctly assessed is another cause of negative output, and results in the return to the previous step and in a reassessment of the state of play.

The categorization of situations and the experience of their processing and outcome imply a cultural system which provides the 'players' with scripts, roles and common wisdom; but restricting the analysis to this latter level without taking into account the biosemiotic dimension of encounters precludes any possibility of reaching a comprehensive theoretical understanding of human patterned interactions. Indeed all experience, let it be positive, negative or neutral, presupposes a dynamic situation and its outcome. If the notion of situation is taken for granted, then situations can only be described intuitively and qualitatively as a given rather than as a theoretical object, that is, an explicitly constructed model. The lack of such a model prevents one from apprehending the systematic way in which situations are experienced within a given society. This is not to say that an acute perceptiveness combined with a talented expressive capacity cannot produce valuable accounts which set forth informative verbal copies of introspected or empathetically observed situations. But such descriptions are bound by the limits of the individual instances to which they apply, and can claim at most a literary universalism, that is, a generality restricted to a cultural area, and even, probably in most cases, to a socio-cultural subset of it. Such descriptions cannot integrate historical and cross-cultural dimensions, except in the form of anecdotes. Goffman himself acknowledged the limits of both this approach and his own method (1961: x). However, there does not seem that compelling reasons exist for such self-imposed restriction.

It is indeed possible to distinguish subjective and objective definitions of situations. A first-person perspective can only attend the distinctive features, those which characterize the situation on a phenomenological level and in view of a culture-dependent system of relevance. It is in this sense that "being a part of a situation" demands that the participants work out a definition, or rather a categorization of the situation so that it can be negotiated by relying on an appropriate script. This, of course, does not always succeed: some situations need to be clarified; tentative interpretations must be tested; sometimes ambiguous states prevail, generating anxiety or even panic; some scripts prove to be the wrong ones, etc. This leads to the notion that subjective definitions of situations may be only partially congruent with a given state of play whose exact form and substance can prove elusive for the players' attention. It should be noted here that a third-person approach is not necessarily the exclusive privilege of the social scientist, but also corresponds to the attitude of someone who would bet on the outcome of a confrontation, or speculate on the result of an encounter by assessing the mutual chances of the actors in a political debate or business negotiation, situations that also aptly describe the attitude of a circus audience which tries to assess the probability of a successful outcome whenever artists are confronted with physical challenges. Some degree of detachment must enable them to scan and weigh the various elements in the situational configuration, and to relate individual instances to general rules of thumb or folk statistical wisdom. This is to point out that a social scientist adopting a third-person, objective position with respect to a situation is not attempting something unusual or impossible; moreover, momentarily removing oneself from a situation and taking the part of an observant witness is, if time allows, a strategic advantage toward the maximizing of one's gains. Taking advantage of a situation involves such a third-person vantage point analysis. Naturally the assessment of situations is not an exclusively human characteristic. All organisms whose survival depends on some form of social interaction must have ways of appreciating both intra-specific and inter-specific situational configurations. Surviving is coterminous with correctly defining situations within the temporary sharing or overlapping of two or more territories.

Goffman at times edged toward a third-person definition of situations. In *Behavior in Public Places*, for instance, he states: "By the term situation, I shall refer to the full spatial environment anywhere within which an entering person becomes a member of the gathering that is (or does then become) present. Situations begin when mutual monitoring occurs and lapse when the second-last person has left. In order to stress the full extent of any such unit, I will sometimes employ the term situation at large" (1963: 18). But a part or even the totality of the situation may escape an individual's awareness by necessity (e.g., perceptual impairment, unconscious cognitive dimensions) or by accident (e.g., delayed information, deliberate masking or transmogrification of some components), thus making monitoring incomplete, irrelevant or impossible. Moreover, as has been pointed out earlier in this chapter, monitoring is probably always only partial and mutual monitoring may be, in addition, misconstrued by perceptual, social or species-specific biases. Finally, the very notion of monitoring implies a situation which exceeds the monitoring process since its fallibility is demonstrable. Therefore even if monitoring were meant to include unconscious cognitive processes, the possibility of an objective definition of situation is implied. Only an idealist philosophical background can sustain the illusion of multiple, equipotential realities within which situations could be defined if not *ad libitum*, at least across an open range of possibilities.

Biosemiotic, social, and cultural constraints combine hierarchically to form objective frames within which the negotiation space is very tight, a world in which "the rules are no game", as Anthony Wilden so rightly claimed (1987). However, the irrepressible human propensity to build models – a drive which probably serves both immediate survival and long-term inclusive fitness – can sometimes sort out those rules which are arbitrary in the sense that they could be replaced by other, equally productive rules. Cultural comparativism amply demonstrates that ethological and ecological constraints can be interpreted, exploited or negotiated in a variety of ways (e.g., kinship systems, control and manipulation devices, semiotic organizations of worldviews). This leads some to expose the nature of the rules, a move that is both dangerous for the stability of a society and a precious commodity in terms of flexibility and adaptability. Those specializing in such meta-cultural reflections appear to be stigmatized within the culture to which they belong but from whose absolute conditioning they escape, to a significant extent. In our society, some categories of entertainers, in various specialties, form, it seems, such a group. It is some of their productions that Goffman marshals in his chapter on "The Manufacture of Negative Experience" but the all-purpose metaphor he uses for describing or rather categorizing these performed events (that is, breaking the frame) does not do justice to the high degree of technique that is implied in the term "manufacture". Although his skimming of a variety of shows is useful for demonstrating the diversity and centrality of these particular contrived disruptions as representative of social situations, it raises some important questions which remain unanswered. Is the breaking of frames an end in itself? Is exposing the frames' fragility a form of decadent or deconstructionist pleasure or does it serve some function as has been hinted above? How do these performed acts of deviance relate to their constructed context and to the cultural systems within which they are observed? The example of George Carl has shown that in some cases the concept of frame breaking can be generalized and applied to a whole code through a systematic transformation of its rules; but if Carl's act makes obvious both the phenomenon of negative experience and the fact that great expertise is involved in its manufacture, the 'breaking' metaphor seems to be less apt at illuminating the operative process that is at play. More than the conceptual apparatus proposed by Goffman is needed to come to grips with the generality and complexity of this obviously deeply motivated behavior: the manufacture of negative experience, an expression whose affective connotation may detract from the full consideration of what can be more abstractly characterized as meta-cultural or meta-semiotic operations. If the frame metaphor is to be preserved, it could be said that the operations performed consist of framing the frames rather than breaking them. For this, a notion of objective situation is needed on two levels: a system of cultural rules without which there would be no frame, and a biosemiotic system without which the rules would have nothing to regulate. It is the contention of this chapter that Goffman's insights demand to be developed to their full extent by focusing on more precisely contextualized data and in view of wider theoretical grounds. The circus is a prime terrain for such an inquiry and semiotics provides the means needed for this kind of epistemological endeavor.

8.8. A lady in danger

A subjective approach to the definition of situation unavoidably leads to accounting for negative experiences in terms of uneasiness, disappointment, upsetting circumstances and disturbing surprises. It would amount to producing tautological statements such as defining negative experience as a state of mind related to some events or behavior which do not meet a subject's expectations. But what actually matters is the nature and structure of expectations in relation to biosemiotic programs, social strategies, and worldviews. A negative experience is only a node in a network of strategic paths, a point at which alternative strategies are devised, or at which plans bifurcate. The negative experience is always a potential event in any strategy to the extent that if there were not anticipated failure, there would not be any strategy. A strategy is always a form of expectation of a possible shortcoming that is conceptualized as something to be negotiated if it cannot be avoided (both with respect to self- and public-image). Here, also, stocks of sayings such as the claim that 'every cloud has a silver lining' or that 'to err is human' are provided by cultures for the benefit of their members whose re-entry in the system is thus facilitated by a semiotic shock-absorbing device.

Negative experiences have been categorized, as can be expected, given their importance. A cross-cultural examination of this phenomenon will not be attempted here. For the purpose of this chapter only three central concepts in the English language will be taken into consideration: incident, accident and failure. Each one can be assessed in view of an objective definition of situations and as conceptual devices which play a part in the negotiation of negative experiences in as much as they assign responsibilities with respect to an objective frame of reference. 'Incident' denotes some unexpected variation in the input of an action which modifies one or several of its parameters and temporarily jeopardizes the successful outcome of this action. It implies that the disturbance is controllable or has been controlled. This categorization is often used symbolically to reduce the magnitude of a disturbance and to suggest controllability in order to reduce anxiety (Hochschild 1983). As noted earlier, Goffman relished in creating incidents in order to test the resistance of the frames; most of his examples of 'manufactured' negative experience are of this sort but the testing of the resistance, or fragility, of frames for its own sake could hardly be the actual motivation of a society which engineers such a wide range of contrived incidents in its public performances. The systematicity and regularity of this cultural phenomenon call for functionalist or structuralist hypotheses. For instance, a society could explore the degree of adaptability of its regulatory scripts by varying their parameters on models simulating real situations (e.g., literary fictions or public performances) or could train in this way its members to tolerate some degree of variability and deviance without collapsing into anomy. A structuralist approach could, on the other hand, interpret these variations as the algorithmic unfolding of the potential of structures, the effect of unconscious dynamism or *semiosis* which systematically transforms these structures, generating negative versions, mirror symmetries, and dissymmetrical variations as if model building were an unbound activity of the collective mind. This latter view can naturally be easily framed within an inclusive functionalist perspective in as much as free-wheeling model construction may ultimately provide the best adaptive response to sudden, catastrophic variations of the environment, although the eventual success can be claimed to be only a matter of choice. Whatever the theory which may be deemed the most credible in view of the data available, the necessity of a theory going beyond Goffman's suggestive metaphors and phenomenological descriptions should be obvious.

'Incident' is semantically defined in contrast to 'accident' which refers to the inability to control a disturbance, and denotes a resulting outcome which is the opposite of the goal being sought. In the introductory anecdote to this chapter, the dropping of the elephant hook was an incident but the fall of the trapeze acrobat was an accident. 'Accident' suggests indeed that, because of the idiosyncratic circumstances, the disturbance was uncontrollable. It puts the immediate blame upon the magnitude or randomness of the disturbance. 'Failure', on the other hand, refers to the same sort of outcome but tends to assign the responsibility to the agent who has failed to control the disturbance or to achieve his goal; this could be, for instance, because of a lack of energy, determination, skill, financial resources or technological potential (in the case of an inanimate object), all circumstances in which the agent's competence is at stake. The three categories of negative experience (incident, accident and failure) can be analyzed in terms of variations of inputs and control at some nodes of a model of dynamic situation. But when these dynamic events are represented they may signify or point to some cognitive contents quite different from what they would mean if they were witnessed in a non-represented situation. For instance, George Carl's failure is a masterful demonstration of his competence at laying bare the system of performance which is a constitutive part of the culture to which he belongs as a performer. The capacity of producing innovative variations of models presupposes that cultural realities are symbolically manipulated in such a way that their rules of production become apparent, cognitively explicit, and eventually dispensable or replaceable by different rules. Indeed, 'negative experience' of the sort described by Goffman cannot be taken at face value when they are parts of larger 'texts' in which they effectuate some specific semiotic operations; in other words, the negative experiences which Goffman described are not ends in themselves but means to other, more general ends. The point of George Carl's getting entangled in the microphone wires rather than efficiently handling the microphone is to manipulate the rules of performance, not just behaving in a way contrary to expectations.

Another example will now be presented in some detail in order to show how a negative experience does function in the context of the larger unit within which it is observed. The description that follows is based on several observations of the act of Johnny, Mario and Betty Zoppe, which was performed as a part of the Ringling Bros. and Barnum & Bailey Circus (Blue Unit) in 1980. It was the centerpiece of the production display that concluded the program's first part. Its title, *The Circus Galaxy*, was defined in the printed program and in the announcement as 'The Spectacular Space Saturnalia that Spans the Spectrum of the Splendiferous!' It involved space-age paraphernalia such as spinning satellites, robots, clowns and dancers dressed and masked as alien beings, science fiction imagery, music from films dealing with space adventures, flashing lights, and the like. A double page in the printed program shows a 13 x 14 inch photograph of the acrobats in action with a 4 x 4 insert of Johnny and Betty Zoppe with their twelve year old son Mario, all in their circus gear but posing as if it were for a happy family photograph. The left third of the double page contains a text which starts with an accurate description of the way in which the act begins:

> High in the circus stratosphere, two rocketships revolve. Suddenly, airlocks open and from one moving rocket a young man descends to a lofty perch beneath the ship. From the other vehicle a lovely young woman emerges to take her place below the craft. Thus begins a spectacular aerial sensation, devised and performed by Johnny Zoppe jr. and his daring wife, Betty. At ground zero, an equally essential member of the troupe, twelve year old Mario Zoppe, mans a complex control panel that guides the movements of the whirling ships and the fate of his astronautically ambitious parents far above.

The scene is dramatized by the thunderous noise and the flames hurling from the rockets' exhaust as they accelerate their gyration, and by the flashing red lights which adorn the ship. Once the two acrobats have simultaneously performed a series of identical movements, hanging upside-down and holding on to their perch, they undertake to present in turn a variety of feats, with each time a significant increase in the apparent difficulty and danger involved in the movements. The last item is performed by the lady; the perch has been re-entered in the ship and has been replaced by a simple trapeze hanging from the rocket's belly; the young woman is grasping the bar with both hands while the man puts himself on his perch in a resting position but with all his attention focused on his wife. Raising her legs, she places her insteps on the bar, then slowly releases her hand grasp and lowers her torso until she hangs upside-down while the rockets are in full motion. Now, extending one leg backward she remains for a moment hanging by one foot only. Then she replaces her instep on the bar and begins to raise her torso and hands toward the bar in order to grasp it again. But it progressively appears that she has difficulty doing so; she seems to suddenly lack the muscular strength as she reverses to the initial upside-down hanging position. For the audience, something unexpected is obviously happening; the music stops, some circus hands gather in the center of the ring below; the spectators become aware that there is no net, and that she is not secured to her trapeze by a safety lunge; a heavy, tense silence reigns; she tries again, but fails to reach and grasp the bar; as seconds pass, there is a poignant feeling of tragedy, of helplessness in the audience. The situation becomes unbearable: it is not an acrobatic act any more, it is a straightforward accident that is being witnessed, a breaking of frame as Goffman would put it. At last she gathers strength and reaches the bar of salvation. The act can conclude. The audience is much relieved and reacts with intense and sustained applause. It was only a serious incident, probably a sudden fatigue or a cramp, whose consequences could have been fatal but which was eventually overcome through determination and effort. That is indeed the general interpretation of the event by the audience as it can be inferred from their wholehearted applause. More technically this event can be described as a momentary lapse of control at a node of the dynamic situation created by this segment of the act.

Actually it is a represented lapse of control, because the whole event is a carefully staged episode which is repeated at each performance. It is a part of the act. Faking an incident in order to enhance the difficulty or danger of an act – or for other reasons – is indeed a regular aspect, albeit a controversial one, of the circus art. We have seen a mild example of this in the introductory chapter of this book. Such apparent failures fulfill an important function in the semiotic message of the individual acts concerned as well as in the general code of the circus. On the most abstract level it enacts visually two categories of action which cannot be fully implemented in the act as this would be its negation from the point of view of the performance principles but which need to be conjured up in one way or another in order to conceptually delineate the other categories of action whose presence forms the act's core. If any acrobatic act is indeed the implementation of some modeling of a type of dynamic situation, then the representation of the actions which are a part of this modeling are endowed with some abstract, symbolic properties. Not only do they actually control a given concrete situation but they also implement a symbolic function: the visualization of a theoretical possibility against the background of all the logical possibilities. If actions are defined as the controlling of dynamic situations by applying plans with a view to overcome particular kinds of disturbance, actions then can be categorized with respect to two values: the variation of the quantity of disturbance relatively to the controlling capacity of the organism, and the variation of success in plan implementations. Both scales of value can be structured around the theoretical point where a disturbance becomes uncontrollable for a specific organism, thus defining two contrastive categories: the possible and the impossible.

The term 'theoretical point' calls attention to the fact that we are dealing here with binary mental constructs, the sort of stuff which organizes symbolic representations. Indeed, it should be obvious that this 'point' is in fact a fuzzy area because within a given species some individuals can control more disturbance than others, and one and the same individual may be able to control some disturbance at one time and not at the other. Actual competence can vary with age, training, and circumstances. On the other hand, the plans can succeed or fail for a variety of reasons other than the relative quantity of disturbance; for instance, a plan may be inappropriate; the nature of the disturbance may be wrongly assessed; other plans may interfere, and so on. Here also there is a grey area made up of half-successes and relative failures; but plans can be logically divided between those which reach their goal and those which do not. Actions can, therefore, be categorized with respect to these two sets of variables (relative quantity of disturbance and relative implementation of the plans): (1) implementation of the possible, (2) non-implementation of the possible, (3) non-implementation of the impossible, (4) implementation of the impossible. These contrastive values saturate the logical possibilities, and it can be hypothesized that they will be represented in any symbolic representation of action because the complete system is necessarily implied if any interpreted or represented act is construed as meaningful. By systematically increasing the quantity of disturbance, whose nature determines the various types of acts, circus acrobatics suggest that the competence of the acrobats so much exceeds the average competence of their audience that it amounts to implementing the impossible. Hanging by one single instep from a revolving trapeze more than one hundred feet above the ground without any safety device is simply beyond the survival competence of humans who have not undergone an exacting training. Moreover, the chronicle of fatal circus accidents teaches us that such extreme acrobatic behavior is in fact on the borderline of the impossible even for those who have been trained to control the sort of disturbance involved in each specialty.

In the Zoppe act, survival through grasping defines the implementation of the possible although it is pushed to some trying limits by the addition of the height and movement as supplementary inputs in the dynamic situation. However, survival through a form of foot grasping is within the natural repertory of apes and monkeys but not of humans; it visualizes the impossible, so to speak. In order to do so, the logical possibility of the non-implementation of the impossible must also be symbolically represented. The fourth term, i.e., non-implementation of the possible, is usually actualized in any circus program by the clowns, sometimes by the acrobats themselves when they start their acts under the deceptive appearance of incompetent agents (Bouissac 1970: 6, quoted by Goffman 1974: 394–395). The symbolic function of negative experiences and the care with which they are staged as a part of public performance should now appear more clearly. The breaking of frame which suddenly occurs in the Zoppe act is the moment at which the circus performance script (which implies the performer's competence because of the accountability principle) flips into the accident script (which prescribes a different set of behavior as it is the audience which then becomes potentially accountable for whatever emergency measures should be taken). It vividly activates the logical possibility of this particular category: the accident due to the failure of the controlling competence – albeit in the form of a mere passing evocation.

But circus acrobatic acts are not purely formal demonstrations performed on models of dynamic situation, they are always 'embodied' in cultural categories, firstly regarding kinship as we have seen in Chapter 6, secondly with respect to some particular setting. The audience is fed with these two orders of information for the Zoppe act as is usually the case. An analysis of the negative experience which is 'manufactured' in this act cannot gloss over the facts that the acrobatic team is a family and that their theme is space exploration. It provides a sociological and historical context for the potential failure and specifies the cultural relevance of 'breaking the frame'.

Aerial acts performed by a small team involve, as a rule, direct contact between the performers. The successful outcome is the result of the harmonious synchronization of complementary actions which require a great amount of physical contact. This explains why, in the Western circus, these acts are most often introduced as family units (husband and wife, or mother, father and child) or sub-units (father and children, brothers, sisters, etc.). In the 1980 show in which the Zoppes performed, there was another act, earlier in the program, the Grantcharovi, including father, mother and son; a regular cradle act in which the acrobats form various combinations such as the man hanging by his knees from the cradle and supporting his upside-down wife who has one foot secured between his legs and the other in his arm pit. The woman holds her son by a rope ring and the boy revolves on himself in a horizontal position. As the printed program states: 'A dazzling demonstration of "family togetherness" deftly demonstrated by the Grancharovi'.

In the Zoppe act, the same type of family unit is taken apart, each one performing at an unreachable distance from one another. A supplementary characterization of the 'negative experience' which has been described above is that although the act involves the core members of a family, the situation is such that their respective position in space makes it impossible for them to rescue one another in case of difficulty. Moreover, the theme of the act explicitly refers to modern technology applied to space exploration. Consequently, several frames are conjured up when the specter of the fatal accident appears: the family whose traditional closeness was the best strategy for the survival of its individual members, and the technology of transportation which, by facilitating mobility, has been a constant disolving factor for the traditional family unit. Both frames are redundantly expressed in the act and its accompanying printed program: on the one hand the Zoppes are introduced as a family with a supporting photograph which underlines their happy togetherness; on the other hand the travel technology that is selected is the one which covers the greatest distances imaginable. Intimacy and cosmic dispersion are thus superimposed. In this context the evoked 'accident' activates the incompatibility of the two frames – an issue which is at the core of modern cultural anxiety. This 'negative experience' is a representation of a contradiction – a sort of double bind – which at the same time frames the two frames in the wider perspective of a meta-cultural statement. The category of action which is used for articulating this – the non-implementation of the impossible – can be thus considered as the syntactic means of this 'discourse'. It should then be obvious that merely focusing on the fake 'incident' and labeling it a negative experience would preclude the understanding of the complex, yet clearly articulated point made by this act. The development of efficient technologies which enable humans to travel faster and further, at the same time tears apart the social fabric, even its most closely knit unit, the family cell as it is represented in Western cultures. The 'incident' demonstrates indeed the impossibility for such a cell to implement its most basic function: the survival of the individual members of the cell through mutual assistance. Even if, at the end, the act asserts, with typical American optimism, the triumph of the will over apparently insurmountable difficulties and the restoration of the family unit, it nevertheless designates one of the most crucial problems of modern society and demonstrates its lethal potential: the conquest of space implies social dispersion which, in turn, may reduce chances of survival, a cosmic anxiety which the circus brings home in a semiotic nutshell easy to cognitively grasp as well as experience with a rich gamut of emotions, including the happy ending.

Chapter 9
There's no business like show business: the marketing of performance

When I started my own show with a lion trainer as my business partner, we bought a young neutered male that had spent the first two years of his life in a New York wealthy home. He had been brought up with children and was pretty tame. Castrated males do not grow manes. Although professionals can tell their sex from their massive head, they may pass for females in the eyes of the public. We called "her" Malika ("queen" in Arabic), and Gérard Debord, the trainer, developed a routine which consisted of wrestling bare chest with the lion. We were putting up private shows on weekends in order to entice potential investors to buy shares in our business. The stunt was impressive. We had staged elaborate preparations to convey the impression that the performance was more risky than it actually was as long as the lion was in the playing mood. For several minutes, the man and the "wild beast" were rolling over on the ground in a "deadly embrace". The play on gender was spicing up the show. Our only problem was that, from time to time, the lion was raising its tail and exhibited his backside. This could have killed our story. As I was standing outside the cage between the display and the audience, my job was to wave my large circus hat in front of the incriminating spot under any pretext that would come to my mind. This helped the cash flow at the beginning of our venture.

9.1. Marketing the performing arts

The marketing of the arts has been the subject of several important inquiries, both in terms of broad sociological considerations (e.g., White and White 1965; Moulin 1967) and in the form of case studies (e.g., Brody 1971; Peterson 1978; Simpson 1981; Brown and Patterson 2000; Kerrigan et al. 2004). But this research has mainly focused on 'tangible' kinds of art, such as paintings, sculpture, records, that is, objects of one sort or another that can be purchased, owned, transferred, whose marketable value may evolve over time, and that can become endowed with sentimental or social values as heirlooms, collectors' items, status symbols, or national treasures.

By contrast, the performing arts raise a whole range of novel issues. For instance, Zolberg (1980: 219) argued that "structural features of art forms are relatively autonomous, and themselves either limit or facilitate the outcome of arrangements for production and diffusion of these culture products." Through a contrastive comparison of displayed art and performed music, she developed the concept of media attributes and showed that the implications of these attributes entailed aesthetic and economic consequences. In a similar vein the aesthetics and economics of operatic and symphonic music were examined by Riggins (1985) in the context of nineteenth century French musical institutions. The marketing of the performing arts is a challenging endeavor that cannot follow the patterns of regular advertising. On the one hand, the 'object' to be marketed is extremely costly to produce and maintain; contracting performers, hiring qualified staff, training and rehearsing personnel for a show, buying or renting premises or tents with all the necessary technical equipment (lighting, music, props, etc.), promoting and administering the spectacle, and so on, require a relatively massive initial investment. In the case of concerts, ballets, theatres, and circuses, most of the expenses demand continuous and constant cash outflow regardless of the income yielded by the successive performances, or whether they take place or not. Even if they do not perform everyday, people and animals usually cannot be 'stored away' while the producers wait for better days. True enough, the investment required for the performing arts is much smaller than that in most branches of industry and commerce, but the relationship between the investment and the maximum profit it may yield is limited and governed by rigorous time constraints (*viz.* the fate of many Broadway shows), which make show business a volatile and high risk affair. A financially successful spectacle is a jewel of organization and semiotic engineering not only because of all the variables that have to be mastered and kept under control, but also because of the pressing time factor involved.

On the other hand, because the 'consuming' of a performance does not involve a material, durable, exchangeable object, the customers are also required to make a risky, albeit less important, investment when they buy an admission ticket to a concert, a play, a circus show, etc. The advertising messages cannot refer to some tangible goods or services, but to ephemeral social experiences which, by definition, cannot be examined, tried, tested, or tasted before the buyers make their decision. Once the event is over, there is no material commodity upon which to fall back and from which to derive a feeling of reassurance that, after all, one has something to show for one's money – or that the items purchased have been put to good use or have produced the services required, preferably a lasting service or a permanent improvement. Research in marketing has dealt with the concept of play as a consumption experience and has taken into consideration the symbolic and hedonic dimensions of consumer behavior. Holbrook and his collaborators, for instance, used the notions of 'hedonic', 'experiential', and 'playful' consumption (Hirschman and Holbrook 1982; Holbrook and Hirschman 1982); but this research focused exclusively on games in which the consumers played an active role (Holbrook et al. 1984) and was only marginally relevant to the marketing of the performing arts. More recent inquiries have expanded the scope of the approach toward the marketing of the performing arts (e.g., Deighton 1992; Kottler and Scheff 1997; Bourgeon-Renault 2003; Schroeder 2005). However this research is concerned with the marketing of high-brow arts and festivals, not with popular entertainments like the circus whose promotional strategies are elusive and particularly difficult to investigate.

The well-known saying that "there's no business like show business" is true in more than one sense, notably regarding its marketing. In spite of the classical claim that the true nature of the 'object' is not an issue in the devising of the marketing strategies (e.g. Kotler 1976) – an approach that may indeed be innovative and fruitful when applied to industrial and natural products – it seems that performances belong to a markedly different paradigm of 'marketable objects', and that the nature of this 'product' of human activity entails some important consequences when it comes to finding ways of maximizing the profit it can generate.

The concept of performance implies an audience both from the point of view of economics and from that of semiotics. Although it is possible to abstract one of these two aspects and to ignore the other, both are obviously inextricably mixed. Performances are communication processes in which a proportionally sufficient number of potential spectators/listeners are persuaded to allot some time and money through a promise that they will derive some form of gratification from an experience that is strictly limited in time, and that is bound by conventional strictures. This tentative definition applies primarily to the context of modern complex societies, more specifically in a market economy system. But performances in traditional societies or in the context of other types of socio-economic structures also necessarily imply both production expenses and motivated audiences; however, the relationship between the two factors can be mediated in various manners, to the extent that they may even appear to the participants as totally unrelated, as, for instance, in the case of religious festivals. Ideology undoubtedly plays its part in the obfuscation of some aspects of the socio-cultural economy of some performance productions.

Because of the temporal nature of performances, a considerable social anxiety is generated at both ends of the communicative act, that is, the performers and the audience. This anxiety can indeed be considered social not only because it emerges from fairly complex social structures, but also because it is generally patterned in the form of culturally defined feelings such as stage fright and superstitious beliefs that motivate various rituals and other prophylactic actions. Disclaimers printed in programs are such contingency plans as are the securing of understudies and insurances. The hiring of ushers or security guards for controlling the crowd bears witness to the showmen's anxiety that is translated into legal terms and organizational measures.

On the other side, there always exists in the audience-to-be a mixed feeling of expectation and skepticism, an excitement that can easily turn into disappointment and protest, and which is prone to get carried away toward extreme enthusiasm or sheer violence. Between the fear of being 'taken' and the anticipation of an absolute aesthetic or playful gratification incommensurate with their actual expense, spectators are volatile and unpredictable factors, even if statistical averaging usually prevents sudden and extreme reactions on a mass level. But if the promises made in the advertising of a spectacle are pushed to the highest degree in order to maximize the potential income, the anticipation it creates also raises the intensity of the excitement, skepticism, and anxiety, and exacerbates the risk involved in the completion of the process. The public at large cannot ignore that the possibility always exists of being cheated in a commercial exchange in which the buyer cannot see in advance what he/she is buying. There are examples of shows that were duly announced and advertised in the most regular and confidence inspiring manner but which never materialized even though proper arrangements were made in advance.

The following excerpts from the weekly local newspaper *The Shoals News* of Shoals, Indiana (USA) are symptomatic. On 2 October 1985, a front page item proclaimed: Circus Coming to County Saturday!

> Ford Bros., billed as America's largest performing wild animal circus, will appear at the Martin County 4-H Fairgrounds, this coming Saturday, October 5 (for one day only) for two performances under the big top. The circus is one of only two 5-ring circuses in the world. The first show will begin at 2:30 p.m. and the second and final performance will be given, starting at 5:30 p.m. Tickets will be $ 6.00 for adults and children, ages 11 and under, will be admitted free. Get free children's tickets at your area merchants or cut the coupon which appears in today's edition of *The Shoals News*. The circus features over 150 wild animals, including elephants and also has the usual clowns, aerialists and acrobats. It has over 150 employees and is housed under a giant tent, the size of a football field, with seating capacity of 5,000. According to the man in charge, Richard Brown, Ford Bros. Circus travels 60,000 miles per year and entertains crowds in 250 cities. They have just returned from a three-month tour of Northeastern Canada, Newfoundland and Nova Scotia and are now en route to Las Vegas, Southern California and Hawaii. Next year's itinerary calls for visits to Alaska, and the Yukon and they will wind up in Puerto Rico and Miami, Florida. The public is invited to come and watch the setting up of the circus from 8:30 to 9 a.m. Saturday. For 90 minutes of fine

entertainment, make your plans now to attend the Ford Bros. Great Circus at the Fairgrounds Saturday afternoon!

This information was supported by a quarter-page picture showing a female tiger trainer holding one of her charges.

The following week's issue (October 9) featured another front page story titled: Circus Does Vanishing Act Saturday.

The old adage 'No news is good news' was not the case last Saturday in Martin County. The biggest news Saturday, however, was no news. No news of the circus, that is. Ford Bros., billed as America's largest performing wild animal circus, failed to perform. In fact, they even failed to show. The incident was a major disappointment to countless numbers of little countians, not to mention the 'fast talking' that all the mommies and daddies had to do when the big tent didn't go up at the 4-H Fairgrounds. The circus vanished. It didn't show, and no one knows why. *The Shoals News* spent Monday morning trying to find out why, but every avenue or question ended in a dead-end road. A man named Richard Brown was in *The News* office a week ago Saturday to place an ad for the circus, as well as supplying us with info. He said that he had secured the 4-H Fairgrounds as the site, which in fact he had done. As of Monday afternoon, Carl Wampler, Extension Agent here, also had no answers to the no-show. 4-H officials were never contacted about the problem. There was no 'sponsor' of the circus; the 4-H was only renting them the space for the event. *The News* called the phone number listed on Mr. Brown's calling card, but only received an answering service, with a nice lady saying she'd have Mr. Brown return our call. No call yet. We then tried the operator for Ford Bros. at Cut and Shoot (that's right), Texas, and she had no listing. Not even the town! We told her we had a zip code for Cut and Shoot, and she directed us to the Postal Service. After looking in the big zip code book, we found that Cut and Shoot was a sub-station of Conroe, Texas... We found that the circus didn't have a phone listed.

We're sorry for any inconvenience to our readers, but it really wasn't our fault. Anyway – it would have been a nice afternoon for a circus...

In some other cases, the 'merchandise' itself is not quite what the potential audience was led to believe. There are countless reports of such behavior in the tradition of circus and fairground entertainments. P.T. Barnum got his fame from the magnitude of his deceptive industry.

The producer's anxiety is no less intense in view of the numerous failures that are chronicled in the history of show business: the specter of thinner and thinner audiences, the dreaded sounds of a crowd demanding a refund, frustration turning into vandalism, panic, stampede and other calamities that can occur when a large number of people is gathered within an enclosure – all these potential outcomes keep haunting the showman's mind.

These preliminary considerations concur to differentiate the issues involved in the market of performance, both in degree and in kind, from those connected with the marketing of goods and services. But before examining the strategies traditionally used in the marketing of performance and ways of optimizing these strategies, a reflection on the nature of performance is in order. It is indeed essential to form a clear conceptual representation of the semiotic structure of this particular object before one can hope to understand its functional relationship with the very semiotics of advertising.

9.2. The golden rules of performance

From a systematic examination of some examples of performance failures, it is possible to formulate at least five principles that govern a felicitous, that is, successful performance, and whose violation explains partial or total failures. We will examine them in detail in the next chapter when we discuss the pragmatics of performance but let us summarize these rules here as they have to be kept in mind when addressing the issues involved in the specificity of the marketing of performance.

Let us call these the principles of *accountability*, *semanticity*, *rhetoric*, *social congruency*, and *timeness*.

Timeness is undoubtedly the most complex of all, because it involves both psycho-physiological factors, such as rhythm and timing, and socio-cultural ones such as the time of day at which the performance takes place along with its duration and segmentation. The rate of the information input must also be taken into consideration. The importance of these factors is quite obvious although they are usually taken for granted.

Social congruency concerns the 'proper' social behavior of the performers toward their audience. Each culture has its own conventions with respect to the etiquette regulating the social interaction occurring at the beginning and at the end of a performance, sometimes in the course of it.

Rhetoric refers to the structure and economy of the delivery of information as the performance unfolds. It involves phenomena such as the creation of expectation and suspense, and the building up of a climax. It could be defined as the semiotic management of the spectator's interest. It aims at avoiding any slackening in the action lest redundancies or excessive conciseness result in boredom and obscurity. It deals with the organization and transmission of the message.

The principle of *semanticity* addresses the issue of the contents of the message, which must be relevant to the culture in which the performance takes place, or at least relevant to a sufficiently large portion of the culture such as an organized subculture, an affluent minority, or a special interest group cutting across other social categories. Violations of this principle are often observed nowadays in cultural exchanges between countries whose cultures are markedly different and whose performing arts are met with curiosity rather than with deep interest outside their cultural boundaries.

However important they may be, these four principles are not sufficient for the conceptual definition of performance (in the sense of spectacle), because they apply to a vast range of other social behavior and communicative acts such as conversation, face-to-face interaction, play and games, and the like.

More fundamental is the principle of *accountability* and its correlative concept of risk. All performance is the implementation of a program of action here and now, and however well-rehearsed it may have been (even how often it may have been repeated before) the degree of preparedness is irrelevant to the performance situation in which one or several persons are meeting the challenge of capturing the attention and the emotions of a group of their congeners during a determined period of time. Naturally, it must be kept in mind that time as such is a valuable commodity, but in modern complex societies the tension implied in this situation is increased by the fact that cash is paid in advance on the faith of a promise.

In view of the latter characteristics, it is obvious that the performance itself implies its announcement, which must specify the nature of the challenge, emphasize its 'interest' or relevance, and establish the credibility of the promise. There are circumstances in which goods and services are in short supply and hardly need any marketing effort beyond the indication of the places where they can be obtained on a "first come, first served" basis. But such a situation is unthinkable when it comes to performance because its advertising is a functional part of the performance itself. This characteristic may be the most crucial difference existing between the marketing of performance and the marketing of other objects, including artistic ones. This property entails some consequences that will now be examined.

9.3. How to capture an audience

The following considerations are based primarily upon a careful examination of the ways in which circus and other performances are traditionally promoted. From these observations, it is possible to extrapolate two simple principles that can be formulated as follows: (1) in order to efficiently market a performance, one must tell an incomplete story; and (2) the narrative must explicitly stage, or at least clearly imply, the notion of risk. For instance, when I was inviting potential investors to attend the demonstration of a sample of the kind of performances my show would put on the road, I was announcing that the trainer would attempt for the first time to wrestle bare chest with a full grown lioness. "Attempt" was the key word to suggest an incomplete narrative and "full grown lioness" as well as "bare chest" implied the necessary risk.

It seems indeed that it is principally through a cognitive strategy than an audience is enticed into the premises where the performance is to take place. In terms of the grammar of story, the narrative must be interrupted at an episode node; it must not reach any end node that would bring the story to a state of completion or even to a temporary stability by suggesting a mere uneventful and safe repetition of the same routine. It is also necessary that the narrative stop at some crucial point at which the perception of a risk structures the whole situation. The notion of the 'perception of risk' has been scrutinized from an anthropological point of view by Mary Douglas (1982, 1985). Her analysis of this neglected aspect of everyday life decision-making processes is particularly relevant here. The determination of the concept of risk is largely a cultural construct, mainly when it comes to the categorization of various degrees of acceptability on both the individual and collective levels. In other words, what counts as risk in a given culture depends on the cognitive organization particular to this culture, its system of values, and its socio-economic structure. The perception of risk cannot be taken for granted because it depends on many cultural variables, and applies to several domains of action: private and public, collective and individual, social classes, age classes, etc. Douglas pointed out that important differences existed between the 'objective' evaluation of various kinds of risks and the evolution of their semiotic treatments within given cultures over a period of time. Not only does the content of risks change but also the ways in which risks are framed, experienced, and eventually institutionalized.

This general perspective casts an interesting new light upon the notion of the institution of performance. Taking as a working hypothesis that, because of the accountability principle, the perception of risk is at the core of any performance from the point of view of both the performer and the audience, it would ensue that the marketing of performance must focus on the *risks taken* rather than on the *skill* used to control the risk-generating situation. In the case of the lioness Malika, the main risk for us was that the lion would resist the trainer's enticements to play with him and would stubbornly keep lying down and growling. Then, provoking it to move could have indeed triggered an attack. The trainer's skill involved being able to read the mood of the lion and creating the context in which it was very likely that the wrestling would happen and be safe. No matter how safe (at least statistically speaking) a performance may be, some inherent risk must be enhanced in order to build up its interest for a potential audience. But how is it possible to achieve this if not by means of narrative? After all, this is semiotically congruent with the explicit content of any performance and not only of the circus in which it could be claimed that all situations are construed 'icons of risk'. Admittedly, the circus is an extreme case, but in as much as any kind of performance implies some skill, it also implies a kind of challenge that this skill is destined to overcome. Even storytelling requires memory and face-to-face interactive skills; capturing and sustaining an audience's interest by whatever means is never a small affair.

This is why it is not possible to market performance as one would market a finished product whose output or result is presented as completed (well done, demonstrated to be perfect, functional, guaranteed to cause no surprise to the buyer, etc.). True enough, the credibility of the challenger must be built up in order to arrest the potential spectator's or listener's attention, but focusing on the certainty of the outcome would miss the point as far as performance is concerned because the life character of the performance implies a risk of failure, although, even in the case of daring circus acts, the outcome is usually safely under control in normal circumstances. However, the announcement of these acts – as in most other types of performance – emphasizes the difficulty of the task and frames it in a narrative whose linear development stops at the performance-to-come, thus hinting at the possibility that no future lies beyond it. In this respect, the performance is information. It is as if the strategy consisted in starting a story and stopping short of its conclusion while convincing a potential audience that they can learn about the next step only by witnessing the performance, which alone can provide the missing information, and so on. This prevents the marketing of performance from making use of sampling in the full sense of the term because it would amount to presenting the performance as a past event: something that would degrade its information value and would be contradictory, as it would be the negation of the very essence of performance. The strategy that is the closest to sampling is parading through the city or in front of the premises where the performance will take place, but in that case the audience is teased and lured inside rather than given an opportunity to really sample the performance. However, even in the form of teasing, the strategy often backfires because the parade can be considered by the public as a free spectacle, and it is extremely difficult to convince a sufficient number of people that the company has indeed much more to show inside than it freely displays outside. In this case what was meant to establish credibility is perceived as a deceptive strategy. This is why this form of marketing requires the services of an excellent speaker (a 'barker' in the circus jargon) able to produce a narrative of the sort mentioned above. When modern circuses advertise their spectacle through television, they do so by showing at a fast rate snapshots of the most daring acts, heavily emphasizing situations involving an obvious risk. They attempt to produce a dazzling impression focused on challenge, daring, and heroism and, correlatively, they give glimpses of an obviously intense audience.

9.4. The power of stories

The hypothesis presented here is that the marketing of performance essentially consists in textual narrative strategies. This applies of course to all sorts of live performance, including a singer's concert. In his pioneering work Kotler (1988) pointedly described the stages through which a popular singer is 'discovered' and 'marketed' by talent agencies and emphasized that a crucial step in the process is 'to story' the person, that is, fabricate an 'interesting' narrative that will be assumed to be the true life story and previous adventures of this person. It generally involves changing his/her name, inventing some unusual circumstances, and producing a fiction whose linear development leads to the present through a succession of episodes that stage ever increasing challenges. This strategy has now become common practice to spice up talent shows such as 'American Idol' and the derivatives it has spawned world wide.

An examination of circus promotional material such as the press releases which public relations persons provide for journalists shows that their general strategy is indeed based upon narratives. When Ringling Brothers, and Barnum & Bailey Circus visited Philadelphia in June 1986, *The Philadelphia Inquirer* (June 2) featured an article revolving around the life story of the tiger trainer Wade Burck, a divorced single father with two young sons. The reader soon learns that Burck 'has been mangled by tigers an average of six or seven times a year' and that 'the worst incident occurred three years ago, when one of the cats attacked with such force that it broke Burck's jaw and collarbone... "I had lost a lot of blood", Burck recounted, "and as soon as the act was over, I passed out."' The reader also learns that on that day his elder son, who was six years old, was watching the performance: information that puts the story on a par with horror films. The newspaper's front page displayed Burck in front of six tigers with a caption reading: 'Wade Burck is not just an animal trainer with Ringling Bros. and Barnum & Bailey Circus, which appears today at the Spectrum. He's a single father of two boys who travel with the circus. Story and more pictures on page 1-C.' The other pictures printed with the article show, in parallel, Burck kissing his younger son Eric, 'who has hurt a finger', and kissing one of his tigers, 'the object of his affections', during the performance, thus exemplifying the trainer's dilemma and raising to an unusually high degree the tension involved in his life of permanent danger.

Another case in point is the article published in the *Globe and Mail* (Toronto) on 21 June 1986, on the occasion of the coming to town of Circus Vargas. The pictures include a female contortionist and two brothers – David Polke, kissing a tiger, and Ted Polke, sitting on the tusks of one of his elephants. The pictures show beautiful samples of circus skills; however, the caption reads: 'Anytime something happens, it is the human's fault.' The article sets the theme right at the outset:

> It was Mother's Day and Joy Polke had gone to the circus to see her only two sons perform… While in the cage David Polke accidentally bumped into Ramar the cat. Ramar leapt up and grabbed him. One claw dug into his right thigh, the other had him by the back. If Joy Polke thought she had lost her youngest, she wasn't alone. David instinctively brought his whip and stick up to protect his face. For some inexplicable reason, Ramar eased his death grip. "You have to have a healthy respect for them," David says later, pointing at a dozen restlessly pacing Siberian Tigers… He knows that the frisky felines are really furballs with razor blades strapped to their paws… David nervously exhales after every trick. He even risked his life so that the audience could go home and say they saw three tigers pirouette to the tune of *My Favorite Things*.

Written from interviews or from press releases, these stories are printed in various forms, from town to town, and play their part in arousing a potential audience's interest. The stars of rock concerts are treated similarly in stories that raise high expectations for the forthcoming event. The numerous magazines devoted to various brands of contemporary popular music perform an important marketing function in two capacities: first, by their narrative focused on the stars and second, by construing audience behavior as a source of uncertainty.

It seems obvious that the actual practice of marketing performances is congruent with the hypothesis developed earlier. The performance is designated as the point of convergence of one or several linear text(s) and will be textualized in turn, while it is experienced, then told, recounted, and reminisced to others as well as among those who participated in it. It happens that performers introduce a fake accident as a part of their routine in order to enhance the difficulty of one of their tricks and capture the intense attention of their audience during the eventual successful completion of the act. It is also an event that is reported after the show by spectators who will claim to have almost witnessed a real accident and will thus contribute to the on-going narrative that sustain the performance. Therefore, it seems that the key factor is to set up a context, a cognitive frame within which the performance to come is the missing and crucial piece because there appears to be a real possibility that the story may bifurcate at this precise point possibly, in the case of rock concert, through a disruptive input from the audience. Naturally, the performance itself is overwhelmingly likely to be eventless but its perception is largely determined by the pre-existing narrative and will be cognitively integrated by the audience as a subsequent part of the narrative when the performance is narrated to those who did not attend it. This can create a tremendous cumulative process that leads some performers to stardom. This strategy of marketing performance must accordingly fulfill a third requirement: besides creating an open-ended story to motivate an audience to converge toward the implementation of the next episode, and suggesting a situation that involves some form of risk, it is essential to frame in advance as much as possible the perception of this episode – including the perception of the risk involved – so that the audience can extract 'the semiotic juice' so to speak, that is, the story-relevant features, from an experience that is at best ambiguous.

Other factors are obviously at play in motivating potential audiences to attend a performance: social status, peer pressure, erotic gratification through voyeurism, desire to overcome boredom, and so on. However, even these other factors can be shown to entertain some complex relationship to the narrative that carries the performance. The quest for status or identity is basically a concern for not being left out of the picture (or the story), for sharing in a cognitive stock; erotic motivations are narrative fantasies that can be seen as private digressions branching out of the main story. Finally, stories are the best medicine against boredom as they secrete information through the thread of their successive episodes.

Refinements and improved efficiency in the marketing of circus performances certainly could derive from a better understanding of the distinctive nature of performance and a close examination of the ways in which performers have instinctively handled the problem ever since human beings have performed for a living or for a profit. More empirical research should be undertaken in this field. Given the paucity of serious inquiries in the marketing of live performances, as bears witness the latest review of the field by Bourgeon-Renault (2003), Peterson remarks are still valid:

> Marketing the performance acts requires distinctive skills, skills that are difficult to develop through traditional means such as commercial production management experience or formal education. The former involves different, often conflicting skills, while the latter currently does not possess as adequate underlying body of knowledge. Indeed, little has been written about performing arts marketing; smaller still is the number of useful articles in the area of market analysis, segmentation and targeting (1980: 199).

The approaches developed in this chapter could provide a few suggestions for a systematic inquiry into the interrelated problems of the nature of performance, its semiotic characteristics, and the way in which it can be most successfully marketed in a society whose sheer dimensions and inner complexity make the mediation of its institutions a basic necessity. Given the fact that Europe in particular has witnessed over the last decades an extraordinary revival of the circus both in the form of successful traveling shows and in the guise of festivals, it is possible that the Internet and the instant communication networks it fosters are playing a determining role in this phenomenon through the fractal dissemination of pertinent micro-narratives.

Chapter 10
The researcher as spectator: the pragmatics of circus performances

As the Director of a small circus, I once introduced the grand equestrian display that was the opening act of the program of our first season on the road. The trainer appeared and stood ready in the center of the ring in his elegant, formal attire while the recorded music flooded the tent and the four Shetland ponies (Sarah, Judith, Rama, and Blackie) were led from the backstage and started trotting along the curb. It was a hot afternoon of July and we had half-lifted the side walls of our modest big top in order to let some drafts cool down the atmosphere. The meadows that could be seen in the distance proved to be irresistible to the miniature horses which instantly jumped the curb and dashed through an aisle toward the green pasture. The trainer and the presenter looked helpless and had no other choice but to run behind the ponies while the clown kept the public laughing by stating that this was actually a magic vanishing act. For the general circus audience it is very rare to witness such extreme failures because half-baked acts usually are not given a second chance. The next day, Sarah, the head horse, was kept on the training lunge and all went well although, admittedly, it was not one of the greatest achievements of the equestrian art.

A few years later, I witnessed another embarrassing performance. The act was billed as "The first riding lion ever presented in a circus". A big horse was led to stand along the curb of the ring, wearing a heavy cover on its back. Then a wooden crate was wheeled to the center. A young tame lion was inside. The trainer held the leash that had been fixed to its collar and opened the crate's door as the band played a triumphant music. The lion refused to get out. The leash was pulled. The crate was banged. A piece of meat was dangled in front of the animal. Nothing could compel nor entice the lion out.

While the trainer was sheepishly pleading for pity with his open palms, the crate was wheeled back out of the ring followed by the horse. The next act was not ready to start. A dreadful silence followed until the conductor decided to save the show with a popular tune.

10.1. Toward a theory of live performances

In modern societies, the performing arts form a distinct category of public entertainment in opposition to the mass distribution through the media of expertly staged performances which have been recorded and edited. By contrast, theater, ballet, circus, concert, rodeo, puppetry, storytelling, etc., unfold their signs in real space and time, and engage spectators who respond cognitively and emotionally on the spot. Performers and spectators are involved in reciprocal gratifications. But sometimes frustration occurs within the boundaries of such ritualistic events. In industrialized and computerized cultures, the performing arts become economically fragile because the institutions which sustain them increasingly depend on public and corporate funding. However, they retain their power of fascination for large, if not massive audiences, which prize the experiential, risk-loaded and one-time event quality they afford. In traditional and local cultures, performances still strive and provide their spectators with a unique fulfillment in smaller scale, economically sustainable institutional settings.

All performing arts are two-way communicative processes involving crafted signs in ideally noise-free channels. They embody the values of the societies in which they are perpetuated, and often reflect cultural changes and social tensions while trying to symbolically negotiate and overcome such disturbances. For all these reasons, the performing arts, both in traditional and modern settings, are of prime interest to semioticians who can observe, in quasi experimental conditions, the crafting, combining and trading of signs in well defined contexts. But conducting a semiotic inquiry in any of the performing arts is a daunting task because the observer is necessarily at the same time a spectator. It ensues that the difficulties in establishing some measure of post-positivistic objectivity are compounded. Can a semiotic analysis of a performance be anything more than a mere hermeneutic account of its reading from the spectator/observer point of view? Or is it possible to construct a consensual theory of the performing arts and elaborate a reliable method which would allow the observer to distance himself/herself from this engrossing experience and reach a semiotic understanding of both the pleasure of the 'text' and the structural details of such cultural productions? There are, expectedly, some differences depending on whether the observer operates within his/her own culture, and whether the performance considered belongs to self-styled 'high' (formal, elitist, textual, mainstream) culture or to so-called 'low' (popular, oral, traditional, marginal) cultures.

The study of traditional performances, in particular, poses a host of challenges to the researchers. As we have seen in the previous chapters of this book, observing circus acts is a methodological endeavor that is rife with problems. A clear assessment of these problems in the cases in which they are most obvious can help develop a more acute sensitivity to a general condition which may easily be glossed over when one deals with performances in one's own culture. We have seen in Chapter 4, for example, how easy it is to take some crucial aspects for granted. Another difficulty comes from the fact that all observation perturbs to various degrees the event that is observed. There is the risk, for instance, that the observed performance has been somewhat tailored by the performers in view of what they assume to be the investigators' specific goals and interests. Traditional performing groups are increasingly coming into contact with people external to their social environment through global tourism and cultural exchanges. Consequently, a set of marketing constraints such as the location and duration of the performance, or the contents of dialogues and gestures of performers may be modified in order to meet the real or supposed expectations of spectators whose standards of acceptable behavior may be markedly different from those prevailing in the culture in which the traditional performances originated. If some traditionally accepted elements are considered too crude or offensive, or politically incorrect, they can be changed through a process of self-censorship to suit the taste of the outsiders who may be in search of exotic experiences as long as these experiences remain within the limits of their sense of decency. Furthermore, when traditional performances are closely linked to religious or ritualistic values, as it is often the case, their secularization implies a transformation into spectacles governed by the laws of entertainment. Their purely aesthetic reception and the feedback this sort of reception generates, such as clapping of the hands or *ad libitum* photographing, adulterate the experience of the performers themselves and have a definite impact on the performance. When I was observing ragged Indian circuses in small towns in Kerala, I could not really blend in the audience. I was perceived as a 'tourist' and my local assistants noticed that some performers tended to use more English words, tended to focus the performance toward me and my camera, and refrained from spicing up their comic displays with gross sexual jokes.

With respect to the understanding of traditional performances in their original context, there is indeed always a danger that the 'scientific' observers can be considered by the performers as just another kind of outsider toward whom the same rules of behavior apply as toward the tourists and cultural events' audience in general. Performers have learned how to negotiate such situations in which they are confronted to audiences which do not share their cultural background and values. Economic necessities do not leave much choice to the traditional performers besides complying with customers' expectations, mainly at a time when urbanization and industrialization transform their own society into a population of tourists whose taste and attention have been molded by the constraints of city life and the narrative patterns of popular film industry, let they be from Hollywood or Bollywood. In some circumstances, the researchers may be perceived by the performers as a particularly desirable kind of outsiders who have often precious connections with official agencies and whose expectations should be satisfied because of their potential support in facilitating access to the market structures of tourism and the political arcane of cultural exchanges.

For example, in research on the circus, some anthropologists who have conducted interviews with the performers in order to gather information about circus performances have discovered that, whatever their efforts to establish their status as academic researchers, they have been lumped with journalists and used as a public relation commodity. In a highly competitive social and economic context such as the circus, 'being written about' may confer both symbolic and material advantages. Moreover, a researcher's interaction with individual performers always has a political dimension with respect to the power structure of the group. At the beginning of her career, anthropologist Mary Douglas experienced the pitfalls of fieldwork precisely in the circus. Her point of entry in this social microcosm – that is, whoever had given her access to the performers – determined all further modalities of her interfacing with them, including the kind of information she could gather (Douglas 1991: 201–204).

Whatever a performance researcher may fancy about his/her 'scientific neutrality' with respect to an 'object of study', his/her very presence and the circumstances of the initial contact can distort the production and subsequent perception of the performance and its ensuing documentation. Even when researchers chose to conduct their observation as mere member of an audience, their presence is immediately noticed. Performers are indeed extremely sensitive to the composition of their audience. Any unusual person or behavior is instantly scrutinized and must be ascribed to a category of spectators. Although it is true that the presence of investigators in the audience does not always alter in major ways the usual proceedings of the performance, the impact of outsiders must be taken into account. Even in the best cases of participant observation the mere visible presence of some recording device often changes the nature of the event by bringing a measure of enhanced self-awareness in the performers as well as in the audience. Although, in theory, a circus act can be displayed in the absence of an audience, a public performance is always of a dialogic nature. Both people and animals are sensitive to any variation brought about by unfamiliar behavior or equipment.

Conversely, an observer can become so involved in the event that the entrancing experience itself overpowers all her or his efforts to stick to a pre-established analytical program. The anecdote that introduced Chapter 2 provides such an example. Although it might appear that such an experience from inside, so to speak, provides a privileged insight into the nature of the performance, it also opens the way to heterogenic interpretations, that is, interpretations conditioned by another cultural context than the one in which the observed traditional performance originated and now functions, principally if there is a great cultural distance between the participant-observer and the regular audience. Cultural perceptions and values may drastically transform such an experience and make it incommensurable to the form and meaning of the traditional event, let it be story telling, dance, drama or music, whose relevance to the culture goes well beyond the immediate context to involve broad societal factors and the whole spectrum of other cultural artifacts.

In brief, any student of performance must keep in mind that, even within his or her own culture, the gaze of the observer always has an impact on the performance that is observed. This general phenomenon does not necessarily invalidate a systematic observation but indicates that one should always attempt to evaluate the perturbing factor of the outsider's gaze, mainly, but not only, if recording equipment is present. A pragmatic solution to this general problem is to ensure that more than one performance of the same act is observed. With time it can be expected that the degree of perturbation declines and even totally disappears. Moreover, if the observer succeeds in establishing his or her status as friend of the performers and connoisseur of their art, and can also become sensitive to the perturbations caused by other outsiders, it can be confidently assumed that the study and analysis of the performance which are achieved in such conditions have some validity. However, the potential for the manipulation of the researchers by the performers which such relations of intimacy imply should never be underestimated.

10.2. The predicaments of description

The second challenge confronting the student of performance comes from the temporal mode of traditional cultural events, their usually multi-linear unfolding, which requires a great deal of methodological ingenuity of the part of the observer if most of it is not to be lost through selective, untrained attention. Even if the first sort of challenge which has been discussed above has been successfully met, or at least taken into consideration and assessed, the second one remains intact. An apparently easy solution such as sound or video recording is in fact loaded with methodological fallacies. First, the film of the event does not solve the problem of how to analyze the event. Not only it merely postpones the challenge (the film or video remains to be analyzed), but also it makes the challenge more formidable because the recording freezes the performance as a single instance from a single visual point of view, which is further transmogrified by the framing, distance, focusing and rhythm of the cameraman. The resulting footage can be at most an accessory element for the final analysis. In fact, it could be claimed that only a performance which has been thoroughly analyzed can be usefully filmed and preserved. Moreover, with the exception of "happenings", performances are repeatable events, which can be observed again and again, and it seems impossible to build a reliable model of such performances unless they are closely observed several times through their variations across different contexts. It is indeed important to understand what can vary in a traditional performance, and how much the variable elements can vary, without jeopardizing the performance's integrity; what is context-sensitive and what is not so; at which nodes can improvisation take over, and within which limits; how much it can be condensed or expanded depending on what circumstances: and so on.

But the greatest challenge, which is the subject of this chapter, is the transformation of the performance experience into a single code: its "textualization". Even if iconographic elements are introduced in the researcher's descriptive output, such diagrams and drawings are useful only in as much as they are framed by a text which gives them meaning by specifying their representative status. For instance, a waving line whose direction is marked by an arrow is meaningless by itself unless it is specified that it represents the trajectory of a dancer, or of a group of dancers, or the motion of a dancer's hand. It could also be a decorative motive, or even a melodic line. Only a verbal message is able to disambiguate such a graphic representation. Because a performance is by definition a temporal object which unfolds more or less rapidly, sometimes with a succession of various speeds, it challenges the attention and memory capacities of the investigators. Because it is characterized by a flow of events whose various streams blend with each other in time at various rates, it cannot be functionally sliced into still frames except for the identification of particular components such as costumes, make-up, or postures that are held for some minimal time. But once again, the latter need to be integrated into an explanatory text. Therefore the main problem is to devise a method for reliably textualizing the performance.

There are several reasons why "description" is not a sufficient concept for determining and guiding such a process of textualization, that is, the transformation of a multi-linear and multi-sensorial temporal experience into a uni-linear verbal object: the text upon which further analysis of the performance will be conducted, and the form in which it will be preserved. If we want this new object to encode all the information relevant to the performance so as to be able to serve as a self-sufficient score for recreating it, we must develop a demanding method which cannot be characterized as a mere description, unless we redefine the word 'description' for our purpose. This is why it may be useful to use a different expression such as 'verbal copy' to designate the methodical transformation on the performance into a new object which will encapsulate all the relevant information pertaining to the performance which is to be studied and preserved. The notion of verbal copy of an object or situation has been thoroughly discussed in logical semiotic terms by Maria Nowakowska (1979) who provides the following definition:

> A verbal copy is a description of the situation, in the form of a conjunction of sentences of the form '*x* is such and such'. [...] [T]he successive bits of information contained in sentences '*x* is such and such' cannot be completely arbitrary; they must concern the attributes specified in the system, which, of course, is a natural requirement. There is, however, another requirement, namely that the successive bits of information must be expressed in an 'admissible' way, that is, by using only those expressions that are allowed. (Nowakowska 1979: 142)

The question which can be asked then is the following: under which conditions are exact verbal copies possible at all? The answer is that it depends on the richness of attributes and labels which have been elaborated concerning any possible objects. In practical terms, this means that a heuristic matrix must first be drafted, in which each slot corresponds to a potential kind of information. The verbal copy will consist of filling each slot, including those that will receive a zero value. Then each slot will be transformed into a proposition of the sort indicated by Nowakowska's formal definition. For a clown act, for instance, Chapter 7 could be used to draft such a matrix for the purpose of producing a verbal copy of any make-up. It will ensure that all relevant information is recorded. It is important not to take anything for granted. We saw in Chapter 4 how taking the plumes of the circus horses at face value could blind the semiotician in front of crucial information. A mere photo of a clown face is not the solution to the analytical problem but it can be used as an intermediary object for the observation that leads to the elaboration of the verbal copy as long as it is methodically scanned with respect to the matrix. The semiotic understanding of a circus act is a cognitive process that is necessarily mediated by an adequate verbal copy of a formal nature. Like for any other scientific inquiry, this is the condition for uncovering counter-intuitive knowledge.

However, as was pointed out earlier in this book, usual linguistic resources at times may prove to be insufficient for encoding all information in a reasonably economical manner. This is why researchers must include in their repertory of descriptors the technical vocabulary used by the various specialties comprising the circus art. But, of course, their exact meaning should be made explicit. For example, the term 'signature' is used by white-face clowns to designate the particular configuration and design of the eyebrows which are painted on their whitened forehead. This can be further broken down using anatomical terminology to precisely locate the black curve with respect to the muscle system of the face. Only such accurate verbal copies can make possible productive comparisons and reliable elaboration of the system of signs that accounts for the meaning effects or *semiosis* of the white-face clown make-up.

The abstract definition given by Nowakowska in logical terms will be made still more user friendly in the last section of this chapter, when it is applied to actual instances of performance. But, for the time being, it is important to understand the advantages of adopting a well-defined logical model, rather than the ill-defined, fuzzy notion of "description" in the recording and study of performance.

"Description" is indeed a dangerous word because it conveys a false sense of objectivity and because it is associated with literary tropes and social practices which include their own implicit norms. It is neutral only in appearance. Students are instructed how to make "good" descriptions when they learn how to write creatively with respect to some particular literary models. Original metaphors are thus encouraged in some pedagogical contexts. On the other hand, "scientific" description promotes the use of quantitative data and particular rhetorical devices such as the distancing of the describing subject from the described object, and the elimination of all emotional components. Therefore there is a risk that the researchers who undertake the daunting task of "describing" actual performances fall upon one or the other kind of descriptions mentioned above and use as guidelines a set of implicit norms which were devised for completely different purposes. Literary descriptions must be vivid and entertaining, and often play a distinct function in narratives and poetry. The scientific description must be quantitative and dispassionate, and meet some well defined pragmatic requirements. A "verbal copy" must be far more inclusive and must obey a different set of selective constraints. Unless we want to investigate exclusively the naïve reception of a performance by asking spectators to provide spontaneous descriptions of what they have seen and experienced, such texts are not valid objects for a study of the complex socio-cultural events formed by traditional performances. Furthermore, their high degree of selectivity and their usual reliance on descriptive stereotypes could not serve for the effective recreation of these complex objects.

In order to produce an effective verbal copy it is first necessary to construct an exhaustive model of performance, and to derive from it a set of classes and their corresponding labels. Only then can we devise methodical strategies of textual representation and verbal encoding. Naturally the goal is not to create the equivalent of a performance with words. This can be achieved with greater or lesser success by literary descriptions which may indeed convey similar values and emotions for a sensitive reader. The goal is rather to encode and order all the information which is sufficient for a reconstruction of the performance (its objects, situations and transformations). The verbal copy is an artifact elaborated through implementing a series of tasks which are determined by an abstract model of performance, and which consists of laying out on a two-dimensional space a three-dimensional event. All the constants and variables of the model must be determined in the verbal copy of the particular performance which is the object of research. The first step is therefore to elaborate a model which is sufficiently general but whose parameters are at the same time very finely determined. It must be like a net cast upon the performance, which actually captures all the essentials. In order to build such a model we must specify the general pragmatic conditions which define a performance, as well as the rules of implementation of the performance itself.

10.3. The rules of performance

The term "rules" should not be taken here in a strict normative sense but instead refers to a set of general pragmatic conditions which seems to account for the differences which we experience between a successful performance and a failed one. This sort of difference is not a matter of all or nothing but rather a question of degrees. One or several of these "rules" can be more or less respected by the performers whose level of professionalism can vary. They are similar to the "felicity" conditions, which Paul Grice (1975) called "maxims", of linguistic communication, in particular conversation. In fact these "rules" are relatively easy to uncover by simply reflecting upon bad performances, an experience which is actually more common than unqualified successes. It is through trying to locate the source of the failure – that is, as we have seen in Chapter 8, what Erving Goffman (1974) called a "negative experience" – that we can pin-point violations in the implementation of the performance, and become aware of the extent to which success depends on the respect of these "maxims".

The first maxim could be informally expressed as "meet the audience expectations". This is the principle of accountability. All performers are in a contractual relation to their audience. Any advance announcement of a scheduled performance constitutes the terms of a proposed contract bearing upon the kind of skill of the performers, the genre of work they will perform, the place, time and duration of the event. In the anecdotes introducing this chapter, the trainers were supposed to deliver proofs of their excellence, let alone competence in controlling their charges. Usually an audience is requested to pay an admission fee before the performance, but even when the attendance is free, as it is often the case in traditional performances, the members of the audience are providing their own time during which they abstain from any productive activities. Sometimes the performance is commissioned by a donor for religious, corporate or political reasons. Whatever are the form and modality through which a performance is produced, there is always a give and take process which binds the performer to live up to the terms of a contract. This general condition may remain implicit and be regulated by oral tradition, or it may be explicitly stated, sometimes in great details and in legal jargon as it is the rule in modern societies in which performance has been industrialized, and involves considerable financial risks.

The second maxim deals with the act of communication which a performance fundamentally is. It could be stated as "communicate effectively". Any member of the audience must be able to clearly see, and/or hear the performer(s) as the performance is implemented, and this unfolding must be clearly articulated in all the media it involves. This is the rhetorical rule. It demands that the desired effects of the performance upon the audience be taken into consideration by the performers as they produce it. This rule has also important consequences for the organization of the semantic contents of the performance. In acrobatic acts, for instance, there must not be any doubt about what the artist intends to achieve. Sometimes, a double or triple somersault is outlined by a hand gesture of the acrobat or a partner before the act itself in order to guide the audience's perception of what will happen so fast that it might not be accurately perceived.

The third maxim concerns the semantic contents of the performance. It can be expressed by the injunction: "Be relevant". There is always a certain semantic gap between the way in which a performer understands an artistic or ritualistic tradition and the reception of the corresponding performance by an audience. Even within a particular culture the semantic mapping of experience is not perfectly homogeneous, much more so naturally across cultures. A century or so of anthropological efforts to comparatively map the semantic universes of a large sample of world cultures has revealed marked discrepancies in the ways natural objects and social behaviors are classified and lumped together in constructive cognitive categories. Given the fact that traditional performances make sense in the most absolute manner within the cultural areas in which they originated and continue to strive, culture-specific semantic categories and their mutual relations form necessarily the core of these performances. Performers cannot engage an audience whose system of cognitive relevance does not overlap, at least to some extent, with the system upon which the meaning of their performance rests.

The fourth maxim is "Be proper", that is "Behave properly toward the audience according to the social conventions of the culture". A performer acts indeed on two registers at the same time, or at least successively, since there is a logic of actions which belongs to the message intrinsic to the performance, and in addition there is a form of social behaviors toward the audience, a sort of performers' etiquette correlative to the conventional behavior of the audience which is expected to show various degrees of appreciation. Admiring whistling in North America is not congruent with the European code according to which aggressive whistling in the context of performance is a strong mark of disapproval. These social behaviors, or their absence, are an important part of performance because they frame the whole experience in a way which has an impact on the deep meaning of the performance. Are the performing identities spirits who possess the performers for the time of the performance, or are the performers skilled artists who manufacture the illusions of the personae they represent and gleefully take credit for their performing success?

The fifth maxim concerns time. It actually involves so many aspects that it is difficult to express it with a single injunction. It comprises "Be in time", "Be timely", "Keep time in mind", "Keep the tempo". It has to do with time structure and duration, tempo and rhythm, speed and intervals. It could be called the rule of "timeliness" to include all the above aspects which must be taken into consideration when a performance is analyzed.

The above considerations bearing upon the pragmatic conditions of performances provide a tentative framework which should help a researcher to conceptualize performance in a more comprehensive manner than a naïve approach could afford. By "naïve approach" I mean the frame of mind of an observer who studies the performance by focusing on what is happening in the performing area without questioning the assumptions which make this experience possible. Any performance presupposes an institution produced by, and embedded within, a culture, and a set of implicit rules whose observations ensures the felicitous implementation of the patterned event. It is only once a particular performance has been assessed with respect to these pragmatic conditions that a verbal copy can be productively undertaken.

10.4. How to make a verbal copy

It is not possible to start making a verbal copy of a performance until a cognitive matrix has been developed. A cognitive matrix is a structure or a conceptual graph which determines which kind of information is relevant to the performance and should be entered as a part of the copy. It lists the choices which can be made by the performers in the implementation of the performance. For instance, a performer must make a first contact with the audience for the performance to start. The contact can be sudden or progressive. It can involve the *dramatis persona* right at the onset of the performance, or it can first introduce the civil identity of the performer who, after having been acknowledged as the real substrate of the character will then endow her/his performing identity and will initiate the performance. It is obvious that further choices are involved in each one of these modes of starting points. Is a social contact established with the audience, or only with the other performers, or even with some deity as it is the case in many Hindu performances through the burning of incense or the reciting of a mantra? It may be that, in some cases, the three types of contacts will be present in a particular order. A performer may represent the transition from civil to performing identity, or adopt the epiphany mode of appearance, hence possibly never relinquishing the performance identity to the extent that the audience cannot relate the *dramatis persona* to any known real person, as it has often been the case with circus clowns for the general audience of their performances. As we saw in Chapter 7, many traditional performers use masks or make-up which so transform their face that the two identities cannot be intuitively related.

In view of the above, a descriptive proposition such as: "at the beginning, performer *x* enters the stage and walks toward its center" cannot be considered a verbal copy because it leaves out a large amount of relevant information. There are many ways of walking, some indicating that the performer walks as an ordinary person who goes and takes the place he/she is supposed to occupy at the beginning of the performance, some other signifying that it is the *dramatis persona* who walks for some performance related purpose to this particular spot of the stage area. Therefore the gait is one of the relevant parts of the cognitive matrix which must be specified in the verbal copy. Other such parts are the visual and auditory attributes of the performing identity. These attributes belong to identifiable categories either as categories which are functional in the contextual culture and may denote social class, age, mood, etc., or as categories pertaining to the code specific to a particular genre of performance such as a princess, a warrior, a monster, a clown, etc. What is said, and how it is said, the music being performed, if any, the reaction of other characters, whose attributes have also been specified, are equally relevant parts of the cognitive matrix. Such a matrix can be conceived as a fairly wide-mesh net whose purpose is to catch selectively the information which could be used later for reconstructing the performance rather than duplicating it with a perfect match including elements which are not perceived by the audience and therefore are not relevant to the performance such as the real age of the performers, their blood pressure, the color of their undergarments, and the like. The descriptive matrix is exclusively sensitive to the cognitive categories through which the meaning of the performance is produced for its audience. For instance some colors may or may not be relevant as an attribute of a performer's clothing. Similarly, some qualities or modifications of the voice, some accompanying tunes, or some identifiable sounds may be indicative of social categories or shifting of registers.

It should be obvious at this point that a verbal copy is a methodical enterprise which requires first the careful elaboration of an appropriate cognitive matrix. This elaboration can be achieved only through multiple reflexive experiences of the kind of performances one wants to study. The all-purpose matrix which has been sketched above cannot be directly applied to any type of performance. It must first be fine tuned. There is in this process a degree of circularity, but it is a constructive circularity since the researcher is led to start with tentative verbal copies which can be compared to further experiences of the same performance. At first the researchers must train their observation skill with the general matrix in mind. Next, a tentative copy is made through taking notes and using short term memory. Then, it must be formatted, so to speak, that is, the propositions must be standardized and made readable by a larger community of researchers. This first stage will reveal many gaps in the information collected. Only further experiences of the same performance, or the complementary memory of the other research team members, will make it possible to saturate the matrix. Naturally, drawings, diagrams and sketches can be inserted in the verbal text to economically specify some stable or dynamic patterns.

The final verbal copy will be the result of a consensus. It will take the form of a lengthy text in which natural syntax will indicate clearly what is perceived simultaneously and what is perceived successively. Which attributes are permanent for the duration of the performance, which ones are changing at which points in the process. The fine tuning of the copy is facilitated by the numerous analyses of human communicative behavior which have been produced over the last fifty years, both in the auditory and visual channels. The works of human ethologists such as Irenaus Eibl-Eibesfelt (2007 [1989]) or psychologists such as Paul Ekman (1982) have provided a standardized terminology which can be very effectively used, and several researchers have produced ways of noting in great detail gestures, postures and choreographic movements (e.g., Rudolph Laban 1974). On the other hand, the semiotic attention given to the function of structured space in determining meaningful positions, social categories, etc., (for instance Edward Hall 1969), represents an essential methodological commodity. The same applies to the analysis of the rich repertory of non-linguistic vocal qualities and other bodily produced sounds observed by researchers such as Fernando Poyatos (1976). Objects, theatrical and circus props, tales and dances, music and natural noises have also been extensively studied from a semiotic point of view, that is, according to their capacity to produce constructive meanings (e.g., Poyatos 1992, 1993). The research skill involved in the production of successful verbal copies presupposes an advance level of "semiotic literacy" which provides both non trivial cognitive classes (what counts as information in a type of situation) and their labels (that is, admissible terms to be used as descriptors).

10.5. From rules of performance to rules of description

The functional relations that exist between the pragmatic conditions of performance as they have been outlined in the third part of this chapter and the classes of descriptors which are used to complete a verbal copy of a particular performance should now be obvious. In fact it would not be possible to determine *a priori* those classes of descriptors in the absence of a theoretical model of performance encompassing the whole situation with the audience and performers embedded in the socio-economic structure of a particular culture. The initial situation is an unstable relation characterized by a more or less confident expectation on the part of an audience. The performers have been credited in advance, so to speak, and their task will be to restore the equilibrium by meeting their commitments. Their currency is purely symbolical since it represents the meanings and values upon which the social system rests. This is why the classes of descriptors are intimately related to the maxim of relevance and the maxim of propriety, and their rhetorical arrangement by the maxim of communication which both must combine in order to achieve the effective manipulation of the audience's interest and bring it to a state of semiotic satiety. The verbal copy cannot merely produce lists of descriptors' labels but must reconstruct their dynamic relations and retrace the trajectory of the performance from its initial situation to its terminal state within the spatial and temporal frames which are dictated by cultural conventions.

This approach provides the student of performance with the theoretical and practical means to cope with cultural diversity since verbal copies are not meant to be the results of the blind application of a universal method, but rely on the prior elaboration of a descriptive matrix which is context-sensitive. However, the conceptual tools through which such an elaboration is possible belong to the metalanguage of semiotics without which performance researchers would probably be unable to free themselves from the taken-for-granted situation which our culture labels "the audience", and they would be restricted to produce "descriptions" which would be mostly redundant with respect to their feelings as an audience, that is, with respect to the blind effects of the cognitive manipulations engineered by the performers. This is why a description, in the usual uncritical sense of the term, cannot be the basis for a reconstruction of the performance "described", whereas a verbal copy, in the technical sense specified by Nowakowska, should be able to achieve such a goal.

Conclusion
Circus in perspective

Where does circus come from? A deep time perspective

All cultural events, and particularly the performing arts, are grounded not only in popular tradition and historical societal forms, but also in human physiology and psychology as both have evolved over hundreds of millions years through natural selection. Circus has a remarkable status in this respect because its basis, its building blocks so to speak, is a set of typical actions that can be assumed to have been essential for human survival in the deep time of the species when extreme situations offered constant challenges not yet mediated by cultural artifacts. Such situations are now modeled in the circus ring, mostly in the form of devices such as trapezes, fixed bars, and high wires, and enable acrobats to demonstrate their capacity of surviving the dangers they involve through appropriate actions. We have reviewed in Chapter 2 some of these artifacts which are much more than mere props since each one generates a type of survival through actions which form the core of the circus specialties. These actions are often combined in particular circus acts.

These core actions include (1) balancing and progressing on narrow surfaces; (2) grasping hanging supports that prevent deadly falls; (3) clearing obstacles by jumping or climbing; (4) throwing or catching objects in a way that allows a person to reach targets or keep a number of valuable items intact; (5) controlling animals both to exploit the resources afforded by some and neutralize the aggression of predators; and, (6) no less important for a social species, negotiating social situations. The wire walkers, the aerialists, the jumpers, the climbers, the sharp-shooters, the jugglers, the trainers of domestic and wild animals, and the clowns are true icons of survival in these respective categories. They implement the successful overcoming of extreme versions of the modern challenges with which we are familiar in the constructed environment of our everyday life: keeping our upright balance when we stand or walk, grasping a hand rail fast enough or tightly enough to prevent a fall; avoiding collisions with obstacles that lie in our path or clearing gaps; reaching for targets or not letting objects slip through our hands; keeping our dogs, cats or cattle under control; and maintaining good joking relationships with our fellow humans, sometimes even in testing situations. We take all these common competences for granted until we witness or experience their selective disruption through physical impairments or mental illnesses. We also become acutely aware of them when our usual environment is temporarily changed: the ground is slippery and there is no bar to be grasped; we have to handle too many objects at the same time; we are confronted with an aggressive dog or uncooperative family members or neighbors who lack a sense of humor. In brief, all circus acts are based on the artificial constructions of extreme situations, and on the corresponding acquired skills that are necessary to meet the challenges they offer, but these skills are not alien to those we need to negotiate at every step in our physical and social lives.

The point of these remarks is that whatever the circus artists perform in front of us resonates in our own body and mind. This physical and moral empathy has been recently explained by the discovery of mirror neurons in our brains (Stamenov and Gallese 2002; Hurley and Chater 2005). These are visuomotor neurons which fire both when we perform a particular action, such as lifting an arm, and when we see the same action performed by someone else. It can be assumed that such neurons fire with a particular intensity when we witness extreme actions. This, to my knowledge, has not been tested yet on subjects attending circus performances. However, a plausible hypothesis could be that circus is so special and so involving because it reaches out to the deepest part of our body, that is, our primal brain, and activates an ancestral visuomotor memory which is inscribed in our genome and is at the very basis of our sociality in as much as it sustains dynamic empathy. It has been shown that sounds made by the mouth or hands activate brain regions involved in planning the movements that produce such sounds (Miller 2006).

This is undoubtedly the basis of what is meant when the circus is claimed to be timeless, that is, not dependent on a particular historical period defined by its cultural make-up and technology. Of course, this claim should be qualified as we have seen in Chapter 4, for instance, that the implementation of some acts is context-sensitive and follows socio-cultural evolution. Nevertheless, the circus displays fundamental actions that are rooted in our deepest evolutionary past, actions that were necessarily vital for the common ancestors of all primates who are generally considered to have been social tree-dwelling mammals (e.g., Beard 2004; Walker and Shipman 2005; White et al. 2009).

The visuo-motor competencies that now constitute the complete repertory of circus specialties were present two hundred millions years ago, and enabled these ancestral mammals to successfully survive and reproduce in the trees in which they lived and from which they were getting their subsistence. From the analysis of their fossilized anatomy it is possible to infer that these competencies included for instance: keeping their balance and progressing on tree limbs, climbing vertical trunks, hanging from branches and jumping from one branch to the other, catching insects and birds, picking up fruit and seeds, and carrying them around to a safe place, fending off predators, and maintaining essential social bonds without which individual survival would not be ensured. Some of these competencies became somewhat less vital once these ancestral primates, under some evolutionary pressures which are still debated, started to walk and run upright on the ground, and evolved toward fully bipedal modern humans in a different, mostly terrestrial environment (Stanford 2003; Bramble and Lieberman 2004). However, the human species still carries in itself fossil behaviors and fundamental potentials that a determined training can develop and refine, and which can be relied on whenever some circumstances force human groups to seek refuge in trees.

An example of such a fossil behavior that is often cited is the grasping reflex observed in newborn infants who can support their own weight hanging by their hands from a rod, a precious life-saving behavior when one is born in a tree from a hairy mother (Peiper 1963). Apparently, some individuals preserve this capacity in adulthood and some circus aerialists are credited with the conservation of this fossil ability. It is also well known that grasping feet and opposable toes have survived in some modern humans. There is also other evidence that some genetic lineages have fully conserved atypical biological features that are not any longer commonly found in humans today. These genetic variations, that are now considered to be pathological in otherwise healthy individuals, may have proved to be adaptive in particular contexts. Interestingly, such a rare phenotype was recently discovered in three consanguineous families from northern Pakistan in which some individuals completely lack the ability to sense pain. These families derive their living from entertaining audiences by performing feats that are beyond the scope of those who possess a fully functional sense of pain. It is undoubtedly a liability not to be selectively informed by neuron paths of specific danger warnings transmitted from the skin to the brain, such as sharpness or excessive heat, but a marked advantage if one's means of survival consist of impressing other humans by driving nails through one's tongue or walk on live charcoals (Cox et al. 2006; Pearson 2006). These remarks are not meant to lessen the achievements of circus artists, whose exacting training usually starts early and requires constant maintenance and fine-tuning, but to point out that under certain socio-cultural circumstances some genetic variations may prove to be adaptive, which otherwise could be devastating. Circus and associated activities can offer such opportunities.

This perspective casts an interesting light on the possible reasons that explain why the Olympic Games, as originally revived by Pierre de Coubertin and Michel Bréal, did not include any of the body techniques associated with the circus arts. First, of course, is the ideological principle that excluded professionals from being qualified. One had to be an amateur (a "gentleman for whom sport is a hobby") to be allowed to compete in the games. Secondly, all the Olympic specialties, rooted in Classical Greek traditions that the modern founders of the games fancied to perpetuate, concern bipedal competencies, that is, what makes humans what they are as opposed to animals which run on their fours or hang out in trees. The Olympics typically display the abilities of a savannah hunter: running (and occasionally swimming), throwing weapons as far and as precisely as possible, lifting heavy weights, wrestling, jumping (from the ground), etc., and horsemanship which, historically, requires most of the above abilities. Of course, there is some degree of overlapping with circus displays, in which case the style of delivery is markedly different so as not to confuse one with the other. In any case, even when fixed bars or jumps are involved, the Olympic athletes start from the ground.

But there may be more to this. The fascination for the circus is ambiguous: the mastery of all these extraordinary physical feats is potentially dangerous if it were taken out of the performance ring and used in the service of criminal goals. This dimension has been very effectively exploited in a *007* thriller directed by John Glen (*Octopussy*, 1983). Set in the context of the Cold War, circus artists demonstrate the military value of their art: walking over walls on a stretched wire, throwing knives accurately, controlling the force of elephants to force fences, and the like. In more general terms, the fitness and charm of the performers exert an irresistible seduction on their audience, sometimes well beyond the appreciation of their artistic skills. This is why, in spite of its occasional foregrounding of "family values" or "educational purposes", circus has always been perceived as a threat to the social order because of this subversive attraction. Running away to join the circus is a popular literary *topos* but usually is not the kind of situation that families dream of for their children. These aspects also belong to the timelessness of the circus as warfare and seduction are rooted in our deep past.

Therefore, the timelessness of circus does not refer to a kind of non-temporal status but rather to its firm grounding in the very deep time of evolution as opposed to historical time through which cultures changed at a much faster rate, notably with the domestication of the horse which, as we have seen in Chapter 4, is the backbone of its spectacle from the very origin of this spectacular institution. Structuralist approaches to the understanding of circus performances can reveal the subtle semiotic mechanisms through which cultural codes exploit and transcend the biosemiotic resources of the human species.

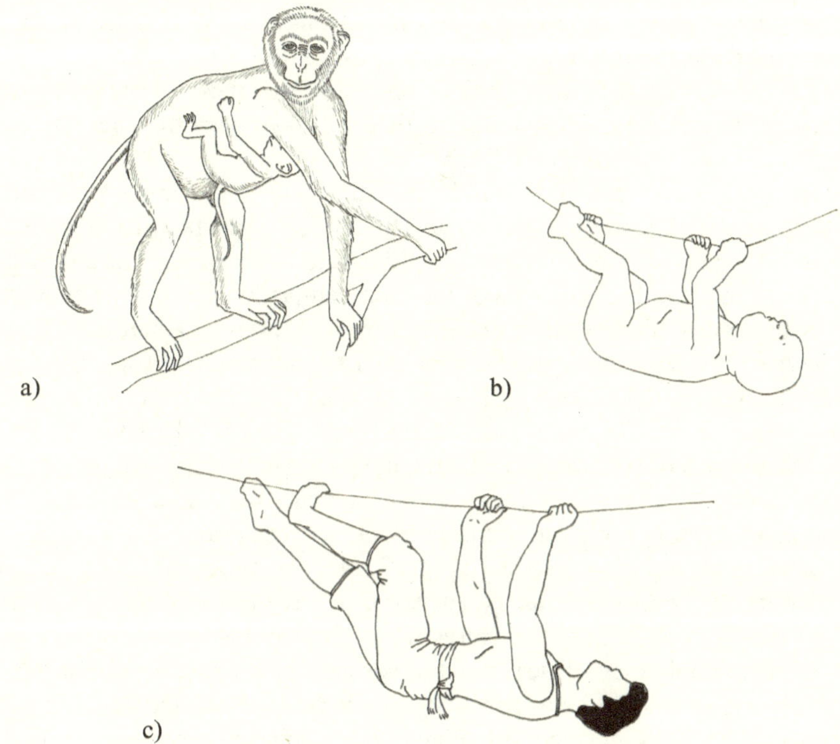

Figure 6. More than four millions year ago, the common ancestor of apes and humans had adapted to arboreal life by evolving vital grasping and balancing reflex. Modern circus artists exploit through intensive training these primal competences which have not completely disappeared from our behavioral repertory. The survival value of grasping is obvious in tree-dwelling primates (a) and this reflex persists in new-born humans (b). Whenever a high wire walker loses his/her balance, spontaneous grasping may prevent a fall and make it possible to return to the initial position (c). Trapeze acrobats rely on their gripping power to perform their acts.

Where is the circus going? Challenges and opportunities

Circus always takes place within a particular culture and displays through its own prism ethical values and social norms, historical and political references, esthetic standards, the memory of the circus tradition itself, even sometimes direct allusions to local issues involving social justice or deeper ideological struggles (Bouissac 1991; Carmeli 2003). This can be achieved by the acting and personae of the performers, their symbolic props, and the dialogues of the clowns. The circus of the Soviet Union made massive use of these means of conveying ideology for inner consumption. When the Moscow Circus started traveling to Western countries during the Cold War, it was wont to include discreet propaganda elements in its artistically crafted performances. We have encountered such an example in Chapter 6.

Circus can indeed articulate, either unwittingly by conforming to the mood of the time or deliberately in the context of struggles for political awareness, definite contents referring to the body politics and other issues. The alternative circuses of the last three decades of the 20th century were not-shy about their activist agenda, at times to the point of self-irony. Alexander Kluge's 1967 film, *Die Artisten in der Zirkuskuppel: Ratlos* [Artists under the Big Top: Perplexed] which received the 1968 Golden Lion at the Venice Festival, bears witness to this socio-cultural trend. The main character is a woman, Leini Peikert, who attempts to create a new utopian circus in which animals are neither trained nor dressed up, and artists explain the physical laws which rule their acrobatic acts. This film is an interesting symptom of the interface between circus and activism that was brewing during the rebellious 1960s. This was a time when the perceived marginality of the circus attracted European middle-class youths who saw it as a window of opportunity for expressing their anarchistic utopia. They were also prone to apply their critical stand to the very medium they were using. In 1970, Hilary Westlake founded in London *Circus Lumiere*, "a show for adult audiences", which performed in England and in some European cities. In this circus the "liberty horses", as we noted in Chapter 4, were a group of harnessed men driven through their routine by a dominatrix, and the magician extracted a top hat from a rabbit. Its socio-artistic mission was continued by *Son of Circus Lumiere* in the 1980s. In 1976, Austrian André Heller created with Bernhard Paul *Circus Roncalli* to honor a pope who was seen as a bold mover and shaker of the Catholic Church, and allegedly a circus fan himself. In France, *Cirque Aligre* made light of the traditional pomposity of the circus code and idiom with its rat trainer who was "putting the rat head in his mouth", a feat which seemingly had more impact on the audience than the worn out "trainer's head in the lion's jaws", and other antics. Later on, *Circus Archaos* went much further in breaking taboos with, for instance, its circus hands miming masturbation in front of the closed-circuit TV screens that were showing the couple engaged in a classical acrobatic act on a pedestal in the center of the ring. This and other extreme features were censored (or self-censored) in certain cities. Obviously, this brief survey is not meant to review the whole movement of the "new" circus but merely to illustrate this trend while pointing out that the core of these spectacles ultimately were traditional acrobatic acts staged in a provocative way.

Many examples of such-short lived circuses appeared in Europe. The extent to which they succeeded in raising socio-political awareness or deeply altering the very essence of the circus remains to be assessed. But there is no doubt that they ushered in an esthetic revolution in the circus. Traditional circuses, whose owners were first flabbergasted by the success of these technically mediocre spectacles, soon started adopting some of their gimmicks. The new wave had been, for the most part, educated in middle-class families, and brought to the circus their literate and musical culture as well as their familiarity with private and public agencies that support the arts and to which they often had privileged access. They also were media savvy and attuned to the latest technologies.

This esthetic revolution coincidentally happened when animal welfare supporters were gaining some clout with politicians. Campaigns against the use of animals in circuses were well financed and could express themselves in the media as well as summon rather large groups of protesters to harass traditional circuses. The new circus was demonstrating that circus companies could financially prosper without carrying a load of wild animals. These animals were regularly shown in their natural environment on television programs with comments that glossed over the harshness of life in the wild and glamorized freedom in nature with properly euphoric musical scores. The new circus, which of course could have hardly afforded the resources and knowledge demanded by circus animal husbandry and training, appeared as the virtuous harbinger of a new age in "clean" entertainment, and claimed to have reinvented this immemorial art. Many companies found indeed some innovative ways of presenting classical acrobatic specialties and used spectacular technology to the advantage of the performers. Québec's *Cirque du Soleil*, which early had created its legend as being born from a group of street performers, and had secured comfortable governmental subsidies, soon became a multinational company that practically cornered the "new circus" market on a global scale. With the possible exception of the Australian *Circus OZ*, the subversive circus of the 1970s either vanished with the dispersal of the *ad hoc* groups that had brought it to life, or was absorbed into the new forms of the traditional circus that proved to be extraordinarily resilient. On the one hand, traditional circuses adapted to the expectations of their audiences, and on the other hand new circuses devolved toward brilliantly renewed ancient forms.

However, the impact of the "reinvented" circus has been considerably limited in space and time. It can be only locally and sporadically, rather than globally, construed as a post-modern revolution. The new forms spread in Northern Europe, where wild animals had been already banned in some countries. English-speaking countries such as Canada and Australia, more recently India, have joined in this trend. But the traditional circuses in the United States, Mexico,

Central and South America, and Southern and Eastern Europe, continue to perform impervious to these changes. Most German, Russian and French circuses have not altered the substance of their programs, having kept producing wild animal acts or now reintroducing them in the ring in order to meet public demand. What has changed is the style of presentation, and the conditions in which their wild animals are kept and displayed. Ironically, many of the trainers come from British circus families and seemingly can perform almost anywhere in the world except at home (Carmeli 2003) although there are signs that the horses, lions and elephants are coming back as bylaws are rescinded in an increasing number of counties and townships.

It seems that, in the course of the last half century, under a variety of political, socio-economic and cultural pressures, several trends have emerged from the "timeless" circus. They have coexisted with, and influenced each other. Rather than a linear, dialectic development, circus has branched out into at least three genres: the traditional "modern" circus with its complement of acrobats, animal trainers and clowns (e.g. the German circus *Krone*); the purely acrobatic circus with a theatrical and comic component (e.g., *Cirque du Soleil*); and a new genre, the artistic, educational or community circus that takes at times the form of a kind of "studio circus", oscillating between activism and estheticism, with the usual support of various government agencies. These three forms coexist globally as a probe of Internet resources indicates. Indeed, circus fans have created and maintain thorough listings of routes and programs, as well as archives and blogs that show the robustness of the traditional circus. Most circuses now have their own homepages through which they can communicate effectively with their audiences, and address any issues they may have. There are, of course, regional variations that reflect the political economy of cultural policies and the differential political powers of lobbyists who oppose or support the circus on a diversity of ideological grounds.

The resilience of the circus through the process of globalization and its adaptation to changing cultural contexts keeps providing a rich domain of inquiry for semiotics. The playing out of the primal repertory of human survival behaviors cast in signs borrowed from all the cultures of the world achieve in the crucible of the ring a unique and challenging fusion between nature and culture. The resources of both biosemiotics and cultural semiotics, as we have attempted to show in this volume, are required if one is to come to grips with the circus's symbolic complexity and the pleasures it affords.

References

Alderson, F.
1972 *Bicycling, a history*. New York: Praeger.

Altman, S.A.
1965 Sociobiology of Rhesus monkeys. *Journal of Theoretical Biology* 8. 490–552.

Assael, B.
2005 The Circus and Victorian Society. Charlotteville: University of Virginia Press.

Balzac, H. de
1975 [1835] *Le Père Goriot, La Comédie humaine,* vol. 3, 874–875. Paris: Gallimard/Pléiade.

Baudry de Saunier, L.
1891 *Histoire générale de la Vélocipédie*. Paris: Ollendorf.

Beard, C.
2004 *The hunt for the dawn monkey: Unearthing the origins of monkeys, apes, and humans*. Berkeley: University of California Press.

Bordez, C. and G. Juliani
2002 *Dernier tour de piste*. Montréal: Editions JCL.

Bouissac, P.
1976a *Circus and culture*. Bloomington: Indiana University Press.

Bouissac, P.
1976b Circus performances as texts: a matter of poetic competence. *Poetics* 5(2). 101–118.

Bouissac, P.
1976c La discursivité non-linguistique. In P. Léon & H. Mitterand (eds.), *L'Analyse du discourse/Discourse analysis*, 203–213. Montréal: CEC.

Bouissac, Paul
1987 The marketing of performance. In Jean Umiker-Sebeok (ed.), *Semiotics and marketing*, 391–406. Berlin & New York: Mouton de Gruyter.

Bouissac, Paul
1990 Incidents, accidents, failures: The representation of negative experience in public entertainment. In Stephen H. Riggins (ed.), *Beyond Goffman. Studies on communication, institution, and*

social interaction, 409–443. Berlin & New York: Mouton de Gruyter.

Bouissac, P.
1991a From calculus to language: the case of circus equine displays. *Semiotica* 85(3/4). 291–317.

Bouissac, P.
1991b The circus: A semiotic spectroscopy. *Semiotica* 85(3/4). 189–199.

Bouissac, P. (ed.)
1991 Semiotics of the circus. *Semiotica* 85(3/4) [Special issue].

Bramble, D. and D. Lieberman
2004 Endurance running in the evolution of *Homo*. *Nature* 432. 345–352.

Brandsträdter, J.
2006 Action perspectives on human development. In W. Damon & R Lerner (eds.), *Handbook of child psychology: Theoretical models of human development*, vol. 1, 516–568, 6th edn. Hoboken, NJ: Wiley.

Breton, A.
1972 [1935] *Manifestoes of surrealism*. R. Seaver & H.R. Lane (eds.). Ann Arbor, MI: Ann Arbor Paperbacks.

Brody, J.J.
1971 *Indian painters and white patrons*. Albuquerque: University of New Mexico Press.

Bruner, J.S.
1990 *Acts of meaning*. Cambridge, MA: Harvard University Press.

Carmeli, Y.
2003 Lion on display: culture, nature, and totality in a circus performance. *Poetics Today* 24(1). 65–90.

Carmeli, Y.
2007 Travelling and family in the 1970s British circus. *Semiotica* 167(1/4). 369–385.

Cervelatti, A.
1961 *Storia del Circo: Questa sera grande spettacolo*. Milan: Carlino.

Circus coming to county Saturday
1985 *The Shoals* (Indiana) *News*, 2 October 1985, 1.

Circus does vanishing act Saturday
1985 *The Shoals* (Indiana) *News*, 9 October 1985, 1.

Cox, J.J., F. Reimann, A.K. Nicholas, G. Thornton, E. Roberts, K. Springell, G. Karbani, H. Jaffri, J. Mannan, Y. Raashid, L. Al-Gazali, H. Hamamy, E.M. Valente, S. Gorman, R. Williams, D.P. McHale, J.N. Wood, F.M. Gribble and C.G. Woods

2006 An SNC9A channelopathy causes congenital inability to experience pain. *Nature* 444. 894–898.

Dawkins, R.

1989 *The selfish gene*. New edn. Oxford: Oxford University Press.

Diez, B.R.

1981 *Las lenguas Especiales. El Lexico del Ciclismo*. Publicaciones 22. Leon: Colegio Universitario de Leon.

Douglas, Mary

1985 *Risk acceptability according to the social sciences*, New York: Sage.

Douglas, Mary and Aaron Wildavsky

1982 *Risk and culture*. Berkeley: University of California Press.

Dundes, A. and A. Falassi

1975 *La Terra in Piazza*. Berkeley, CA: University of California Press.

Eco, Umberto

1976 *A theory of semiotics*. Bloomington, IN: Indiana University Press.

Eibl-Eibesfeldt, I.

2007 [1989] *Human ethology*. New York: Aldine de Gruyter.

Ekman, Paul

1973 *Darwin and facial expression: A century of research in review*. New York: Academic Press.

Ekman, Paul

1979 About brows: Emotional and conversational signals. In J. Aschoff, M. von Cranach, K. Koppa, W. Lepennies & D. Plog (eds.), *Human ethology*, 169–202. Cambridge: Cambridge University Press.

Ekman, Paul

1982 Methods for measuring facial actions. In Klaus R. Scherer & Paul Ekman (eds.), *Handbook of methods in nonverbal behavior research*. Cambridge: Cambridge University Press.

Ekman, Paul

2001 *Telling lies*, 3rd edn. New York: Times Books.

Ekman, Paul and W. Friesen
1978 *Facial action coding system: A technique for the measurement of facial movement.* Palo Alto, CA: Consulting Psychologists Press.
Ekman, Paul, W. Friesen and P. Ellesworth
1972 *Emotion in the human face.* New York: Pergamon Press.
Franke, G., W. Suhr and F. Riess
1990 *European Journal of Physics* 11. 116.
Fréjaville, G.
1923 *Au Music-Hall.* Paris: Editions du Monde Nouveau.
Fridlund, A.
1994 *Human facial expression: An evolutionary view.* San Diego, CA: Academic Press.
Goffman, E.
1974 *Frame analysis. An essay on the organization of experience.* New York: Harper and Row.
Goody, J.
1976 *Production and reproduction.* Cambridge: Cambridge University Press.
Greimas, A.J.
1966 *Sémantique structurale.* Paris: Larousse.
Greimas, A.J.
1987 [1970] *On meaning.* F. Collins & P. Perron (trans.). Minneapolis: University of Minnesota Press.
Greimas, A.J.
1989 [1976] *The social sciences: A semiotic view.* Frank Collins & P. Perron (trans.). Minneapolis: University of Minnesota Press.
Grice, H. Paul
1975 Logic and conversation. In Peter Cole & Jerry L. Morgan (eds.), *Syntax and semantics. Speech acts*, 41–58. New York: Academic Press.
Hacher, Kathy
1986 Daddy, the tiger-tamer. *The Philadelphia Inquirer*, 3 June 1986, 1c–8c.
Hachet-Souplet, P.
1905 *Le dressage des animaux.* Paris: Didot.
Hall, Edwards T.
1969 *The hidden dimension, Garden City.* New York: Anchor Books.

Hawthorn, Tom
1986 It's showtime – 300 days a year. *Globe and Mail* (Toronto), 21 June 1986, D3.
Hediger, H.
1935 Zirkus-Dressuren und Tierpsychologie. *Revue Suisse de Zoologie* 42. 389–394.
Hediger, H.
1955 *Studies of the psychology and behavior of captive animals in zoos and circuse.* G. Sircom (trans.). London: Butterworth's Scientific Publication.
Hediger, H.
1967 Verstehens- und Verständigungmöglichkeiten zwischen Mensch und Tier. *Schweizerische Zeitschrift für Psychologie und ihre Anwendungen* 26. 234–255.
Hediger, H.
1968 *The psychology and behavior of animals in zoos and circuses.* New York, NY: Dover.
Hirschman, Elizabeth C. and Morris Holbrook
1982 Hedonic consumption: Emerging concepts, methods and propositions. *Journal of Marketing* 46. 92–101.
Holbrook, Morris B. and Elizabeth C. Hirschman
1982 The experiential aspects of consumption: Consumer fantasies, feelings and fun. *Journal of Consumer Research* 9. 132–140.
Holbrook, Morris et al.
1984 Play as a consumption experience: The roles of emotions, performances, and personality in the enjoyment of games. *Journal of Consumer Research* 11. 728–739.
Hugo, V.
2002 La vache [1837]. In *Selected poetry in French and English.* Translated by Steven Monte. London: Routledge (p. 41).
Hurley, S. and N. Chater (eds.)
2005 *Perspectives on imitation*, Vol. 1. Cambridge, MA: MIT Press.
Jakobson, R.
1960 Linguistics and poetics. In T.A. Sebeok (ed.), *Style in language.* Bloomington, IN: Indiana University Press.
Jeanes, R.W.
1949 *Les origins du vocabulaire cycliste en France.* Paris: Sorbonne doctoral dissertation.

Kern, S.
1983 *The culture of time and space 1880–1918*. Cambridge, MA: Harvard University Press.

Knoblich, G. and J.S. Jordan
2003 Action coordination in groups and individuals: Learning anticipatory control. *Journal of Experimental Psychology: Learning, Memory, and Cognition* 29(5). 1006–1016.

Kotler, Philip
1976 *Marketing management: Analysis, planning, and control.* 3rd edn. Englewood Cliffs, NJ: Prentice-Hall.

Kotler, Philip
1980 Foreword. In Michael Mokwa et al. (eds.), *Marketing and the arts*, xiii–xv. New York: Praeger.

Laban, Rudolph
1974 *Choreutics. The language of movement.* Lisa Ullman (ed.). Boston: Plays Inc.

Leach, E.
1964 Anthropological aspects of language: animal categories and verbal abuse. In E. Lenneberg (ed.), *New directions in the study of language*, 23–63. Cambridge, MA: M.I.T. Press.

Leroi-Gourhan, A
1965 *Le geste et la parole*. Paris: Albin Michel.

Lévi-Strauss, C.
1962 *La pensée sauvage*. Paris: Plon.

Lewin, R.A.
1999 *Excursions in scientific, cultural, and socio-historical coprology*. New York: Random House.

Lloyd, B.B.
1972 *Perception and cognition, a cross-cultural perspective*. London: Penguin Books.

Lorenz, K.
1981 *The foundations of ethology*. New York: Springer.

Lotman, J.
1977 *The structure of the artistic text.* R. Vroom (trans.). Michigan Slavic Contributions. Ann Arbor, MI: University of Michigan Press.

Luria, A.
1973 *The working brain, an introduction to neuropsychology*. London: Penguin Books.

Luria, A.
1976 *Cognitive development: Its cultural and social foundations*. Cambridge, MA: Harvard University Press.

Maddox, J.
1990 Bicycling about to be explained? *Nature* 346. 407.

Mair, M.W.
1978 *Steps towards principles of text regulation*. Toronto Semiotic Circle 2, 24–34. Toronto: Victoria University.

Mair, M.W.
1980 The melody of the text. *Semiotica* 32(1/2). 119–138.

Mair, M.W.
1986 The eye in the control of attention. In J.-L. Nespoulous, P. Perron & A.R. Lecours (eds.), *The biological foundations of gestures: Motor and semiotic aspects*, 123–146. Hilsdale, NJ: Lawrence Erlbaum Associates.

McDougal, C.
1977 *The face of the tiger*. London: Deutsch.

Messinger, D., A. Fogel and K.L. Dickson
1999 What's in a smile? *Developmental Psychology* 35(3). 701–708.

Mey, M. de
1976 The structure of behaviour and action. *Communication and Cognition* 9(3/4).

Mick, David Glen
1986 Consumer research and semiotics: Exploring the morphology of signs, symbols and significance. *Journal of Consumer Research* 13. 196–213.

Miller, G.
2006 Probing the social brain. *Science* 312. 838–839.

Miller, G.A. and P.N. Johnson-Laird
1976 *Language and perception*. Cambridge, MA: Harvard University Press.

Miller, G.A., E. Galanter and K. Pribram
1960 *Plans and the structure of behavior*. New York: Holt, Rhinehart and Winston.

Mokwa, Michael, William Dawson and Arthur E. Prieve (eds.)
1980 *Marketing and the arts*. New York: Praeger.

Moulin, Raymonde
1967 *Le Marché de la peinture en France*. Paris: Les Editions de Minuit.

Nowakowska, Maria
1979 Foundations of formal semiotics: Objects and their verbal copies. *Ars Semeiotica. International Journal of American Semiotics* 2(2). 133–148.

Nowakowska, Maria
1980 An empirical approach to foundations of formal semiotics. *Ars Semeiotica. International Journal of American Semiotics* 3(3). 313–349.

Palmer, A.J.
1956 *Riding high. The story of the bicycle*. New York: Dutton.

Pearson, H.
2006 Freaks of nature? *Nature* 444. 1000–1001.

Peiper, A.
1963 [1961] *Cerebral function in infancy and childhood.* B. Nagler & H. Nagler (trans.). New York: Consultant Bureau.

Peterson, Richard A.
1978 The production of cultural change: The case of contemporary country music. *Social Research* 45. 292–314.

Peterson, Robert
1980 Marketing analysis, segmentation, and targeting in the performing arts. In Michael Mokwa et al. (eds.), *Marketing and the arts*, 182–200. New York: Praeger.

Piaget, J.
1971a *The construction of reality in the child.* M. Cook (trans.). New York: Ballantine Books.

Piaget, J.
1971b *The child's perception of time*. A.J. Pomeranz (trans.). New York: Ballantine Books.

Piaget, J.
1976 *The child and reality*. A. Rosin (trans.). London: Penguin Books.

Pivato, S.
1990 The bicycle as a political symbol: Italy, 1885–1955. *The International Journal of the History of Sport* 7(2). 172–187.

Pond, I.K.
1937 *Big top rhythms*. New York: Willett Clark.

Ponge, F.
1961 Le cheval. *Le Grand Recueil*, 146–150. Paris: Gallimard.

Poyatos, Fernando
1976 *Man beyond words: Theory and methodology of nonverbal communication*, Oswego, NY: NYCEC Monographs.

Poyatos, F.
1993 *Paralanguage: Interdisciplinary approach to interactive speech and sounds.* Amsterdam: Benjamins.

Poyatos, F. (ed.)
1992 *Advances in nonverbal communication: Socio-cultural, clinical, esthetic, and litarary perspectives.* Amsterdam: Benjamins.

Pribram, K.
1971 *Languages of the brain: Experimental paradoxes and principles in neuropsychology.* Englewoods Cliffs: Prentice Hall.

Riggins, Stephen Harold
1985 Institutional change in nineteenth-century French music. *Current Perspectives in Social Theory* 6. 243–260.

Ritchie, A.
1975 *King of the road. An illustrated history of cycling.* London: Wildwood Press.

Sebanz, N., H. Bekkering and G. Knoblich
2006 Joint action: bodies and minds moving together. *Trends in Cognitive Sciences* 10(2). 70–76.

Simpson, Charles R.
1981 *SoHo: The artist in the city.* Chicago: University of Chicago Press.

Smith, R.A.
1972 *A social history of the bicycle. Its early life and times in America.* New York: American Heritage Press.

Stamenov, M. and V. Gallese (eds.)
2002 *Mirror neurons and the evolution of brain and language.* Amsterdam: John Benjamins.

Stanford, C.
2003 *Upright: The evolutionary key to becoming human.* New York: Houghton Mifflin.

Strehly, G.
1903 *L'Acrobatie et les Acrobates.* Paris: Delagrave.

Tarachow, S.
1951 Circuses and clowns. In G. Roheim (ed.), *Psychoanalysis and the social sciences*, 171–185. New York: International University Press.

Thétard, H.
1928 *Les Dompteurs*. Gallimard: Paris.
Tinbergen, N.
1989 [1951] *The study of instinct*. Oxford: Oxford University Press.
Turner, V.
1974 *Dramas, fields, and metaphors*. Ithaca: Cornell University Press.
Wainwright, S.A.
1988 *Axis and circumference. The cylindrical shape of plants and animals*. Cambridge, MA: Harvard University Press.
Walker, A. and P. Shipman
2005 *The ape in the tree: An intellectual and natural history of proconsul*. Cambridge, MA: Harvard University Press.
Watson, O.M.
1970 *Proxemic behavior*. The Hague: Mouton.
Whipple, F.J.W
1899 The stability of the motion of a bicycle. *Quarterly Journal of Pure and Applied Mathematics* 30. 312–348.
White, Harrison and Cynthia White
1965 *Canvases and careers*. New York: John Wiley.
White, T.D., B. Asfaw, Y. Beyene, Y. Haile-Selassie, C.O. Lovejoy, G. Suwa and G. Wolde Gabriel
2009 *Ardipithecus ramidus* and the paleobiology of early hominids. *Science* 326. 75–86
Wilson, D.G.
2004 *Bicycling science*. 3rd edn. Cambridge, MA: MIT Press.
Wilson, M. and G. Knoblich
2005. The case for motor involvement in perceiving conspecifics. *Psychological Bulletin* 131. 460–473.
Woodforde, J.
1970 *The story of the bicycle*. London: Routledge.
Zolberg, Vera L.
1980 Displayed art and performed music: Selective innovation and the structure of artistic media. *The Sociological Quarterly* 21. 219–231.

Subject index

Acculturation 26
Acrobats 83ff.
Action, concept of 31–37
Aerial acts 96, 147
Alberto Zoppe 46
Apollo Circus 8, 101
August (clown generic) 103–119

Barnum 153
Bears 68
Bicycle 70–81
Biomorphology 108–111
Biosemiotics 106–108
Blackpool Tower Circus 1, 11, 92
Burger Sisters 92–95

Charlie Cairoli 11, 115
Chorus girls 60–62
Chris Christiansen 21
Circus Archaos 182
Circus Busch-Roland 21
Circus Krone 184
Circus Lumiere 66, 182
Circus OZ 183
Circus Roncalli 182
Circus Vargas 8
Cirque Alexis Gruss 100
Cirque du Soleil 72, 183
Clowns 5, 26, 38–41, 104–117, 132–134
Clown make-up 103–119
Cognitive maturation 25
Context 45
Crazy Horse 64
Cultural change 65, 69, 71
Cultural transmission 37
Cycles 68

Daniel Suskow 120
Description 166, 170
Duchesne smile 112

Elephants 120
Eloize Berchtold 120
Eyebrows 107–108

Firmin Bouglione 44
Fornasari clowns 39–42

Gender economy 95–100
George Carl 112, 128–136
Gerard Debord 68
Glottocentrism 57
Grantcharovi 147
Great Jai Bharat Circus 101

Horses 55, 63, 162

Indian circuses 6, 101

Juggling 2–4, 21
Jumping 88–89

Leuco-signals 111
Liberty horse acts 55, 69
Lions 48, 49, 54, 150, 156, 162

Meme 72
Monkeys 46

Negative experience 125–128, 137–138
Neoteny 108

Objects 22
Octopussy 180
Olli and Illi 18–20

Palio 65
Performance (rules of) 151–155, 163–166, 170–172
Pragmatics of performance 163–176
Punakawan 118–119
Pyramid 82–90

Ringling Bros and Barnum & Bailey Circus 144, 158

Rudy Dockey 42
Russian Soviet Circus 91
Russian State Circus 90

Semiotic square 17–18
Social metaphors 89–92
Spatial algorithm 14
Spatial semiotics 11–16
Staged failure 4–5, 93, 141–147

Tangier troupe 86
Ted Polke 159
Text 22, 38
Tigers 44, 49–51, 111
Time 29–34
Trampoline 90–92

Ursula Boettcher 46–48

Venus Circus 101
Verbal copy 2, 168–170, 172ff.
Vidushaka 118

Wade Burk 158ff.
Walk on the ceiling 93
White-face (clown generic) 103–119

Zoppe aerial act 146

Author index

Balzac, H. de 64
Cocteau, J. 64
Dali, S. 65
Douglas, M. 156, 165
Dundes, A. 66
Ekman, P. 107, 127, 174
Falassi, A. 66
Gautier, T. 7
Goffman, E. 121–128
Greimas, A.J. 64
Grice, P. 170
Hediger, H. 49–52
Hugo, V. 54, 65
Jakobson, R. 44–45
Jeannes, R.W. 79
Kluge, A. 182
Leach, E. 63
Levi-Strauss, C. 59–60, 63
Luria, A. 35
Mair, M.W. 38–39
McDougal, C. 51
Narayan, K. 82
Novakowska, M. 168
Piaget, J. 34
Pond, T.K. 28
Ponge, F. 65
Poyatos, F. 174–175
Pribram, Karl 35
Tarachow, S. 26
Wilden, A. 140

www.ingramcontent.com/pod-product-compliance
Lightning Source LLC
LaVergne TN
LVHW050956080826
845145LV00006B/1513

* 9 7 8 3 1 1 0 2 1 8 3 0 5 *